Mrs Oliphant

The Two Marys

Mrs Oliphant

The Two Marys

ISBN/EAN: 9783741199202

Manufactured in Europe, USA, Canada, Australia, Japa

Cover: Foto ©Andreas Hilbeck / pixelio.de

Manufactured and distributed by brebook publishing software (www.brebook.com)

Mrs Oliphant

The Two Marys

BY

MRS OLIPHANT

AUTHOR OF "THE CHRONICLES OF CARLINGFORD," "THE WIZARD'S SON,"
"THE PRODIGALS," ETC.

METHUEN & CO.
36 ESSEX STREET, W.C.
LONDON
1896

CONTENTS

THE TWO MARYS—
                                                  PAGE
    I. MY OWN STORY   .   .   1
    II. HER STORY   .   .   85

GROVE ROAD, HAMPSTEAD   .   .   127

THE TWO MARYS

I. MY OWN STORY

CHAPTER I

MY name is Mary Peveril. My father was the incumbent of a proprietary chapel in that populous region which lies between Holborn and the New Road—a space within which there is a great deal of wealth and comfort, and a great deal of penury and pain, but neither grandeur nor abject misery. I like those streets, though I know there is no loveliness in them. I feel that I can breathe better when I come out into the largeness and spacious width of the squares, and I take a pleasure which many people will laugh at in the narrow paved passages—crooked and bent like so many elbows, with their bookstalls and curious little shops. How often have I strayed about them with my father, holding on by his coat-skirts when I was little, by his arm when I grew tall, while he stood and gazed at the books which he

THE TWO MARYS

could so seldom afford to buy. When he found a cheap one that pleased him, how his face brightened up! While he looked at them I was not often thinking what the thoughts might be in his mind. What was I thinking of— swinging by the skirts of his coat, or by his arm when I grew a great girl? How can I tell? Thinking how bright the twinkling lights were; how funny life was, so full of people passing whom we never saw again—of paving-stones and shop-windows; and droll with whispering airs that blew round the corners, and always seemed to want to tell you something; and again more lights and more faces and more shop-windows. In winter these passages always felt warm and comfortable, and I had some theory about them which I scarcely remember now—something like the theory of the poor man whom I once heard saying that he went into the streets by night because the gaslights made them so warm. The desolateness of such a forlorn being, seeking warmth in the lighted streets, did not strike me when I heard that speech; I only felt I understood him, and had frequently been conscious of the same feeling. But I remember very well how once, when I was swinging back a little upon papa's arm, clinging to him, proud of showing that I belonged to him and was old enough to take his arm, yet separate from him, as youth so often is, thinking my own thoughts, living in another

THE TWO MARYS

world, I all at once caught the illumination on his face as he fell upon a book he wanted which was cheap enough to be bought. To think he should really care about such a trifle—he—papa, the clergyman whom everybody looked up to; that he should look as pleased about it as Ellen our servant did when she got a new dress! I was half humiliated, half sympathetic. Poor papa! What a pity he could not buy a great many books when he cared so much for them! But yet, I think, there was a little sense of shame on his behalf, and of humiliation, mingled with that more amiable thought; that he should care so much about anything, seemed somehow a derogation from his dignity, a descent on his part into a less lofty place.

We lived in Southampton Street, in the end where there are no shops. We had two very white steps before our front-door, which was the brightest point about us. When anyone asked in that street where the clergyman of St Mark's lived, the house was always pointed out by this: "No. 75, the house with the white steps." I used to think for years and years that they were a natural feature, and had nothing to do with any work of man, or rather, woman. It was a shabby house inside. There were two little kitchens in the basement, two little parlours on the ground-floor, two little bedrooms above that, and on the top storey I think there were three divisions instead of two. One of the little parlours—the back one, which looked out upon a little square yard about the same size—was papa's study. It was not a cheerful room, with that outlook upon four brick walls, and a little square bit of mouldy black soil in which flourished some poor tufts of grass, and the big water-butt in the foreground, where the water was black with soot—when there was any water at all. The room had a writing-table in it, always covered with books and papers, and papa's chair—black haircloth, beginning to wear white at the edges—between the table and the fire, and two other black chairs standing against the opposite wall. It was divided by folding doors from the parlour, in which we lived. This room was furnished with a haircloth sofa, half-a-dozen chairs, a round table with a close-fitting oilcloth cover, and, thrust up into a corner, an old piano, upon which I practised sometimes, and which on other occasions served as a sideboard. There was a short Venetian blind at the lower part of the window to keep people from seeing in, and a chair in the recess, on which I used to sit and darn papa's stockings and dream. Sometimes I read, but, generally, dreaming was more fun. I made out such nice new lives for myself and papa. Sometimes I would dream that we were quite different people from what we appeared to be—great people, rich and noble, with all kinds of grandeur belonging to us, though no one knew; and how it would be found out all of a sudden, to the confusion of everybody who had ever been uncivil. I used to trace out, as minutely as if I had seen it, every detail of what we were to do. I was Lady Mary in these visions; and if anyone had called me so I should have been, I am sure, more shocked to think that *it* had been prematurely discovered than struck by the unreality of the title. It was not unreal to me. Sometimes it would take other shapes, and my imagination would content itself with the notion of someone dying and leaving us a fortune, and how we would wear mourning and do our very best to be sorry; but the other idea was much the favourite. It was very sweet to me to think that, for all so humble and so unknown as we were, things would appear very different *if people but knew!* The old life comes round me as my thoughts go back to it, the afternoon sounds in the street—vulgar sounds, but softened by summer air as much as if they had been the sweetest; the drowsy tinkle of the muffin-man's bell, the prolonged cry of "water-cre-e-e-sses!" the sound of children's voices and dogs barking, and distant wheels that always ground out an accompaniment; and myself in the window, poor Mr Peveril the clergyman's daughter, to my own knowledge Lady Mary, and a very great, small person. I wonder which was the real Mary—she or I.

I have heard that in poor mamma's time we were so fine as to have a drawing-room upstairs on the first floor, like Mrs Stephens next door; but that splendour was long, long over, for mamma died soon after I was born, and I was left all alone—a small baby, with papa on my hands to look after. I do not think, however, that I was at any time very sorry for this. I was sorry for her, who died so young, but not for myself; I felt instinctively that, had she been there, always poking between papa and me, I should not have liked it, and that on the whole things were best as they were. The room which had been the drawing-room was papa's bedroom, and I slept in the room behind, over his study. Ellen had the three little places up above all to herself, though one of them was called—I don't know why—the spare room. In this little place we lived, and never asked ourselves whether it was dingy or not. The walls were dark, with papers which had not been renewed so long as I could remember; and the curtains were dark, and always had the look of being dusty, though, thanks to Ellen, they never were so in reality. We had no pictures, except two old prints from Raphael's cartoons. One was the "Miraculous draught of fishes," and the other "Peter and John at the beautiful gate of the Temple." How I remember those twisted pillars, and how many dreams have they twisted through! But I never admired them, though they were part of my life. I should have liked a landscape better, or some pretty faces like those one sometimes sees in the shop-windows. When the people who went to St Mark's talked of having a lithograph of papa the thought made me wild with excitement; but the lithograph was never done.

It must not be supposed, however, that papa and I lived in that state of ecstatic delight in each other's society which one hears of often in books. There were no great demonstrations between us. I led my own life by the side of his, and he, I suppose, lived his by me, like two parallel lines which never meet whatever you may please to do. I do not know that it occurred to me to think articulately that the happiness of my life depended on him. I did not seek to sit in his study or to be near him while he worked, as I have heard of girls doing. I was quite satisfied to be in the parlour while he was busy on the other side of the closed doors; indeed, until he ceased to be all mine, I accepted papa as calmly as I did the other accessories of my life. When he went out to dinner, which was a very rare occurrence, yet happened sometimes, I would make myself very comfortable with a book over my tea. I was fond of going out with him; but then, he was the only person who ever took me out, through amusing places, where there were shop-windows and crowds of people passing. I had not been brought up to have my walk regularly every day, like well-educated children. I walked when I could. Sometimes I had an errand to do—something to buy or order, which I did by myself in one of the shops of the neighbourhood; but this was an office I hated, for I was too shy to go into a shop with any pleasure; and sometimes old Mrs Tufnell would send for me to walk in the square, which was fine, but not very amusing. I liked the passages about Holborn with the bookstalls a great deal better. But we did not talk a great deal even in these walks. Sometimes I would be seized with a fit of inquiry, and would pester papa with a torrent of questions; but at other times I fell back into my dreams, and would be making some splendid expedition as Lady Mary all the time, while I hung, always a little behind him, on his arm, leaving him as undisturbed as, generally, he left me. I think of this calm of indifference now, when I look back upon it, with very odd feelings. Is it that one does not care so long as one has those whom one loves all to one's self? It is only, I suppose, when your rights are interfered with that you grow violent about them. I suppose it was the fact that we loved each other —I him,—and he me—that made us happy; but it was so natural to love each other that we thought little about it, and I am afraid it would have surprised me a little in my secret heart if any one had told me that my happiness depended upon papa.

The way in which this tranquil ease of possession was disturbed was a very gentle and gradual one—

THE TWO MARYS

at least, so I can see now, though at the time it appeared to me most abrupt and terrible. My idea of my father was that he was old, as a child's ideas generally are; but he was not old. He was about five-and-forty when I was fifteen. He was not tall—and he stooped, which made him look still less so. At fifteen I was as tall as he was. He had a handsome, refined face, with very clear features, and a sort of ivory complexion. His hair was worn off his temples, and there were a great many lines in his face—partly with trouble, partly with work; but his smile was the sweetest smile I ever saw, and he had a way of captivating everybody. I have heard it said since that this power of fascination did not last, and that he grew melancholy and monotonous after the first few times you had seen him; and though I was very angry when I heard this first, I can with an effort believe that it might be true. I suppose it was the same faculty which showed itself at church, where there were always new people coming, who attended closely for a few weeks and then went away. He was like a man who gives you everything he has at once, and then has nothing more for you. At home he was silent, always kind, but never saying much. I scarcely recollect ever to have been scolded by him. Ellen scolded me, and so did old Mrs Tufnell, and even Mrs Stephens next door; but papa only said, "Poor child!" with the air of a compassionate spectator, when I was

THE TWO MARYS

complained of to him. Our chief conversation was at meals, when he would sometimes talk a little, and tell me of things he had seen or heard; and it was at tea one evening that he first brought forward the name of the other person who was henceforward to stand between us. No such thought was in his mind then, I am sure; but he was more communicative than usual. He told me that he had seen a young lady on one of his visits, in a very strange place for such a person to be found—in the back parlour of a small grocer's shop which I knew quite well. He told me quite a long story about her—how she was an orphan and had been left destitute, and had been obliged to go back to her mother's family, who had been a governess in her day, and married much above her. Her father, too, was dead, having been of no use whatever in the world or to her, and there was no prospect before her but that of going out to be a governess—a thing which papa seemed to think a great hardship for her. I had been trained to believe that some such place would have to be mine as papa got older and I grew a woman; therefore I was not at all shocked by the suggestion. I said: "Has she heard of any nice situation, papa?" with the quietest matter-of-fact acceptance of his words.

"Heard of a situation! You talk very much at your ease, Mary,—but if you saw this elegant, accomplished, refined girl," said my father. "Poor thing, I cannot bear to think that she should be driven to such a fate."

I did not make any answer. I was surprised. It had never occurred to me that it was "such a fate." Most girls, it seemed to me, who were not great ladies were governesses, both in the little real world with which I was acquainted and in books.

"Poor thing!" he said again. "Poor thing! how I wish there was any possible way of saving her. What a thing it is to be poor!"

"But any situation would be better than staying with the Spicers," I said. "Think, papa—the Spicers! I should not mind being a governess—I suppose I shall be, some day or other—but I should hate living in a parlour behind a shop."

"Well, Mary, I hope you will see her some time, and when you do see her you must be very kind to her," said my father with a sigh; and that night he drew his chair to the fire and tried to talk, which was a thing that took me very much by surprise. But, unfortunately, I had a new book which was very interesting, and instead of responding to this unusual inclination, as I ought to have done, I kept on reading, making pettish and uncertain replies, until he grew tired of the attempt and gave it up, and got a book too, as usual. He sighed a little as he did so, with a sort of disappointed air; and through my reading and my interest in the story somehow I perceived this, and

THE TWO MARYS

felt guilty and uncomfortable all the rest of the evening. When I had finished my volume I was very conciliatory, and tried all I could to bring him back to the point where he had given it up, but it was of no use. I have always found it exactly so in my experience. If you are too stupid, or too much occupied with yourself, to take just the right moment for explanations, you never can recover the thread which you have allowed to slip through your fingers. Even to this day I often wonder what papa would have said to me that night had I let him speak. I have invented whole conversations, but they never were much satisfaction to me. To think out what perhaps some one might have said is very different from hearing them say it. I was not at all pleased with myself that evening when I went to bed; but perhaps this was partly because I had finished my novel and it was not satisfactory, and seemed, now it was over, such a poor sort of thing to have preferred to a conversation with papa.

Nothing, however, happened for some time after this to put me on my guard. I went on in my old careless way. If he was out a little more than usual, I paid no attention. All that was quite natural. Of course he had his duties to attend to. He dined at Mrs Tufnell's once during this time, and was very particular about his tie, and about having his coat brushed. "It is quite nice," I said; "it was well brushed on Monday morning before it was put away. Why, papa, I thought you did not like a fuss: how you laughed at me for being so particular about my sash when we went to the party at Mrs Overend's. Shouldn't you like to have a sash too?"

He laughed, but he did not look like laughing; and I remember stopping short in the middle of my tea, and laying down my book to ask myself if anything could be the matter with him. One or two odd people whom I did not know had come to see him of late. Was it possible he could be ill? But no, he ate as usual, and he had looked quite ruddy when he went out. So I took up my novel again, and helped myself to jam, and thought no more of it. I believe the whole business was decided, or the next thing to decided, that night.

I could if I liked have heard a great deal of what was said in the study while I sat at work in the parlour, and this was a thing which Mrs Tufnell and Mrs Stephens had often remarked. They thought it "not quite nice:" for, to be sure, people might say things to papa as their clergyman which they did not wish to be overheard. But it could not well be helped, for there was no other room where I could sit. I have said too that I could have heard if I liked; but the fact was I did not care, and I never heard. When you are perfectly indifferent and used to everything, and know there is no mystery in it, it is astonish-

THE TWO MARYS

ing how little you hear. I had got accustomed to the hum of voices from the study just as I had to the cries in the streets and the muffin-man's bell. Sometimes, I suppose, a word must have caught my ear now and then, but I paid no attention, and heard as if I heard it not: I was thinking of such very different things. One day, however, I did catch a few words which surprised me. It was a summer day. The back-door into the little yard and all the windows everywhere were open. The noises in the street came into the house exactly as if we were living out of doors, but so softened by the warm air and the sunshine that they were pleasant instead of being disagreeable. The day was not hot, but only deliciously, genially warm. We had put up white curtains in the parlour, and the wind blew them softly about, flapping the wooden stretcher in the blind against the window-frame. I was in a muslin dress myself; and I was happy without any reason, not in the least knowing why. I came downstairs singing, as I had a way of doing, and went into the parlour and sat down in the window. I gave up singing when I sat down, partly because it might have disturbed papa, and partly because people stopped to listen as they were passing. I was running up the breadths of my new frock, a blue print, which was as bright and pretty as the day, and, to tell the truth, did not care in the least what the voices were saying on the other side of

THE TWO MARYS

the folding doors. I had made noise enough to demonstrate my presence, and, as nothing was ever hid from me, it never came into my head to listen. It was Spicer the grocer's voice, I think, which attracted my ear at last. It was a strange, little, harsh, snappish voice, so unharmonious that it worried one like a dog barking; and by degrees, as he talked and talked, some sort of vague association came into my mind—something which I had half forgotten. What was it I had heard about the Spicers? I could not recollect all at once.

"Governessing ain't paradise," said Spicer, "but it's better perhaps than other things. Marrying a man as is in poor health, and at a troublesome time o' life—and nothing to leave to them as comes after him; that ain't much, Mr Peveril. A woman's best married, I allow; but marriage has consekenses, and when there's no money——"

I did not hear what my father said in reply, and indeed I did not care to hear. I was half annoyed, half amused, by Spicer's queer little barking voice.

"Forty-five, sir? no, it ain't old—but it ain't young neither. I've known many a man carried off at forty-five. Them things have all got to be considered; though for that matter twenty-five would make little difference. The thing is, here's a young woman as has a trade she can make her living by. A man comes in, marries her right off: they have a child or two in natural course, and then he goes and dies. Nothing more natural or more common. But then you see, Mr Peveril, sir, here's the question: what's to become of her? And that's the question I've got to consider. I've a family myself, and I can't put myself in the way of having to support another man's family; and a woman can't go out and be a governess, it stands to reason, with two or three young uns on her hands."

My father said something here in a very earnest, low, grave voice, which really attracted my curiosity for the first time. Whatever he was saying, he was very serious about it, and his tone, though I could not hear what he said, woke me up. Perhaps he warned Spicer to talk low; but at all events I heard nothing more for some time, except the grumbling and barking of the grocer's voice, in a much subdued tone. They seemed to argue, and Spicer seemed to yield. At last he got up to go away, and then I heard him deliver his final judgment on the matter, whatever it was, standing close to the folding doors.

"You speaks fair, sir. I don't say but what you speaks fair. Granting life and health, it's a fine thing for her, and a honour for us. And taking the other side of the question, as I'm bound to take it, I wouldn't say but the insurance makes a difference. A woman with a thousand pounds and a babby is no worse off than if she hadn't neither—and Missis is better nor Miss in the way

THE TWO MARYS

of setting up a school or such like. I may say, Mr Peveril, as the insurance makes a great difference. A thousand pound ain't much for a dependence; and if there was a lot of little uns—but to be sure, in them matters you must go on providence to a certain extent. I'll think it over, sir—and I don't see as I've any call to make objections, if her and you's made up your minds." Then there was a step towards the door, and then Spicer came to a stand-still once more. "First thing," he said, "Mr Peveril, is the insurance. You won't put it off, sir? I've known them as meant it every day o' their lives, and never did it when all was done; and died and left their families without e'er a——"

"It shall be done at once," said my father peremptorily, and almost angrily; and then there was a begging of pardon, and a scraping and shuffling, and Spicer went away. I saw him go out, putting his hat on as he shut the door. I never liked Spicer—of course he was one of the parishioners, and papa could not refuse his advice to him or to any one; but I made a face at him as he went away. I felt quite sure he was the sort of man one sometimes reads of in the newspapers, who put sand in the sugar, and sell bad tea to the poor people, and have light weights. This was in my mind along with a vague, faint curiosity as to what he had been talking about, when to my surprise papa came into the parlour.

He came in quickly, with a flush on his face, and the most uneasy, uncomfortable look I ever saw a man have. Was he ashamed of something?— ashamed! he—papa!

"I suppose you have heard all that Spicer has been saying, Mary," he said to me, quite abruptly. He gave me one strange look, and then turned away, and gazed at the Beautiful gate of the Temple which hung over the mantelpiece as if he had never seen it before.

"Yes," I said; and then it suddenly flashed upon me that Spicer's talk had not been exactly of a kind to be overheard by a girl, and that this was why poor papa looked so embarrassed and uncomfortable. He felt that it was not proper for me. "I heard a little of it," I said instantly, "but I never listen, you know, papa, and I don't know in the least what he was talking about."

Poor papa! how delicate he was; how shocked I should have heard anything I ought not to know —though it was not so dreadful after all, for of course everybody knows that when people are married they have babies. But he did not like to look me in the face; he kept his back to me, and gazed at the twisted pillars.

"Mary," he said, "I have a little explanation to make to you."

"An explanation?" I looked at him over my blue print, wondering what it could be; but it did not seem worth while to stop working, and I threaded my needle and made a knot on my thread while I waited for what he was going to say. Then suddenly my heart began to beat a little fast, and the thought crossed my mind that perhaps my dreams were about to become true, and that he knew all about it as well as I, and was just going to tell me I was Lady Mary, and he Earl of———. I had never been able to choose a satisfactory title, and I could not invent one on the spur of the moment; but instinctively I gave a glance from the window to see whether the beautiful carriage was in sight, coming to take us to our splendid home.

"Perhaps I ought to have taken you into my confidence before," he said, "for you have been brought up a lonely girl, and ought to feel for people who are lonely. I have been very lonely myself, very desolate, ever since your poor mother died."

Here my heart gave a slight stir, and I felt angry, without knowing exactly why. Lonely? Why, he had always had me!

"When you are older," he went on nervously, "you will feel what a dreadful thing the want of companionship is. You have been a good child, Mary, and done all you could for me. I should not have been able to live without you; but when a man has been used to a companion of—of his own standing, it is a great change to him to fall back upon a child."

THE TWO MARYS

I grew angrier and angrier; I could scarcely tell why. A feeling of disappointment, of heart-sinking, of fury, came over me. I had never made much fuss about adoring my father, and so forth; but to find out all at once that he had never been satisfied—never happy——

"Do you mean me?" I said, quite hoarsely, feeling as if he had wronged me, deceived me, done everything that was cruel—but with no clear notion of what was coming even now

"Whom else could I mean?" he said, quite gently. "You are a dear, good child, but you are only a child."

Oh, how my heart swelled, till I thought it would burst! but I could not say anything. I began to tap my foot on the floor in my anger and mortification, but still I was so stupid I thought of nothing more.

"Don't look as if you thought I blamed you, Mary," said my father; "on the contrary, you have been a dear little housekeeper. But—do you remember, dear," he went on, with his voice shaking a little, "that I told you once of a young lady who lived with the Spicers?"

It began to dawn upon me now. I turned round upon him, and stared at him. Oh, how pleased I was to see his eyes shrink, and the embarrassed look upon his face! I would not give him any quarter; I felt my own face growing crimson with shame, but I kept looking at him,

THE TWO MARYS

compelling him to keep opposite to me, preventing him from hiding that blush. Oh, good heavens—an *old* man—a man of forty-five—a clergyman—my father! and there he sat, blushing like some ridiculous boy.

He faltered, but he kept on, not looking at me, "I see you remember," he said, with his voice shaking like a flame in a draught of air. "She has no prospect but to go out as a governess, and I cannot see her do that. I have asked her to—to—share—our home. I have asked her to—to be your—best friend; that is, I mean, I have asked her to marry me, Mary. There! You must have seen that I have been disturbed of late. I am very glad there is no longer this secret between my little girl and me."

And with that he kissed me quite suddenly and trembling, and went off again to the mantelshelf, and stared up at Peter and John by the Beautiful gate.

For my part I sat quite still, as if the lightning had struck me. What ought I to do? I did not realise at first what had happened. I was struck dumb. I knew that I ought to do or say something, and I could not tell what. My lips stuck together—I could not now even open my mouth; and there he stood waiting. I suppose if I had possessed my wits at that moment I would have gone and kissed him or something. Even, I suppose, if I had stormed at him it would have been less idiotic—but I could say nothing; I was bewildered. I sat staring into the air with my mouth open, over my blue print.

At last he made an impatient movement, and I think said something to me, which roused me out of my stupefaction. Then—I do not know what impulse it was that moved me—I asked all at once, frightened, feeling I ought to say something, "What is her name, papa?"

"Mary Martindale," he said.

CHAPTER II

I REMEMBER quite distinctly how people talked. They did not think I observed or listened, for I had always been a dreamy sort of girl, and never had attended much to what was said about me. At least so everybody thought. They said I had always to be shaken or pulled when anything was wanted of me, to make me listen—which is true enough, I believe; but nevertheless I was not half so absent as people thought at any time, and heard a great deal that I was not supposed to hear. And now my senses were all shaken up and startled into being. How well I recollect hearing old Mrs Tufnell and Mrs Stephens talking in the quiet front drawing-room in the Square, while I was in the little room behind, taking no notice, as they thought. They had given me a book and got rid of me, and though they all pretended to deplore my dreamy ways, I think on the whole it was rather a relief to get rid of a quick, inquisitive, fifteen-year-old girl, and to be able to talk in peace. It was twilight of the summer evening and we had taken tea, and the two ladies were seated at one of the windows looking out upon the

THE TWO MARYS

Square. The windows had long, full, white curtains, hanging and fluttering from the roof to the carpet. They were seated against that soft white background in their black silk dresses, for Mrs Tufnell was old, and Mrs Stephens was a widow and always wore black. It was like a picture: and I, not being so happy as I used to be, sat with my book and read and listened both together. You may think this is nonsense; but I could do it. I see them now approaching their caps to each other, with little nods and shakes of their heads and the white curtains fluttering softly behind them. Mrs Tufnell was a great patroness of papa's, and always went to St Mark's regularly, and Mrs Stephens was our very nearest neighbour, living next door.

"I hope it will turn out the best thing that could happen for *her*," said Mrs Tufnell, nodding her head at me. They would not say any more lest they should attract my attention. "She has been greatly neglected, and left alone a great deal too much,—and I hear *she* is accomplished. Dear, dear, who would have thought that he, of all men in the world, would have taken such a step."

"I don't quite see that," said Mrs Stephens; "he is a young man still, and nobody could suppose he would always be contented with his child's company: besides, she is so cool and indifferent, as if she never thought it possible anything could happen: and I am sure she never did anything to make herself necessary or agreeable——"

"Poor child!"

"You may say 'poor child!' but yet I blame her. A girl of fifteen is a woman to all intents and purposes. She ought to have seen that there was a great deal in her power by way of making him comfortable and herself pleasant. It's rather hard to say the plain downright truth about it, you know, he being a clergyman and all that. Of course, when there is a young family one can say it is for their sake; but in this case there's no possible excuse—he only wanted a wife, that's all. I don't blame him; but it's a coming down—it's a disturbance of one's ideal——"

"I don't know much about ideals," said Mrs Tufnell; "what surprises me is, if the man wanted to marry, why he didn't marry long ago, when the child was young and he had an excellent excuse. As for being a clergyman, that's neither here nor there. Clergymen are always marrying men, and it's no sin to marry."

"It disturbs one's ideal," said Mrs Stephens; and, though Mrs Tufnell shrugged her shoulders, I, sitting behind over my book, agreed with her. Oh the inward humiliation with which one sees one's father in love!—I suppose it would be still worse to see one's mother, but then, I never had a mother. I blushed for him a great deal more than he blushed for himself, and he did blush for himself too. If he was happy, it was a very uneasy, disturbed sort of happiness. He took me to see her—to Spicer's; and he went often himself and sat in the parlour behind the shop, and suffered, I am sure, as much as ever a man who is having his own way could suffer. Mrs Tufnell, who was a thoroughly kind old lady, at length came to his aid, and invited Miss Martindale to stay with her the rest of the time, and to be married from her house, which was a thing which even I was grateful for. And the night before the wedding-day the old lady kissed me and said, "Things will turn out better than you suppose, dear. It is hard upon you, but things will turn out better than you suppose."

I am not sure that this is ever a very effectual kind of comfort, but to me it was exasperating. Had I been told that things would turn out worse than I supposed, I should have liked it. It seemed to me that nothing could be half bad enough for this overturn of all plans and thoughts and life. For you must recollect that it was my life that was chiefly to be overturned. Papa liked it, I supposed, and it was his own doing—but the change was not so great to him as to me. All the little offices of authority I used to have were taken from me—my keys, which I was proud of keeping—my bills and tradesmen's books, which I had summed up since ever I can remember. I was turned out of my room, and sent upstairs to

THE TWO MARYS

the spare room beside Ellen. In the parlour I was never alone any more, and not even my favourite corner was mine any longer. I had no more walks with papa, swinging back from his arm. She had his arm now. She made the tea, and even darned his stockings. I was nothing in the house, and she everything. If you suppose that a girl bears this sort of dethronement easily, I am here to witness to the contrary. I did not take it easily; but the thing that went to my heart most was, I think, that she was called Mary, like me. For the first few days when I heard papa call Mary I used to run to him and find her before me, and get sent away, sometimes hastily (one time I ran in and found them sitting together, he with his arm round her waist. I wonder he was not ashamed of himself, at his age!); and another time with a joke which made me furious: "It was my other Mary I wanted," he said, looking as vain and foolish as—as—. I never saw anybody look so foolish. *My* father! It humbled me to the very ground. And then I took to never answering to the name at all, which sometimes made papa angry when it was really me he wanted. I soon came to know very well which of us he meant by the sound of his voice, but I never let him know that I did so. His voice grew soft and round as if he were singing when he called her. When he called me, it was just, I suppose, as it always had been; but I had

THE TWO MARYS

learned the other something now, the different accentuation, and I resented the want of it, though I knew that it never had belonged to me.

All this time I have not spoken of her, though she was the cause of all. When I saw her first, in the grocer's back shop, working at frocks for the little Spicers, I could not believe my eyes. Though I had already begun to hate her as supplanting me with my father, I could not but acknowledge how very strange it was to see her there. She had on a very plain black alpaca dress, and she sat in the back parlour, amid all that smell of hams and cheese, with a sewing-machine before her; and yet she looked like a princess. She was tall and very slight, like a flower, and her head bowed a little on its stem like the head of a lily. She was pale, with dark eyes and dark hair. I believe she was very handsome — not pretty, but very handsome, almost beautiful, I have heard papa say. I allow this, to be honest, though I cannot say I ever saw it. She had a pathetic look in her eyes which sometimes felt as if it might go to one's heart. But, fortunately, she always looked happy when I saw her — absurdly happy, just as my poor foolish father did — and so I never was tempted to sympathise with her. I do not understand how anybody but an angel could sympathise with another person who was very happy and comfortable while she (or he) was in trouble. This was our situation now. She had driven me out of everything, and she was pleased; but I was cross from morning till night, and miserable, feeling that I scarcely minded whether I lived or died. Her smiles seemed to insult me when we sat at table together. She looked so much at her ease; she talked so calmly, she even laughed and joked, and sometimes said such merry, witty things, that it was all I could do to keep from laughing too. It is painful to be tempted to laugh when you are very much injured and in a bad temper. Reading was forbidden now at meals, and neither papa nor I ever ventured to prop up a book beside us while we ate. I suppose it was a bad custom; yet my very heart revolted at the idea of changing anything because she wished it. And then she tried to be "of use" to me, as people said. She made me practise every day. She gave me books to read, getting them from the library, and taking a great deal of trouble. She tried to make me talk French with her; but to talk is a thing one cannot be compelled to do, and I always had it in my power to balk that endeavour by answering *Oui* or *Non* to all her questions. But the worst of it all was that I had no power to affect either her or papa, whatever I might do to make myself disagreeable. I suppose they were too happy to mind. When I was sulky, it was only myself I made miserable, and there is very little satisfaction in that.

I cannot but say, however, looking back, that

she was kind to me, in her way. She was always good-natured, and put up with me and tried to make me talk. She was kind: but *they* were not kind. As soon as my father and she got together they forgot everything. They sat and talked together, forgetting my very existence. They went out walking together. Sometimes even he would kiss her, without minding that I was there; and all this filled me with contempt for his weakness. I could not support such nonsense—at his age, too! I remember one day rushing to Mrs Stephens' to get rid of them and their happiness. She was well off, and I don't really know why she lived in such a street as ours. She kept two servants all for herself, and had a nice drawing-room on the first-floor very beautifully furnished, as I then thought, where she sat and saw all that was going on. Without Mrs Stephens I think I should have died. I used to rush to her when I could bear it no longer.

"What is the matter, Mary?" she would say, looking up from her Berlin work. She had a daughter who was married—and she was always working chairs for her, and footstools, and I don't know what.

"Nothing," said I, sitting down on the stool by her wool-basket and turning over the pretty colours; and then, after I had been silent for a minute, I said, "They have gone out for a walk."

"It is very natural, my dear; you must not be

jealous. It might be a question, you know, whether you liked your papa to marry; but now that he is married, it is his duty to be attentive to his wife."

"He had me before he had a wife," cried I; "why should he love her better than me? Why should he be so much happier with her than with me? He has always something to say to her: he is always smiling and pleasant. Sometimes with me he will be a whole day and never say a word. Why should he be more happy with her than with me?"

Mrs Stephens laughed. "I can't tell you how it is, Mary, but so it is," she said; "and by and by, when you are older, you will have somebody whom you will be happier with than you ever were with your papa. That is the best of being young. When my Sophy married, it was very hard upon me to see her happier with her husband than she had been with her mother, and to know that all that sort of thing was over for me, and that I must be content with my worsted-work. But you will have a happiness of your own by and by, when you are older; so you must not grudge it so much to your poor papa. I think he is looking pale. I thought he coughed a great deal on Sunday. Is she doing anything for that cough of his, do you know?"

"I never noticed that he had a cough."

"Well, I hope *she* does," said Mrs Stephens,

with a strange look, as if she meant something. "Your papa never was strong. He has not health to be going out of nights, and to all those concerts and things. She ought to look after his cough, Mary. If she does not, it will be she who will suffer the most."

I did not in the least understand what this meant; I had never remarked papa's cough. Yes, to be sure, he always had a little cough —nothing to speak of. I had been used to it all my life, and it was not any worse than usual —it was nothing. I told Mrs Stephens so, and then we talked of other things.

What a long year that was! When the wedding-day came round again they had a party, and were quite gay. It was a very odd thing to see a party in our house; but, though I would not have owned this for the world, I almost think I half enjoyed it. I had got used to papa's foolish happiness, and to Mrs Peveril's ways. By mere use and wont I had got more indifferent; and then there began to be some talk of getting a situation for me as a governess. Papa did not like the idea, but I myself pressed it on, with a feeling that something new would be pleasant. I took most of my ideas of life from novels; and if you will think of it, young ladies who are governesses in novels, generally come to promotion in the end, though they may have to suffer a great deal first. I did not much mind the suffering. Whatever it may be that makes one superior to other people, one can bear it. I made up my mind to a great deal of trouble, and even persecution, and all kinds of annoyances, feeling that all this would come to something in the end. All my dreams about being Lady Mary, and a great personage, had been dispersed by my father's marriage. But now I began to dream in another way; and by degrees the old nonsense would steal back. I used to sit with a book in my hand, and see myself working in a schoolroom with the children; and then some one would come to the door, and I should be called to a beautiful drawing-room, and the lady of the house would take me in her arms and kiss me, and say, "Why did not you tell me who you really were!" and there would be a lawyer in black who had come with the news. All this I am sure is intensely silly, but so was I at the time; and that is exactly how my mind used to go on. Sometimes a gentleman would come into it, who would be intensely respectful and reverential, and whom I would always refuse, saying, "No; I will allow no one to descend from their proper rank for me!" until that glorious moment came when I was found out to be as elevated in rank as in principles. Oh, how absurd it all was! and how I liked it! and what a refuge to me was that secret world which no one ever entered but myself, and yet where so many delightful people lived whom I knew by their names, and could talk to for hours together! Sitting there under Mrs Peveril's very nose, I would have long argumentations with my lover, and he would kiss my hand, and lay himself at my feet, and tell me that he cared for no one in the world but me; and the scene of the discovery was enacted over and over again while papa was talking of parish matters, quite unaware that by some mysterious imbroglio of affairs he was really the Earl of —— So and So—(I never could hit upon a sufficiently pretty name). Thus, instead of weeping over my hard fate and thinking it dreadful to have to go out as a governess, I looked forward to it, feeling that somehow the discovery of the true state of affairs concerning us was involved in it, and that, without that probation, Fate would certainly never restore me to my due and native eminence in the world.

But, however, I must come back to the night of the anniversary, and to our party. I had on a pretty new white frock—my first long one: and I half, or more than half, enjoyed myself. Everybody was very kind to me, everybody said I was looking well; and Mrs Tufnell and Mrs Stephens petted me a good deal behind backs, and said, "poor child!" And then papa's curate, who was one of the guests, kept following me about and trying to talk to me; whenever I looked up I met his eyes. I did not admire him in the least, but it amused me very much, and pleased me, to see that he admired me. When I wanted anything he rushed to get it for me. It was very odd, but not at all disagreeable, and gave me a comfortable feeling about myself. When the people went away, papa stood a long time in the hall between the open doors, saying good-night to everybody. He went back into the parlour after they were all gone; he went up to the fireplace, I don't know why, and stood there for a moment as if there had been a fire in the grate. Then he called "Mary!" I might have known it was not me he wanted. He held out his hand without turning round. "I never thought I could be happier than I was this day last year," he said, "and yet I am happier to-night. What a delightful year you have given me, my darling——Oh, is it you? What did you mean by not telling me it was you, when you must have perceived that I thought I was talking to my wife?"

"There was no time to tell you," I said. It gave me a pang I can scarcely describe when he thrust my hand away which I had held out to him. He was ashamed; he sat down suddenly in the big chair, and then all at once a fit of coughing came on, such a fit of coughing as I never saw before. It frightened me; and he looked so pale, and with such circles round his eyes! When he could speak he said, hurriedly, panting for his breath, "Be sure you do not tell her of this——." That was all he thought of. It did not matter for me.

But, as it happened, it was not long possible to

keep it from *her*. When I look back upon that evening, with its little follies, and the laughter, and the curate, and my new dress! O, how little one knows! That very night papa was taken ill. He had caught cold in the draught as he shook hands with the people. It was congestion of the lungs, and from the first the doctor looked very serious. The house changed in that night. The study and the parlour and the whole place turned into a vestibule to the sick room, which was the centre of everything. The very atmosphere was darkened; the sun did not seem to shine; the sounds outside came to us dulled and heavy. I was not allowed to be very much in the room. She took her place there and never left him, day or night; and if I were to spend pages in describing it I could not give you any idea of my dreariness, left alone down below, not allowed to help him or be near him while my father lay between living and dying. I could not do anything. I tried to read, but I could not read. To take up a novel, which was the only thing I could possibly have given my attention to, would have seemed like profanation at such a time. It would have been worse than reading a novel on Sunday, which I had always been brought up to think very wicked; and as for my dreams, they were worse even than the novels. I dared not carry them on while papa was so ill. I felt that if I allowed my thoughts to float away on such useless currents, I never could expect God to listen to my prayers. For this reason I made a dreadful effort to think "as one ought to think," to think of religious things always and all day long—and this was very difficult; but I made the effort, because I thought God was more likely to listen to me if I showed that I wanted to do well.

But, oh the dreary days and the dreary nights! The three last nights I sat up in my dressing-gown, and dozed drearily and woke still more drearily, after dreaming the strangest dreams. Sometimes I thought it was the wedding-day again, and he was standing with her hand on his arm; sometimes it was the anniversary, and he was saying how happy he was; sometimes it was a funeral. I dreamed always about him, and always in different aspects. One morning I woke up suddenly and found Ellen standing by me in the grey dawning. She did not say anything; the tears were running down her face. But I got up and followed her quite silent, knowing what it was.

He died, after a week's illness, in the morning, leaving us a whole horrible, light, bright day to get through with what patience we could; and then there was a dreary interval of silence, and he was carried away from us for ever and ever; and she and I, two creatures of different minds as ever were born, with but this one link of union between us, were left in the house alone.

CHAPTER III

SHE and I alone in the house! I do not think that I could express our desolation more fully were I to write a whole book. He who had brought us together was gone. The link between us was broken—we were two strangers, rather hostile to each other than otherwise. No pretence of love had ever existed between us. She had never had any occasion to be jealous of me; but she had known and must have felt that I was jealous of her, and grudged her position, her happiness, her very name. She knew this, and it had not mattered to her so long as he was alive; but now that he was gone, now that she and I, bearing the same name, supposed to belong to each other, were left within our dismal house alone——

We went together to the funeral. I was too much absorbed in my own feelings, I believe, to think of her; and yet I noticed everything, as people do when they are deeply excited. She walked by herself, and so did I. There was no one to support either of us, and we did not cling to each other. The churchwardens were there, and Spicer the grocer, to my annoyance. When

THE TWO MARYS

I saw him all the conversation which I had once overheard came to my mind. Even as I stood by my father's grave it came back to me. I understood it only partially, but it seemed to me as if the time had come on which he calculated, and which he had spoken of. I do not think it had ever recurred to me till that moment. She would be better off with a thousand pounds than with nothing. A thousand pounds——and——what had he said? I thought my heart had been too faint to feel at all, and yet it began to quicken now with excitement. I looked at her as she walked before me. What was to become of her? What was to become of me? But I did not think of myself.

When we got back to the house Spicer came in and the churchwardens with him; they came into the parlour. When I was going away Mr Turnham, who was one of them, called me back. "Miss Mary," he said, "wait a little. It is hard upon you, but there is some business to be settled. Pray, come back."

I went, of course. She had dropped into the chair my father used to sit in. He had given it up to her when they were married, but now death had unmarried them, and I could not bear to see her there. Spicer had gone to sit by her; they were at one side of the room, Mr Turnham and I at the other, as if we were opposite sides. The other churchwarden had shaken hands with us all and gone away.

THE TWO MARYS

"In the present melancholy circumstances it is our duty," said Mr Turnham, "to inquire into our late dear friend's monetary arrangements; there must have been some settlement or other—some explanation at least, as he married so short a time ago."

Then Spicer cleared his throat, and edged still more on to the edge of his chair. Oh, heaven knows. I was as miserable as a girl could be—but yet I noticed all this as if I did not care.

"There was no settlement," he said, "reason good, there wasn't nothing to settle as was worth the while; but being Mrs Peveril's only relation, and responsible like, he spoke very clear and honourable about his means to me. 'I ain't got no money, Mr Spicer,' he said, 'but I've insured my life for my daughter, and I'll do as much for her. They'll have a thousand pounds apiece, and that's better than nothing,' he said; 'it will get them into some snug little way of business or something.' He was a sensible man, Mr Peveril, and spoke up handsome when he saw as nothing was exacted of him. I don't know what office it's in, but I believe as what he said must be true."

"Perhaps if we were to adjourn into the study, and if one of the ladies would get the keys, we might look in his desk if there was a will," said Mr Turnham. "I am very sorry that our late lamented friend had so short an illness, and therefore was unable to say anything as to what he wished."

"Stop, please," Mrs Peveril said all at once. "Stop: neither of us is able to give you any help to-day; and afterwards we will try to manage for ourselves. We thank you very much, but it is best to leave us to ourselves. I speak for Mary too."

"But, my dear Mrs Peveril, you will want some one to manage for you; it is painful, I know, but it is best to do it at once; you will want some one to manage——"

"I do not see the necessity," she said. She was dreadfully pale; I never saw any one so pale; and it went to my heart to be obliged to side with her, and acquiesce in what she said; but I could not help it, I was obliged to give in. She spoke for me too.

"As long as there's me, you may make your mind easy," said Spicer. "A relation; and on the premises, so to speak. I'll do for 'em all as is necessary; you may make your mind quite easy, Mr Turnham—you trust to me."

Then she got up; her head drooped in her great heavy black bonnet and veil. She was not like a lily now, in all that crape; but I could not keep my eyes from her. She was not afraid of these men, as I was. She held out her hand first to the one, then to the other. "Good-bye," she said. "We thank you very much for taking so much interest, but we would like to be alone to-day. Good-bye."

Mr Turnham got up not quite pleased, but he shook hands with her and then with me, and said "Good-bye and God bless you" to us both. "If you want me, you know where I am to be found," he said, with a little look of offence. Spicer stayed behind him, as if he belonged to us.

"I agree with you," he said, putting his hand on her shoulder. "Them as is strangers has no business with your affairs. Trust 'em to me, my dear; trust 'em to me. When your money's safe in a good snug little business you won't be so badly off; at least it's always something to fall back upon;—don't you be downhearted, my dear. I don't see as you will be so badly off."

"Good-bye, Mr Spicer," she said. She pushed past him and left the room with an impatience which I understood. He and I were left standing together, looking at each other. Nobody considered me much. It was the wife who was thought of—not the daughter. He shook his head as he looked after her.

"Bless us all! bless us all!" he said. "That's what comes of turning a woman's head. Miss Mary, I ain't going to forsake you, though she's far from civil. I'll stand by you, never fear. If the money's well invested you'll both get something 'andsome. Nothing pays like business; and as there ain't no babby—which was what I always feared——"

"I don't want to talk about Mrs Peveril," I said.

"Oh, you don't want to talk about her! no more do I. She's very flighty and hoity-toighty. I remember when she was very glad to get a corner at my table. She thinks she's set up now, with her thousand pounds. It's a blessing as there's no family. Miss Mary, I'll take your instructions next time as I comes if you'll put yourself in my hands. I've come to think on you as a relation too; but bless you, my dear, I know as you can't be cheerful with visitors not just the first day. Don't stand upon no ceremony with me."

He wanted me to leave him, I thought, that he might examine everything, and perhaps, get at poor papa's papers; but I would not do that. I stayed, though my heart was bursting, until he went away. What an afternoon that was! it was summer, but it rained all day. It rained and rained into the smoky street, and upon papa's grave, which I seemed to see before me wet and cold and sodden, with little pools of water about. How heartless it seemed, how terrible, to have come into shelter ourselves and to have left him there alone in the wet, and the cold, and the misery! If one could but have gone back there and sat down by him and got one's death, it would have been some consolation. I went up to my

THE TWO MARYS

room and sat there drearily, watching the drops that chased each other down the window panes. It was so wet that the street was quite silent outside, nobody coming or going, except the milkman with his pails making a clank at every area. There were no cries in the street, no sound of children playing, nothing but the rain pattering, pattering, upon the roofs and the pavement, and in every little hollow on both. The house, too, was perfectly still; there was no dinner, nothing to break the long monotony. Ellen came up in her new black gown, with tears on her cheeks, to bring me a glass of wine and a sandwich. I could not eat, but I drank the wine. "Oh, Miss Mary," said Ellen, "won't you go to her now? There's only you two. It ain't a time, Miss, oh, it ain't a time to think on things as may have been unpleasant. And she's a taking on so, shut up in that room, as I think she'll die."

Why should she die any more than me? Why should she be more pitied than I was? I had lost as much, more than she had. She had known him but a short time, not two years; but he had been mine all my life. I turned my back upon Ellen's appeal, and she went away crying, shaking her head and saying I was unkind, I was without feeling. Oh, was I without feeling? How my head ached, how my heart swelled, how the sobs rose into my throat; I should have been glad could I have felt that it was likely I should die.

THE TWO MARYS

"Will you go down to tea, Miss Mary," Ellen said, coming back as the night began to fall. I was weary, weary of sitting and crying by myself; any change looked as if it must be better. I was cold and faint and miserable; and then there was in my mind a sort of curiosity to see how she looked, and if she would say anything—even to know what were to be the relations between us now. I went down accordingly, down to the dark little parlour which, during all papa's illness, I had lived in alone. She was there, scarcely visible in the dark, crouching over a little fire which Ellen had lighted. It was very well-meant on Ellen's part, but the wood was damp, and the coals black, and I think it made the place look almost more wretched. *She* sat holding out her thin hands to it. The tea was on the table, and after I went in Ellen brought the candles. We did not say anything to each other. After a while she gave me some tea and I took it. She seemed to try to speak two or three times. I waited for her to begin. I would not say a word; and we had been thus for a long time mournfully seated together before she at last broke the silence. "Mary," she said, and then paused. I suppose it was because I was younger than she that I had more command of myself, and felt able to observe every little movement she made and every tone. I was so curious about her—anxious, I could not tell why, as to what she would do and say.

'Mary," she repeated, "we have never been very

good friends, you and I; I don't know why this has been. I have not wished it—but we have not been very good friends."

"No."

"No; that is all you say? Could we not do any better now? When I came here first, I did not think I was doing you any wrong. I did not mean it as a wrong to you. Now we are two left alone in the world. I have no one, and you have no one. Could we not do any better! Mary, I think it would please *him*, perhaps, if we tried to be friends."

My heart was quite full. I could have thrown myself upon her, and kissed her. I could have killed her. I did not know what to do.

"We have never been enemies," I said.

"No. But friends—that is different. There never were two so lonely. If we stayed together we might get to be fond of each other, Mary; we might keep together out of the cold world. Two together are stronger than one alone. You don't know how cold the world is, you are so young. If we were to keep together we might stay—at home."

Some evil spirit moved me, I cannot tell how; it seemed to me that I had found her out, that it was this she wanted. I got up from my chair flaming with the momentary hot passion of grief. "If there is any money for me, and if you want that, you can have it," I cried, and tried to go away.

THE TWO MARYS

She gave a little moaning cry, as if I had struck her. "Oh, Mary, Mary!" she cried, with a wailing voice more of sorrow than of indignation; and then she put out her hand and caught my dress. I could not have got away if I had wished, and I did not wish it, for I was devoured by curiosity about what she would do and say. This curiosity was the beginning of interest, though I did not know it; it fascinated me to her. She caught my dress and drew me closer. She put her other hand on mine, and drew me down to her, so that my face approached hers. She put up her white cheek, her eyes all hollowed out with crying, to mine: "Mary," she said, in a heartrending tone, "do not go away from me. I have nobody but you in the world." Then she paused. "I am going to have a baby," she said all at once, with a low, sharp cry.

I was confounded. I do not know what I said or did. Shame, wonder, pity, emotion—all mingled in me. I was very young, younger in heart than I was in years; and to have such a thing told to me overwhelmed me with shame and awe. It was so wonderful, so mysterious, so terrible. I dropped on my knees beside her, and covered my face with my hands, and cried. I could not resist any longer, or shut myself up. We cried together, clinging to each other, weeping over our secret. *He* had not known. At the last, when she was aware herself, she would not tell

THE TWO MARYS

him to add to his pains. "He will know in heaven, Mary," she said, winding her arms round me, weeping on my shoulder, shaking me, frail support as I was, with her sobs. This was how the other Mary and I became one. We were not without comfort as we crept upstairs, with our pale faces. She went with me to my room; she would not let me go. I had to hold her hand even when we went to sleep. "Do not leave me, Mary; stay with me, Mary," she moaned, whenever I stirred. And we slept by snatches, in our weariness; slept and woke to sob, and then slept again.

CHAPTER IV

THIS union, following so close upon our complete severance from each other, astonished everybody. We frightened Ellen. When she came to call me next morning, and saw the other sleeping by me, she thought it was witchcraft; but I did not mind that. I rose, and dressed very quietly, not to wake *her*. She was sleeping deeply at last, the sleep of exhaustion. During all papa's illness she had not rested at all, and at last sorrow and watching had worn her out. But I need not go over at length everything that happened. We told kind Mrs Tufnell and Mrs Stephens, our nearest neighbours; and I believe they told it to many in the parish; but Mary and I neither knew nor heard what went on out of our house. I had got to call her Mary, as he did; I liked it now—it no longer seemed to interfere with me. I thought my voice sounded round and soft like his when I said her name: Mary. It is a pleasant name to say, though it is my own. I got to admire it, being hers—I, who had hated her for being so called. But all that was changed now.

I do not quite know how our business was settled, for I know nothing about business. This

THE TWO MARYS

I know, that she managed it all herself, as she had said; she would not let Spicer have anything to do with it. She wrote about the money to an old friend of papa's, and got it invested and all settled. Half was for her and half for me. It brought us in about £85 a year. We settled to let the first floor, two rooms furnished as a sitting-room and bed-room, which would pay our rent; and we got three or four little pupils, who came every day, and whom we taught. Everything was very closely calculated, but we decided that we could manage it. We had never been used to be rich, neither one nor the other: and though when all was well I had dreamed of going away among strangers, yet now I could not help chiming in with that desperate desire of hers to avoid separation and remain together. She used to tell me stories of how she had been when she was a governess. How she had lived upstairs in a schoolroom alone in the midst of a great houseful of people; how when she came downstairs she was in the society without belonging to it; and how when any one in the family was kind to her they got into trouble. What she said was quite vague, but it was not comfortable; and by degrees my dreams and ideas were modified by her experience. But I could not be cured of my follies all in a moment, even by grief. After a while I began to dream again; and now my dreams were of my high estate being discovered somehow when

THE TWO MARYS

I was seated lonely in that schoolroom, trying to get through the weary evening. I used to make a picture to myself of how the lady of the house would come penitent and ashamed, and make a hundred apologies; and how I would say to her, that though her other governesses might not turn out to be Lady Marys, yet did not she think it would be best to be kind and make friends of them? Lady Mary! I clung to my absurdity, though I began to be old enough to see how ridiculous it was. How could I ever turn out to be anybody now—now that papa was gone? But when a girl is but sixteen there are often a great many follies in her head which she would be deeply ashamed of if any one knew them, but which please her in secret as she dreams over them.

My life was altogether changed by papa's death. It is dreadful to say so, but it was not changed for the worse. Perhaps I had been happier in the old days before Mary was ever heard of, when he and I used to sit together, not talking much, and walk together, thinking our own thoughts—together yet without much intercourse. I had been quite content then, having enough to amuse me in my own fancies, as he, I supposed, had in his. But now I began to be able to understand why he had wearied for real companionship, now that I knew what real companionship was. We lived together, Mary and I, in a different way.

THE TWO MARYS

We talked over everything together; the smallest matter that occurred, we discussed it, she and I. She had the art of working everything that happened, into our life, so that the smallest incident was of importance. Even in those very first days, though her heart was broken, she soothed me. "Mary," she said, with her lips trembling, "we cannot be always crying; we must think of something else whenever we can; we must *try* to think of other things. God help us; we must live, we cannot die." And then she would break down; and then dry her eyes, and talk of something, of anything. When we got our little pupils, that was a relief. She went into her work with all her heart. Her attention never seemed to wander from the business, as mine constantly did. We had four little girls; they came for two hours in the morning and two in the afternoon. When they went away we had our walk. In the evening we did our needlework, and she made me read aloud, or sometimes play, and she taught me to sing. We used to stop and cry at every second bar when we began, but by degrees that hysterical feeling passed off. I was never away from her. I had constant companionship, communion,—talk that kept me interested and even amused. I got to be—I am almost ashamed to confess it—happier than I had been for a long time, perhaps than I had ever been in my life.

We had lived like this for about three months,

THE TWO MARYS

and had got used to it, when something came to make a little change. Mary and I rarely spoke of our secret. It seemed to be my secret as well as hers, and I tried all I could to take care of her, with a secret awe which I never expressed. I could not have spoken of it; I should have been ashamed; but the mysterious sense of what was coming was always in my mind. The needlework which we used to do in the evenings filled me with strange feelings. I never dared ask what this or that was for. I was afraid and abashed at the very sight of the little things when they happened to be spread out and showed their form. It was making them which made me a good needlewoman: perhaps you will think that is of no great importance in these days of sewing-machines; but oh, to have let a sewing-machine, or even a stranger's hand touch those dearest little scraps of linen and muslin! Nothing but the finest work, the daintiest little stitches, would do for them. I used to kiss them sometimes in my awe, but I would not have asked questions for the world. This is a digression, however; for what I was going to say had nothing to do either with our work or our secret. All this time we had not let our first floor —and it was with great satisfaction in her looks that Mrs Stephens came in one day and told us that she had heard of a lodger for us. " He is a gentleman, my dears," she said, "*quite* a gentleman, and therefore you may be sure he will give

THE TWO MARYS

no trouble that he can help. He is an engineer, and has something to do, I believe, about the new railway; otherwise he lives at home somewhere about Hyde Park, and moves in the very best society. When I say an 'engineer,' I mean a 'civil' one, you know, which is, I am told, quite the profession of a gentleman. He will want the rooms for six months, or perhaps more. His name is Durham; he is cousin to the Pophams, great friends of mine, and if the lodgings suit him he would like to come in at once."

Mary had given a little start, I could not tell why. There seemed no reason for it. Her work had fallen out of her hands; but she picked it up again and went on. "His name is—— What did you say, Mrs Stephens?—a civil engineer?"

"Yes, my love, a civil engineer—Durham, his name is. He will come with me to-morrow, if you are agreeable, to see the rooms."

Mary made a visible pause. She looked at me as if she were consulting me; it was a curious, appealing sort of look. I looked back at her, but I could not understand her. What did I know about Mr Durham, the civil engineer? Mrs Stephens was not so observant as I was, and probably she never noticed this look. And then Mary said, "Very well. If they suit him, we ought to be very thankful. I should have preferred a lady——"

"My dear, a lady is a great deal more at home

than a man, and gives more trouble," said Mrs Stephens; "very different from a man who is out all day. And then, probably he will dine almost always at his West-end home."

The idea was funny, and I laughed. The notion of the West-end home amused me; but I could not help observing that Mary, who was always ready to sympathise with me, did not smile. Her head was bent over her work. She did not even say anything more on the subject, but let Mrs Stephens go on and make all the arrangements for coming next day. I thought of this after; and even at the time I noticed it, and with some surprise.

Next day, just as we were going out for our walk, Mary, who had been at the window, started back, and went hurriedly into the little room behind, which had once been papa's study. "Mary," she said, "there is Mrs Stephens and——her friend. Go with them, please, to see the rooms. I am not quite well: I would rather not appear."

"I am so stupid; I shall not know what to say," I began.

"You will do very well," said Mary, and disappeared and shut the door. I had no time to think more of this, for the stranger came in directly with Mrs Stephens; and in my shyness I blushed and stammered while I explained. "She is not very well," I said; "I am to show you. Will you please—sit down; will you come upstairs?"

THE TWO MARYS

"You will do very well," said Mrs Stephens, patting me on the shoulder. "This is Mr Durham, Mary, and I don't think he will eat any of us. It is a nice light, airy staircase," she said, as she went up, not to lose any opportunity of commending the house. "A capital staircase," said Mr Durham, with a cheery laugh. I had scarcely ventured to look at him yet, but somehow there was a feeling of satisfactoriness diffused through the air about him. I cannot explain quite what I mean, but I am sure others must have felt the same thing. Some people seem to make the very air pleasant: they give you a sense that all is well, that there is nothing but what is good and honest in the place where they are. This is what I felt now; and when we got upstairs I ventured to look at him. He was tall and strong and ruddy, not at all like any hero whom I had ever read of or imagined. There was nothing "interesting" about him. He looked "a good fellow," cheery, and smiling, and active, and kind. He settled at once about the rooms. He laughed out when Mrs Stephens said something about their homeliness. "They are as good as a palace," he said; "I don't see what a man could want more." The sitting-room was the room papa died in, and it cost me a little pang to see them walking about and looking at the furniture; but when people are poor they cannot indulge such feelings. We learn to say nothing about them, and perhaps that helps to subdue them. At all events, I made no show of what I was thinking, and it was all settled in a few minutes. He was to come in on Saturday, and Ellen was to work for him and wait upon him. I could not help thinking it would be pleasant to have him in the house.

And thus there commenced another period of my life, which I must speak of very briefly,— which indeed I do not care to speak of at all, but which I will think about as long as I live. I did not see very much of him at first. I was nearly seventeen now, and very shy; and Mary watched over me, and took great pains not to expose me to chance meetings with the stranger, or any unnecessary trouble. Ellen managed everything between us. She was a good, trustworthy woman, and we did not require to interfere; she was full of praises of Mr Durham, who never gave any trouble he could help. But one night, when I was taking tea with Mrs Stephens, he happened to come in, and we had the pleasantest evening. He knew a song I had just learned, and sang a second to it in the most delightful deep voice. He talked and rattled about everything. He made Mrs Stephens laugh and he made me laugh, and he told us his adventures abroad till we were nearly crying. When it was time for me to go he got up too, and said he would go with me. "Oh, it is only next door; I can go alone," I said, in my shyness. "It is only next door, but I live there too, and I am going to work now," he said. "To work! when all the rest of the world are going to bed?" said Mrs Stephens; "you will make yourself ill." How he laughed at that! his laugh sounded like a cheery trumpet. He did not mean to kill himself with work. "But I hope you will let me come to tea again," he said. How pleased Mrs Stephens was! She always says she likes young people, and we had spent such a pleasant night.

Many more of these pleasant evenings followed. Sometimes when we were sitting quiet after tea, she would send for me suddenly; sometimes she would write a little note in the afternoon. This expectation filled my life with something quite new. I had never had many invitations or pleasures before: I had never expected them. When we sat down to work after tea I had known that it was for the whole evening, and that no pleasant interruption would disturb us. But now a little thrill of excitement ran through my whole life. I wondered, would a note come in the afternoon? If it did not come, I wondered whether the bell would ring after tea, and Ellen come in saying, "If you please, ma'am, Mrs Stephens's compliments, and would Miss Mary go in, and take her music?" Mary never interfered; never said "Don't go." She looked at me sometimes very wistfully; sometimes she smiled and shook her head at me, and said I was getting dissipated.

THE TWO MARYS

Once or twice she looked anxious, and told me a story, which I only half understood, of girls who met with people they liked, and were very happy, and then lost sight of them ever after. Mary was very clever at telling stories, and I was fond of listening; but she did it so well and delicately that I fear I never thought of the moral—never, at least, till all the harm was done and it was too late.

I would not have any one think, however, that Mr Durham either meant or did any harm. To say so would be very wrong. It was as imperceptible with him as with me. He went quite innocently, as I did, to cheer up Mrs Stephens, and because an evening's chatter with a little music was pleasant; and by degrees we thought less and less of Mrs Stephens and more and more of each other. If any one meant anything beyond this, it was she who was the guilty person. She would nod off to sleep in her easy-chair while we were talking. She would say, with a sleepy smile, "Don't mind me, my dears. The light is a little strong for my eyes. That is why I close them—but I like the sound of your voices even when I don't hear what you say." Alas, if she had heard everything that had been said it might have been better. After a while he began to say strange things to me while she had her doze. He talked about his family to me. He said he hoped I should know them some day. He said his mother was very kind and wise—"a wise woman." These were the very words he used. And then he said——other things; but that was not till the very, very last.

One morning we met in the little hall. It was raining, and it was a holiday, and when he insisted on following me into the schoolroom, what could I do—I could not shut him out. He seemed to fill the whole room, and make it warm and bright. I do not think we had ever been quite alone before. He came to the window and stood there looking out upon the bare bit of smoky grass and the water-butt. And then all at once he came to me and took my hand. "If I had a nice little house out in the country, with flowers and trees about it, a bright little house—Mary—would you come and be my little wife, and take care of it and me?"

Oh, what a thing to have said to you, all at once, without warning, in the heart of your own dull little life, when you thought you were to work, and pinch, and put up with things, for ever! It was different from my old fancy. But how poor a thing to have been found out to be Lady Mary in comparison with this! What I said is neither here nor there. We stood together in the little old study, among the forms where we had our little scholars, as if we had been in a fairy palace. I was not seventeen. I had no experience. I thought of nothing but him, and what he said. It was not my part to think of his father and mother, and what he would do, and what he wouldn't do. He was a great deal older than I was; about thirty, I believe. Of course, I thought of nothing but him.

"Do you know," he said, after a long time, "I have never seen your stepmother, Mary? I have been three months in the house, and I have never seen her. I must go and see her now."

"Oh, wait a little," I said; "wait a day. Let us have a secret all to ourselves one day." How foolish I was!—but how was I to know?

He consented after a while; and then he made me promise to bring her out at a certain hour in the afternoon, that he might meet us at the door and see her. I made all the arrangements for this with a light heart. Though it was very difficult to hide from her what had happened, I did so with a great effort. I persuaded her to come out earlier than usual. She did not resist me. She was kinder, more tender, than I had ever known. She began to say something of a story she had to tell me as we went out. I went first and opened the door, and stood aside on the white steps to let her go out. Her crape veil was thrown back. Though she was still pale, there was a tint of life upon her cheeks. She was more like herself in her refined, delicate beauty, more like a lily, my favourite image of her, than she had been for ever so long.

I had begun to smile to myself at the success of

THE TWO MARYS

our trick, when suddenly I got frightened, I could scarcely tell how. Looking up, I saw him standing on the pavement gazing at her, confounded. I can use no other word. He looked bewildered, confused, half wild with amazement. As for Mary, she had stopped short on the step. She was taken strangely by surprise too; for the first moment she only gazed as he did. Then she dropped her veil, and stepped back into the house. "I have forgotten something," she said; and turned round and went upstairs to her room. He came in, too, and went upstairs after her, passing without looking at me. His under lip seemed to have dropped; his cheerful face had lost all its animation; his eyes had a wild, bewildered stare in them. What did it mean? oh! what did it mean?

I did not know what to do. I wondered if he had followed her to speak to her, or what was the meaning of those strange looks. I lingered in the hall holding the handle of the door, feeling miserable, but not knowing why. In two or three minutes she came downstairs. "I had forgotten my handkerchief," she said; and we went out together as if nothing had happened. But something had happened, that was certain, She did not talk very much that day. When we were coming home she said to me, quite suddenly, 'Was it your doing, Mary, that I met Mr Durham at the door?"

"He said it was so strange he had never seen you," I said.

"Yes: but you should have known I would not do that for nothing. You should not have been the one to betray me, Mary. I knew Mr Durham once. He is associated with one of the most painful portions of my life."

"Oh, Mary dear! I did not know——"

"You did not know, and I did not want you to find out; but never mind, it is done. It need not, I hope, do any harm to you."

That was a very strange day: the excitement of the morning, and then the other excitement; and to feel that I had a secret from her, and that he was seated upstairs giving no sign, taking no notice of our existence all day long. I was so agitated and disturbed that I did not know what to do. At last I settled myself in the schoolroom to do some translations. When one has been looking for a long time for a holiday, and something happens to spoil the holiday when it comes, it is worse even than if that something had happened on an ordinary day. I think Mary was glad to be left to herself, for instead of our ordinary companionship, she sat in the parlour at work all the long afternoon, and I in the schoolroom. One of the doors was half opened between us. She could hear my pen scratching on the paper, and the rustling of the leaves of my dictionary—and I could hear her moving softly over her work. It was autumn by this time, and the days were growing short, and neither of us cared to ring for tea; and I think Ellen was cooking dinner for Mr Durham and forgot us at the usual hour. We still sat as we had been all the afternoon when the twilight came on. I laid down my pen, having no light to write by, when I heard some one knock softly at the parlour door.

Mary made no reply. She sat quite still, never stirring. The knock came again; then I, too, put my paper away from me and listened. The door opened, and some one came into the parlour. How well I knew who it was! I listened now so intently that nothing escaped me. How could it be wrong? He must have come to talk to her of me.

"Mary!" he said. I rose up softly in my excitement, thinking it was me he was calling; but before I could move further a strange consciousness came over me that it was not me he meant. The old feeling with which I had heard my father call Mary came into my very soul—but worse, a hundred times worse. Oh, had he too another Mary besides me?

"Mary!" he said, breathless, and then paused. "How has all this come about? Why do I find you here? What does it mean? There are many explanations which I have a right to ask. You disappear from me—sent away—I know not how; and then—not to count the years that have passed

—after these three months, in which you must have known me, I find you by chance——"

She knew that I was within hearing, and that whatever she said to him must be to me too. If that was a restraint upon her, I cannot tell. I felt sorry for her vaguely in my mind; but yet I did not move.

"I did not wish you to find me at all," she said, very low. "Mr Durham, there is and can be nothing between you and me."

"Nothing!" he said; "what do you mean, Mary? Why, there is all the past between us—a hundred things that cannot be undone by anything in the future. You know how many things there are connected with you which are a mystery to me —things not affecting you alone, but others. How you went away, for instance; and what became of you, and how much my mother had to do with it? You must have known the moment I found you that all these questions remained to be asked."

"All these questions," she said, "are made quite unimportant by two things. First, that I am the wife, though now the widow, of a man I loved dearly—and that you have begun to love, begun to think of, some one very different from me."

"Ah!" he said, with a strange brief utterance of distress. Whether he was grieved to think of the wrong he was doing me, or whether the strange position he stood in troubled him, I cannot tell; but there was pain in the cry he gave—"ah!"

THE TWO MARYS

with a little shiver. "You have abundance of power to pain me," he said, very low, "but it seems strange you should upbraid me. Yes, I have begun to think of some one else; but that does not prevent me from being deeply startled, deeply moved, by the sight of you."

There was a little silence then, and I came to myself slowly. I woke as it were out of a trance. She knew I was there, but he did not. I had no right to hear his secrets without warning him. I tried to get up, but could not at first. I felt stiff and weary, as if I had been travelling for days together. I could scarcely drag myself up from my chair. The sound I made in rising might have warned him, but I do not think he heard. Before I could drag myself to the door and show I was there, he had begun again.

"Mary," he said, lingering upon the name as if he loved it, "this is not a time for recrimination. Tell me how you left Chester Street, and what my mother had to do with it? and then, if you choose, I will never see you again."

"Is it for your mother, or for me?"

I did not hear the answer. I could not stay longer. I got to the door somehow, and threw it open. I was too much bewildered to know what I was doing, or to think. I came out with a little rush as feeble creatures do. "I want to get away. I want to go out. I cannot stay there all day and hear you talking," I said. I was not addressing either her or him. The sound of my voice must have been very piteous, for I remember it even now.

"Mary!" he cried.

Oh, what a difference in the sound! This time his voice was startled, pained, almost harsh, with a kind of reproof in it: not as he said Mary to her. Oh, papa, papa! it was you first who taught me the difference. I gave a hoarse little cry. I could not speak. Millions of words seemed to rush to my lips, but I could not say any of them. "I have been here long enough," I managed to stammer out. "Let me go—let me go!" Next moment I was in the dark, in the silence, in my own little room, kneeling down by the bedside, crying and moaning to myself. I did not know why. I had heard nothing wrong; but it seemed to me that all my life was over, and that it did not matter what came next.

And, indeed, I cannot tell what came next. She came up to me, and told me the whole story, and in a vague sort of way I understood it. She was not to blame. He had been fond of her (everybody was fond of her) when she was the governess in his mother's house; and it had been found out, and his mother was harsh, and she had gone suddenly away. There was nothing in this which need have made me unhappy, perhaps—so people have said to me since—but then I was very young; and I had been happy—and now I was miserable. I listened to her, and made no answer, but only moaned. The night passed, I cannot tell how. I did not sleep till late in the morning; and then I fell asleep and did not wake till noon. Then what was the use of going downstairs? I stayed in my room, feeling so weary, so worn out. It was Saturday, a half-holiday, and there was nothing to do. She came to me and spoke to me again and again; but I gave her very little answer. And he took no notice—he sent no message, no letter—not a word of explanation. He never asked my pardon. In my misery I thought I heard voices all the day as if they were talking, talking—and he never sent a message or note or anything to me. And then, after a long talk, as I fancied, with him, she would come to me. "Mary, this must not be. You must get up. You must be like yourself. Neither Mr Durham nor I have done you any wrong, Mary."

"Oh, don't call me Mary!" I said; "call me some other name. If you knew how different it sounds when it is said to you, not to me."

And then she would look at me with her eyes full of tears, and sit down by me, and say no more. And so passed this bitter day.

CHAPTER V

NEXT day was Sunday. When I woke up, early, I recollected all that had happened with a flush of overwhelming shame. How childishly, how foolishly I had behaved. I was very, very wretched; but I was ashamed, and pride got the upper hand. I dressed myself carefully, and went downstairs, resolved not to show my misery at least, to be proud and forget it. "If he does not care for me," I said to myself, "I will not care for him." I passed his room very softly that I might not wake him. There was early morning service in St Mark's now, for the curate who had succeeded poor papa was very High Church. I stole out and went to this early service, and tried to be good, and to give myself up to God's will. Yes, it must have been God's will—though how it could ever be God's will that anybody should be false, or unkind, or cruel, I could not tell. I know it is right, however, whatever happens that vexes you, to accept it as if it must be the will of God. I tried to do that, and I was not quite so miserable when I went home. Ellen opened the door to me, looking frightened. "I thought you was lost, too, Miss," she said. "I have been to church," I answered, scarcely noticing her words. Breakfast was laid in the little parlour. It was very, very tidy, dreadfully tidy — everything was cleared away—the basket with the work and all the little things, and every stray thread and remnant. All of a sudden it occurred to me how little I had been doing to help of late. Instead of working I had been spending the evenings with Mrs Stephens. I did not even know how far the "things" were advanced, and it seemed strange they should all be gone. Of course it was because of Sunday. After a while Ellen brought in the coffee. She had still the same frightened look. "Missis wasn't with you at the early service, Miss Mary?" "Oh, no," I said, surprised at the question; "perhaps she is not up."

"She's never lain down all night," said Ellen; "she was worrited and worn off her legs going up and down to you yesterday, Miss—you that was quite well, and had no call to your bed. She was a deal more like it, the dear. She's never lain in her bed this blessed night, and I can't find her, high or low."

I scarcely waited to hear this out, but rushed up to her room. The bed had not been touched since yesterday. A little prayer-book lay on it, as if she had been praying. The room was in perfect good order—no litter about it. The little "things" were not to be seen. One of her dresses hanging against the wall made me think for a moment she was there, but it was only an old dress, and everything else was gone. Oh the terror and the pain and the wonder of that discovery! I could not believe it. I rushed through all the house, every room, calling her. Mr Durham heard me, and came out to the door of his room and spoke to me as I passed, and tried to take my hand, but I snatched it away from him. I did not even think of him. I can just remember the look he had, half-ashamed, appealing with his eyes, a little abashed and strange. I scarcely saw him at the time—but I remember him now, and with good reason, for I have never seen him again.

And I have never seen Mary again from that day. Mrs Stephens came in to me, startled by the news her servants had carried her; and she told me she had heard a carriage drive off late on the previous night, but did not think it was from our door. She knew nothing. She cried, but I could not cry; and it was Sunday, and nothing could be done—nothing! even if I had known what to do. I rushed to Spicer's, and then I was sorry I had gone, for such people as they are never understand, and they thought, and think to this day, that there was something disgraceful in it. I rushed to Mrs Tufnell, not expecting to find her, for now it was time for church. The bells had done ringing, and I had already met, as I walked wildly along, almost all the people I knew. One woman stopped me and asked if Mrs Peveril was taken ill, and if she should go to her. "Poor thing, poor thing!" this good woman said. Oh, she might well pity us—both of us! But to my surprise Mrs Tufnell was at home. She almost looked as if she expected me. She looked agitated and excited, as if she knew. Did she know? I have asked her on my knees a hundred times, but she has always shaken her head. "How should I know?" she has said, and cried. I have thought it over and over for days and for years, till my brain has whirled. But I think she does know—I think some time or other she will tell me. It is a long time ago, and my feelings have got a little dulled; but I think some time or other I must find it out.

This wonderful event made a great change in my life. I began at once, that very day, to live with Mrs Tufnell in the Square. She would not let me go home. She kissed me, and said I was to stay with her now. Mr Durham came twice and asked to see me; but I could not bear to see him. Then Mrs Stephens came with a letter. He said in it that I must dispose of him; that he was in my hands, and would do whatever I pleased; that he had been startled more than he could say by the sudden sight of one whom he had loved before he knew me; but that if I could forgive him any foolish words he might have said, then he hoped we might be happy. In short, he was very honourable, ready to keep his word; and I felt as if I hated him for his virtue—for treating me "honourably!" Was that what all his love and all my happiness had come to? I sent him a very short little note back, and it was all over. He went abroad soon after, and I have never heard of him any more.

And thus my story ended at seventeen. I wonder if there are many lives with one exciting chapter in them, ending at seventeen, and then years upon years of monotonous life. I am twenty-three now. I live with Mrs Tufnell. I am daily governess to one little girl, and I have my forty pounds a-year, the interest of poor papa's insurance money. I am very well off indeed, and some people think I need not care to take a pupil at all—better off, a great deal, than I was in Southampton Street; but how different! I heard very soon after that Mary had a little boy. It was in the papers, but without any address; and I had one letter from her, saying that we had made a mistake in trying to live together, and that she was sorry. She hoped I would forgive her if she had been mistaken, and she would always think of me and love me. Love me? Is it like love to go away and leave me alone? Two people have said they loved me in my life, and that is what both have done.

However, after that letter I could not do anything more. If she thought it was a mistake for us to live together, of course it was a mistake. And I had my pride too. "I always felt it was a doubtful experiment," Mrs Tufnell said when people wondered, "and it did not answer—that was all." And this is how it was settled and ended—ended, I suppose, for ever. Mrs Tufnell is very good to me, and as long as she lives I am sure of a home. Perhaps I may tell you her story one of these days; for she has a story, like most people. She tells me I am still very young, and may yet have a life of my own; but in the meantime the most I can do is to take an interest in other people's lives.

CHAPTER VI

I HAD not intended to carry on any further a history which is chiefly about myself; but events are always occurring which change one's mind from day to day, and alter one's most fixed resolutions. I do not pretend to understand people who make unchangeable decisions, and certainly I am not one of them. Besides, common fairness requires that I should allow Mrs Peveril to have the same privilege as myself, and tell things her own way. I could not have imagined, had I not seen it, the difference there was between the aspect of things to her and to me. I suppose it is true after all that everybody has his or her own point of view, which is different from all others. Of course we realise this fact quite clearly in a great poem like "The Ring and the Book;" but to recognise it in one's own small affairs has somehow a much stranger, more surprising effect. What an odd difference it would make in the world if we could all see ourselves now and then with other people's eyes! I confess that the girl in her story, who was Mr Peveril's daughter, is very much unlike the girl in mine—and yet the same somehow, as may be traced out with a little trouble. This is humbling, but it is for one's good, I suppose. When you look at yourself in a mirror, you have so much interest in yourself that your defects don't strike you—you can't help being the first figure—the most important; but to feel that all along you are not important at all—anything but the first figure, a mere shadow, scarcely noticed! it has a very odd effect—sometimes laughable, sometimes rather the reverse; but this was what now happened to me.

I must add, however, that a long time passed over before I could even think that Mrs Peveril might have something to say on her side. It was not because of the rupture between Mr Durham and myself, and the sudden conclusion of that dream and all that it seemed likely to bring with it. No doubt these things embittered all my feelings about her; but yet I was reasonable enough to come to see that it was not her fault—that she had kept out of the way with all her might—and that after all she could not foresee that another complication might arise between him and me. She could not of course foresee this; and even if she had foreseen it, what could she have done? I think it shows I was not unfair in my judgment, for a girl of seventeen, to say that I soon came to see that. But though I did not blame her, of course I was embittered against her, and took refuge in being very angry with her on other grounds. That she should have said our living together was a mistake was the chief of these. Why was it a mistake? Did she mean to say it was my fault? If it was simply her fault, as I felt sure it was, why did she call it a mistake? Why not say plainly out, "I was wrong, and so we got into trouble"? How easy it seems to be for people to acknowledge themselves in the wrong! but not so easy for one's self, somehow. I never met anybody who liked doing it, though I have met with so many who ought to have done it, and to whom it would have been so simple—so easy, I thought; but that never seemed to be their opinion. Mrs Tufnell, who is in some things a very odd old lady, says it never is anybody's fault. "There was never any quarrel yet," she will say, "but there were two in it—there was never any misunderstanding but two were in it. There is no such thing as absolute blame on the one side and innocence on the other. Even in your affairs, Mary, my dear——" But this I never can see nor allow. How could I be to blame? Only seventeen, and knowing so little of the world, and expecting everybody to be good and true, and say just what they thought. When a man said he was fond of me, how was I to put up with his having been fond of somebody else? And when a woman professed to be thinking of me, was it natural that I could be pleased to know she had been thinking of herself? I could not help behaving just as I did. It was the only

THE TWO MARYS

natural, the only possible way; but for them, they ought to have known better, they ought to have thought of me. On the whole that is the thing that hurts one—that goes to one's heart. People think of themselves first—when they ought to be thinking of you, they think of themselves first. I suppose it is the same all over the world.

The way in which I first heard Mary's story was simple enough. After years of a dull sort of quiet life at Mrs Tufnell's—who was very good to me, and very kind, but who, of course, could give to me, a girl, only what she, an old woman, had to give — the quietest life, without excitement or change of any kind—she had a bad illness. It was not an illness of the violent kind, but of what, I suppose, is more dangerous to an old woman, a languishing, slow sickness, which looked like decay more than disease. The doctors said "breaking up of the constitution," or at least the servants said so, who are less particular than the doctors, and shook their heads and looked very serious. I was less easily alarmed than anyone else, for it seemed to me a natural thing that an old lady should be gently ill like that, one day a little better and the next a little worse, without any suffering to speak of. It was not until after she was better that I knew there had been real danger, but she must have felt it herself. The way in which her sense of her precarious condition showed itself was anxiety for me. I remember one evening sitting in her room by the fire with a book; she was in bed, and I had been reading to her, and now she was dozing, or at least I thought so. Things appear (it is evident) very differently to different people. I was extremely comfortable in that nice low easy-chair by the fire. It was a pretty room, full of pictures and portraits of her friends, so full that there was scarcely an inch of the wall uncovered. The atmosphere was warm and soft, and the tranquil repose and ease of the old lady in the bed somehow seemed to increase the warmth and softness and kindly feeling. She was an additional luxury to me sitting there by the fire with my novel. If any fairy had proposed to place her by my side as young and as strong as myself, I should have rejected the proposal with scorn. I liked her a great deal best so—old, a little sick, kind, comfortable, dozing in her bed. Her very illness—which I thought quite slight, rather an excuse for staying in this cosy room and being nursed than anything else—heightened my sense of comfort. She was not dozing, as it happened, but lying very still, thinking of dying—wondering how it would feel, and planning for those she should leave behind her. I knew nothing of these thoughts, no more than if I had been a thousand miles away: and fortunately neither did she of mine. I was roused from my comfortable condition by the sound of her voice calling me. I rose up half reluctantly from the bright fire, and the little table with the lamp and my book, and went and sat by her in the shade where I could not see the fire; but still the sentiment of comfort was predominant in me. I gave my old lady her mixture, which it was time for her to take, and advised her to go to sleep.

"You must not doze this time," I said; "you must go right off to sleep, and never wake till morning. Everything is put right for the night, and I shall not go till you are asleep."

"I was not dozing," she said, with that natural resentment which everybody feels to be so accused; and then, after a moment, "Mary, I was thinking of you. If I were to die, what would you do?"

I was very much shocked, and rather frightened; but when I looked at her, and saw by the dim light that she did not look any worse, I felt rather angry. "How unkind of you!" I said, "to speak so! You frightened me at first. What would it matter what became of me?"

"It would matter a great deal," she said. "It would make everything so much worse. I don't want to die, Mary, though I daresay I should be a great deal better off, and get rid of all my troubles——"

"Oh, it is wicked to talk so!"

"Why should it be wicked? I can't help thinking of it," she said, lying in her warm cosy bed. It made me shiver to hear her. I began to cry, rather with a chill, wretched sense of discomfort in the midst of all the warmth than anything else; upon which she put her hand on my shoulder and gave me a little shake, and laughed at me softly. "Silly child!" she said—but she was not angry. There was a very grave look on her face behind the smile. Dying was strange to her as well as to me, though she was very old.

"But, Mary," she went on, "I want to read you something. I want you to think again about some one you once were very fond of. I have some news of Mrs Peveril——"

"Oh!" I said; and then I went on stiffly, "I hope she is well."

"She is quite well—and—your little brother. I wish you would see them. All that happened was so long ago; I think you might see them, Mary."

"I never made any objection to seeing them," I said, more and more stiffly, though my heart began to leap and thump against my breast. "You forget I had nothing to do with it. It was she who went away. She said it was a mistake."

"You are an unforgiving child. You did not try to enter into her feelings, Mary."

"How could I?" I said. "Did she wish me to enter into her feelings? Did she ever give me a chance? She said it was a mistake. What was there left for me to say?"

"Well, well," said the old lady, "I don't defend her. I always said she was wrong; but still I have been hearing from her lately, Mary. I have three or four letters which I should like you to read——"

"You have been hearing from her without ever telling me!"

"Bless the child! must I not even get a letter without consulting her? But, Mary, I am a free agent still, and I can't be kept in such order," she said, half laughing. "Give me that blotting-book, and my keys, and my spectacles, and bring the lamp a little closer."

Indignant as I was, I was comforted by all these preparations. And when she had put on her spectacles and opened the blotting-book, sitting up in bed, my mind was so much relieved that my indignation floated away. "It is a pretty thing for you to talk of dying, and frighten people," I said, giving her a kiss, "with your cheeks like two nice old roses." She shook her head, but she smiled too: she felt better, and got better gradually from that hour.

But in the meantime I had to listen to these letters. Perhaps if it had not been that my old lady was ill, I should have been offended to find that she had deceived me, and had known about Mary all along. It was a deception, though she did not mean any harm. "She had thought it best," she said, "to let time soften all our feelings, before she told me anything about it." However, I must not enter into all the discussions we had

THE TWO MARYS

on this subject. It is only fair that Mary should have her turn, and tell her story as I have told mine. It is not a connected story like mine, but you will see from it what kind of a life hers had been, and what sort of a woman she was. She is different from the Mary I thought—and yet not different either—just as I am different from the girl I thought I was, and yet very like too, if you look into it. I cannot tell what my feelings were as I read first one bit and then another, and a great deal more which I do not think it necessary to quote here. One moment I was furious with her—the next I could have kissed her feet. These people who send you from one extreme of feeling to another, who do wrong things and right things all in a jumble, take a greater hold upon you, somehow, than better people do, who are placid and always on the same level—at least I think so. I started by calling her Mrs Peveril—and here I am already saying Mary, as of old, without knowing! And Mrs Tufnell wishes me to go and see her. She has even made me promise as a kind of reward to herself for getting better. Since she takes it in this way, I shall have to go—and sometimes I fear it, and sometimes I wish for it. Will it make any difference to me? Will the old love come back, or the still older feeling that was not love? Shall I think of that "Mary" that sounded always so much sweeter to her than to me? Or shall I remember only the time when she was everything to me—when she charmed me out of my grief and loneliness, and told me her secret, and made me her companion, and was all mine? I do not know. I begin to tremble, and my heart beats when I think of this meeting; but in the meantime Mary has a right to her turn, and to tell the story her own way. It is all in little bits taken from Mrs Tufnell's letters, and sometimes may appear a little fragmentary; but I can only give it as it came to me.

II. HER STORY

CHAPTER VII

WHEN I went to be governess at Mrs Durham's I was quite young. I had been "out" before, but only as nursery governess. Mine was not a very regular or, perhaps, a very good kind of education. My mother had been a governess before me, and not one of very high pretensions, as governesses are nowadays. I don't think she ever knew anything herself, except a little music and a little French, which she had forgotten before my time. How my father and she met, and, still more wonderful, how they took to each other, is a thing I never could make out. Perhaps I was most fond of her, but certainly I was most proud of him, and liked to copy his ways, and to believe what my mother often said—that I was a Martindale every inch of me. This, poor soul, she meant as a reproach, but to me it sounded like a compliment. I was very silly and rather cruel, as young people are so often. My father had a great deal of contempt for her, and not much affection; and though I had a great deal of affection, I borrowed unconsciously his contempt, and thought myself justified in treating her as he did. She was wordy and weak in argument, and never knew when to stop. But he—when he had stated what he intended to do—would never answer any of her objections, or indeed take any notice of them, but listened to her with a contemptuous silence. I took to doing the same; and though I know better now, and am sorry I ever could have been so foolish and so unkind, yet the habit remains with me—not to take the trouble to reply to foolish arguments, but to do what I think right without saying anything about it. This habit, I may as well confess, has got me into trouble more than once; but I do not say that I am prepared to give it up, though I know I have taken harm by it, and no good, so far as I am aware.

We were very poor, and I had been a nursery governess and a daily governess when I was little more than a child. When my poor mother died a little money came, and then I got a few lessons to improve me in one or two different accomplishments; and then I took Mrs Durham's situation. My father was one of the wandering men who live a great deal abroad; and I had learned French and enough German to make a show, in the best way, by practice rather than by book. "French acquired abroad"—that was what was put for me in the advertisement, and this I think was my principal recommendation to Mrs Durham. Her eldest son was at home at the time—a young man

THE TWO MARYS

just a little older than myself. She was a kind woman, and unsuspicious. She thought George only a boy, and perhaps about me she never thought at all—in connection with him, at least. I used to be encouraged at first to make him talk French, and great was the amusement in the school-room over his pronunciation and his mistakes. They were all very kind when I come to think of it. They were as fearless and trustful with me as if I had belonged to them. And then by degrees I found out that George had fallen in love with me. I think I may say quite certainly that I never was in love with him, but I was a little excited and pleased, as one always is, you know, when that happens for the first time. It is so odd —so pleasant to feel that you have that power. It seems so kind of the man—one thinks so when one is young—and it is amusing and flattering, and a thing which occupies your mind, and gives you something agreeable to think of. I do not say this is the right way of thinking on such a subject, but it is how a great many girls feel, and I was one of them. I had never thought seriously of it at all. It seemed so much more like fun than anything else ; and then it is always pleasant to have people fond of you. I liked it ; and I am afraid I never thought of what it might come to, and did not take up any lofty ground, but let him talk, and let him follow me about, and steal out after me, and waylay me in the passages. I did this without thinking, and more than half for the amusement of it. I liked him, and I liked the place he took up in my life, and the things he said, without really responding to his feelings at all.

When it was found out, and there was a disturbance in the house about it, I came to my senses all at once, with such a hot flush of pain and shame that I seem to feel it yet. They had been so kind to me, that I had never felt my dependence; but now, all in a moment I found it out. His mother was frightened to death lest he should marry me! She thought me quite beneath him; me—a Martindale all over — a gentleman's daughter — much better than she was! This roused a perfect tempest in me. It was my pride that was outraged, not my feelings; but that pride was strong enough and warm enough to be called a passion. I did what I could to show his mother that nothing in the world could be more indifferent to me than he was, but she would not be convinced; and at last I determined to do what my father often had done when my mother was unreasonable—to withdraw out of the discussion at once and summarily, without leaving any opportunity for further talk. My father was living then. He was at Spa, which was not very difficult to reach. One evening, after Mrs Durham had been talking to me (George had been sent away, but I was not sent away because they were sorry for me), I stayed in the school-room till they were all at dinner, and then I carried all my

THE TWO MARYS

things, which I had made up into bundles, down to the hall with my own hands, and got a cab and went off to the railway station. I bought a common box on my way, and packed them all into it. I tell you this to show how determined I was; not even one of the servants knew how I had gone, or anything about me. It was winter, and the Durhams dined at half-past six; so I had time enough to get off by the night train to Dover. I had not a very large wardrobe, you may suppose, but I left nothing behind me but some old things. I was not particular about crushing my dresses for that one night. I remember, as if it were yesterday, the dark sea and dark sky, and great, chill, invisible, open-air world that I seemed to stand alone in, as the steamboat went bounding over those black waves, or ploughing through them, to Ostend. There was a great deal of wind, but the sea had not had time to rise, and there was the exhilaration of a storm without its more disagreeable consequences. The vessel did not roll, but now and then gave a leap, spurning the Channel spray from her bows. Oh how I recollect every particular! You might think a lonely girl in such circumstances—flying from persecution, if you like to put it so—flying from love; with nothing but a very uncertain welcome to look to from a very unsatisfactory father, and no prospect but to face the world again and get her bread somehow—was as sad a figure as could be imagined. But I was not sad. I had a high spirit, and I loved adventure and change. I felt as if the steamboat was me, going bounding on, caring nothing for the sea or the darkness. The wind might catch at us, the water might dash across our sides, the sky might veil itself—who cared? We pushed on, defying them all. A poor governess as good as turned out of my situation because the son of the house had fallen in love with me—a penniless creature without a home, with not a soul to stand by me in all that dark world. And yet I don't remember anything I ever enjoyed more, than that journey by night.

This will show you—and you may show it to Mary to convince her—how much I cared for George Durham. I suppose he was in love with me—at least what a young man not much over twenty considers love. That is six years ago; and probably he has always had a recollection, all this time, that he was in love with me, and thinks that he ought to have been faithful. I should not wonder if there was a kind of remorse in his mind to find that he had fallen in love with Mary, and cared for me no longer. It is a superstition with some people that, however foolish their first fancy was, they ought to hold by it; but I must say that I think it was very foolish, not to say cruel, of both of them, to make this breach on account of me.

I got another situation after that, and did well enough—as governesses do. I never complained, or thought I had any reason to complain. I taught all I knew—not very much, but enough for most people. As for education, as people talk nowadays —of awakening the minds, and training the dispositions, and re-creating the children, so to speak, intellectually and morally—I never thought of such a thing; and why should I? That is the work of a mother, appointed by God, or of some great person endowed with great genius or influence— not of a young woman between eighteen and five-and-twenty, indifferently trained herself, with quite enough to do to master her own difficulties and keep herself afloat. I was not so impertinent, so presumptuous, or so foolish as to have any such idea. I taught them as well as I could; I tried to make them as fond of books as I was myself—I tried to get them to talk like gentlewomen, and not to be mean or false. I was not their mother, or their priest, but only their teacher. I had no theory then; but after one is thirty, one begins to have theories; and I can see what I meant in my earlier time by the light of what I think now. However, this is not much to the purpose. I was a successful governess on the whole; I got on very well, and I had nothing to find fault with. It is not a very happy life—when you are young, and hear pleasant sounds below-stairs, and have to sit reading by yourself in the school-room; when there is music and dancing perhaps, and merry talk, and you are left alone in that bare place with maps on the walls, and one candle—a girl does not feel happy; though on the whole, perhaps, the schoolroom is better than to sit in a corner of the drawing-room and be taken no notice of—which is the other alternative. There are a great many difficulties in the position altogether, as I can see now that I am older. When the governess is made exactly like one of the family, the eldest son will go and fall in love with her and bring everybody into trouble. It is hard for the lady of the house as well. However, after George Durham, I was careful, and I never got into difficulty of that kind again. Four years after I left the Durhams I had a bad illness —rheumatic fever. My people were very kind to me, but I was too proud to be a burden on them; and as soon as I could be moved I left and went into lodgings, and was ill there till I had spent all my money; it was only then that I had recourse to the Spicers. Perhaps I ought to confess that, though Mr Spicer is my uncle, I was ashamed of him and disliked him. I have felt angry at my poor mother all my life for having such relations; but of course there they were, and had to be made the best of. My money lasted till I was almost well, but not well enough for another situation. My father had died in the meantime; and only then I sent to the Spicers, and asked if they would take me in for a time. I was a good needlewoman; I knew I could repay them well for keeping me. That is how I went to them.

THE TWO MARYS

What followed no one could have foreseen. You know how it was.

I cannot talk about my husband—yet. How could I talk about that which was everything to me, which changed my life, which made me another creature? People may love you, and it makes but little difference to you. It is pleasant, no doubt; it softens your lot; it makes things bearable which would not be bearable. I had known that in my life. But to love—that is another thing. That is the true revelation—the lifting up of the veil. It is as different from simply being loved as night is from day. I suppose few women are, as I was, in circumstances to feel this sudden lighting up of existence all of a sudden. Most women have a great deal to love, and know that condition better than the other. They would not make so much fuss about being loved did they not already possess the other gift. But I had never really loved anybody, I suppose. Various people had loved me. I had liked it, and had done what I could to be kind and agreeable to them. Some (women) I had been very fond of. It seems to me now that the world must have been a most curious, cloudy sort of place in my early youth —a dim place, where nothing moved one very much; where daylight was quite sober and ordinary, and nothing out of oneself was exciting.

THE TWO MARYS

When I saw Mr Peveril first I had no warning of what was coming. I did not feel even interested in him. He seemed too gentle, too soft for my liking. What attracted me was, I think, chiefly the fact that he was the only educated man I ever saw there—the only being, man or woman, who was not of, or like, the Spicers. This was my only feeling towards him for the first two or three times I saw him—but then——.

I am afraid I did not think very much about Mary when we were married. Of course I meant to do my duty by her: that goes without saying. And her resistance and dislike did not make me angry. They rather amused me. It seemed so odd that she should think herself of consequence enough to be so deeply offended. She, a girl, with all her life before her—fifteen—of no present importance to any mortal, though no doubt she would ripen into something after a while. When Mr Peveril distressed himself about what he called her want of respect to me, I used to smile at him. He would have made her love me by force had that been possible—as if her little sullenness, poor child, made any difference! It was quite natural, besides—only foolish, if she could but have seen it. She was a naughty child, and she thought herself a virgin-martyr. I hope it is not wicked of me to be amused by that virgin-martyr look. I know it so well. I have seen it over and over again in all sorts of circumstances. To say a tragedy-queen is nothing. There is a sublime patience, a pathos about your virgin-martyrs, which far outdoes anything else. Poor little Mary! if I had not seen that she was quite happy in her own thoughts, even when she thought herself most miserable, I should have taken more notice of it. I can't tell what she was always thinking about—whether it was some imaginary lover or romance of her own that she kept weaving for hours together; but it kept her happy anyhow. She was very provoking sometimes—never was there such a spoiled child. She balked me thoroughly in one thing, and would not let me be her governess as well as her stepmother; which was what I wished. How often should I have liked to box her little impertinent ears, and then laugh and kiss her into good-humour! But in that point there was nothing to be done. I had to leave all to time, in which I hoped—without, alas! having the least thought, the least provision, how short my time was to be. You will see that I am not one to linger upon my private feelings. I have said nothing to you about my happiness. I can say nothing about my grief. The beautiful life stopped short—the light went out— an end seemed to come to everything. I cannot say more about it. Everything ended—except one's pulse, which will go on beating, and the long hours and days that have to be got through somehow, and the bread that has to be eaten in spite of one's self—and has to be earned too, as if it were worth the while.

I wonder at myself sometimes, and you will wonder, that I did not break down under my grief. It was my first real grief, as that which preceded it had been my first real happiness. I have even envied the people who got ill and who could go to bed, and darken their windows and lie still and let the sword go through and through them in quietness, instead of writhing on it as I did; but that must be nature. My first instinct was to snatch at something, to lay hold upon something, lest I should be carried away by some fiery flood or other. And what I snatched at was Mary. I love Mary. You may think I have not acted as if I did; but that is nothing; and she does not love me. But still I have that distinct feeling for her which I never experienced till her dear, dear father (oh, my God, my God, why is it that my child will never call him so!) showed me the way. I have had a great deal to bear from her; she is not like me; and there are many things I dislike in her. But all that does not matter. And it is not as I loved him—but yet I love her. All I remember about those dark days was that I laid hold upon Mary. She could not escape from me when I seized her so—few, very few, people can. To resist kindness is easy enough, but downright love has a different kind of grasp; you cannot get free of that. It is because there is so much fictitious love in the world that people are not aware of the power of the true.

I secured her—for the time. You may say it did not last very long; but that was not my fault; it was because she too, in her time, woke up from her affection for me, and all the torpor of her youth, and heard the call of love, and got up and left those that did but love her. The time we lived together was a strange dreamy time, between blank despair and a kind of languid happiness. Sometimes I would feel almost happy because of what was coming, and then I would be plunged into that horror of darkness, that shadow of death, which is of all things on earth the most terrible—worse, a thousand times worse, than death itself. I say this with confidence, because I as good as died once. I was so ill that I had floated off into that unconsciousness which would have been death had they left me alone; and it was not unpleasant. Had they left me alone I should have died, therefore I am justified in saying that this was death; and it was not disagreeable—just a soft floating away, a gradual growing dim and shutting out, without any of that sense of desertion and loneliness which one feels must be so strong in the dying. But the shadow of death is very terrible. No one can exaggerate its terror. When it seizes upon the soul, all that surrounds you is lost in one sea of misery. The waves and the billows pass over you. You feel as if you could not endure, could not last through that flood of pain—and yet you do last. The great billow passes over, and there is a calm, and your soul is so fatigued and worn out that it lies exhausted, and a languor of rest, which is almost ease, passes over it. This was how I lived for three months with Mary; until the shock of the other who thrust himself into our life —the stranger, who was no stranger, came.

His first appearance was nothing but an insignificant trouble, a mere annoyance to me,—why should I care? I had not thought of him at all for years; and I never had thought of him much. But still I did not want him there: he annoyed me; he was a kind of constant menace of more annoyance to come. But I don't know what steps I could have taken. It was a long time before I could realise that he would fall in love with Mary. I rather think it is difficult to believe that a man who has loved you will love some one else. That is—if you are quite indifferent to him; it is so much easier then, to believe in his faithfulness. The idea did not occur to me. I feared a little for Mary once or twice, and tried to warn her; but she was always a dreamy sort of girl, and it was hard to tell when a new influence came over her. She had lived in dreams of one kind or other ever since I knew her; and I knew nothing, really nothing, about what was going on, till that unhappy afternoon when he recognised me, and came in and talked foolishly in Mary's hearing, about things that had happened so long before. Poor child!—I don't blame her, for her foolishness was natural enough. She thought I had stolen away her lover, as I had stolen away her father. She would not listen to me, and when she did listen to me she did not believe me; and there on the other hand was he, demanding explanations. Good heavens, what right has a man like that to ask explanations—a man one had never cared for, and would have died of? He worried me so that I could not be civil. What with grief, and what with vexation at the turn things had taken, and disappointment in Mary, and illness in myself, I had no patience with the man, maundering on about things that had happened ages before, that were of no importance to any living being. When he waylaid me on my way to her, keeping me back from her, in her agony of temper and mortification and humiliation, what I could have done to him! I was in a nervous state, I suppose, and easily irritated. I could have struck him when he came out and worried me. And there was Mary turning her face to the wall, shutting out the light, shutting her ears, determined to be miserable. Oh! when I toiled up and down stairs going to her, when I felt ill and knew that nobody cared, when I saw her absorbed in her foolish misery, and him tormenting himself and me about dead nonsense that never had been anything, you may excuse me if I had very little patience. After a night of it I got tired and sick of the whole business. It seemed too hard to be obliged to put up with all this folly on the eve of being ill. And who would care whether I was ill or not, if things went on so?

Then I took my resolution suddenly, as I had done before. It was not with the hope and high spirit that had kept me up when I went off to Ostend that I left Southampton Street, my own house. I was sick and tired, that was all. I could not be troubled to go on. I was worried and impatient and indignant—and then Mary had a friend to take care of her. I went away. I went to an hospital after a while in the same irritated hopeless state, feeling that it did not matter what happened; and there my boy was born. Well! what did it matter? They are for honest, poor women, these hospitals—and Heaven knows I was poor enough, but honest. One cares for one's self only when one has other people who care. I had nobody. I did not lose heart altogether, because that is not my nature. I could not if I would; but what did I care for what people would think or for what they might say? no more than for the buzzing of the flies. I should never even hear of it—there was nobody to tell me, nobody to pay any attention. I thought most likely I should die; but I did not calculate upon dying, for by that time I knew I had strength to go through a great deal. And so I did. My boy was quite strong and well, and I got quite well and strong too. Often I have thought this showed how little heart I must have; but I could not help it. I got quite strong. I reflected seriously whether I should not try for a nurse's place, which was very well paid, and where very little was required; but even if I could have parted with my boy, I had no one to trust with the care of him. So instead of doing this, I made shift to live for a whole year upon my forty pounds of income, with a little more which I earned by needlework. When you are a very good needle-woman, you can always earn something. I did very well; I made baby clothes; my eyes were strong, and my health was good, and I had my own baby to comfort me. There is nothing that comforts like a baby. When the child laughs, you laugh too. You laugh to make him laugh; first it is sympathy, then it is delight, till gradually you grow a baby too, and are amused at nothing, and happy for nothing, and live over again, beginning at the very beginning, in the child.

In this way I grew to be so tranquil, so eased in mind, and happy in heart, notwithstanding my loss, which I never forgot, that I was tempted to remain just as I was always; but then it occurred to me that I should lose all that I knew, that I would never be able to teach him, or to get him education, or to rise in the world, as I wanted to do for his sake; therefore it was clear I must do something else. This was what I did: I found out about a situation in a school after a great deal of inquiry. I went to the lady and told her my story; I said I would go to her for almost nothing if I might have my baby and a little maid to take care of him. When she heard of my "French acquired abroad," my showy bit of German, my music, and how I would make myself as useful as ever she liked, having excellent health and no sort of prejudices about what I did, she closed with me. I had two rooms, and board for myself and the maid and the boy—no more at first—but I managed on that. And then by degrees we improved. She gave me first twenty pounds, then a little more. A baby's white frock and a widow's black gown do not cost much. We did very well. I have fifty pounds now the school has increased so much; and I believe I may have a share soon if all goes well. My French goes for a great deal, and even my name and my widow's cap go for something, and everybody in the school likes to tell the story of the baby. Am I happy, do you say? I never stop to ask myself whether I am happy or not. One must form some idea of change in one's mind, some thought of a possibility which might make one happier, before one would think of asking one's self such a question. And as I have no reasonable prospect of ever being happier than

THE TWO MARYS

I am, I do not think about it. I am not unhappy —of that I am sure.

You talk of bringing Mary and me together again. Would it answer, I wonder? Sentiment is one thing, but practicability is another. Having told you that I loved Mary, I have said all that either woman or man can say. Likings change and alter, but love is for ever. Yet, whether we could live together, whether she could trust me, whether she would understand the past, and feel how little I wished or intended to interfere with her, I cannot tell; unless she could, it would almost be better to leave us as we are. So long as a woman is young, as Mary is, it is doubtful and dangerous, I am afraid, to try any relationships but those that are quite natural. She is with you, you dearest, kind friend, as if she were your own child. You can do her nothing but good; but I am not so very much older than she is. I am older—centuries older—but not to outward appearance; and can you not suppose a state of things in which the last chapter of our lives might be, one way or other, repeated again? I say this not with any sort of vanity, Heaven knows, but with fear and trembling. For I should be happier with her—far happier—but not if she came to me with a single doubt in her mind, a single thought which was uncertain or suspicious. Do not tell her this one difficulty which seems to me to stand in our way, but judge for us both what is best. I want her for myself and for my boy.

THE TWO MARYS

We belong to each other, and no one else in the world belongs to us. How often I long for her when I am sitting alone! How many things I have in my mind to say to her! But not unless it would be well for her, to whom anything may happen. Nothing that I know of, except through her or my baby, can now happen to me.

CHAPTER VIII

I WILL not enter into all the particulars of our discussion after this, for time would fail me. The last part of Mary's letter, which she said was not to be shown to me, made me angry. I thought it was vanity on her part to be afraid of interfering with me again. "In what way?" I could not but ask, and that sharply; how could the last chapter of our lives be repeated? Mrs Tufnell only smoothed my hair and soothed me, and called me "dear" and darling," but would give no explanation. "What does she mean?" I asked. "Oh, she means, my love—probably she means nothing. It is just a way of talking that people fall into," said my old lady. I knew this was said simply to quiet me, but on the whole perhaps I preferred it to anything more definite; and, after a time, I allowed myself to be persuaded to pay my stepmother a visit. What a strange journey into the past it seemed! and yet actually we went far away from the scene of the past, into a place so new and unknown to me, that it could awaken no associations. We drove in the comfortable old fly, with the old sleek horse and the old fat man, which was as good as Mrs Tufnell's private carriage. She did not keep a carriage of her own, but I am sure this fly, in which she drove every day of her life except when she was ill, cost her more than a carriage would have done. She was very apologetic about it always. "I could not undertake the responsibility of a carriage," she would say; "horses are always getting ill, and your coachman drinks, or he gets into trouble with the maids, or something. Old Groombridge and his fly suit me quite well. No, he is not an old rogue. I have to pay him, of course, for all his trouble, and for the loss of customers, and so forth. You know, Mary, he always suits himself to my convenience at whatever sacrifice——."

This was her idea, and nothing would convince her otherwise. So we drove in Groombridge's old fly—which was one of the most expensive vehicles in town—out Hampstead way, but past all the houses, past everything, till we came to new houses again, and skeleton roads and villas growing up like mushrooms, in one of those long straggling arms that London puts out into the country. I had got excited so often thinking that we must be quite close upon the place, that at last I ceased to be excited, and felt as if we had set out upon a hopeless circle, and were going to wind in and out and round and round, till we worked back to the point from which we started. How dreary they look, those new places—roads newly laid out, breaking in upon the fields, which somehow look so superior, so desecrated, and vulgarised by those new muddy

THE TWO MARYS

lines with the unnecessary kerbstones; and then all the half-built houses, each one uglier than the other, with their bow-windows, all made by the gross (I suppose), and their thin little walls that the wind whistles through, and even their monotonous attempt at irregularity. A steady, solid row which is very ugly and nothing more, is endurable. I was saying this, when suddenly the fly made a sharp turn, and immediately the villas and the kerbstones became invisible. We had got within a mossy wall, through a large old-fashioned gate. There was an avenue, not very long nor very grand, but still an avenue, with odd old trees all gnarled and mossed over, and I suppose in a very bad condition, but still old, and trees—trees which our grandfathers might have walked under. The house was an old red-brick house, very dark red, and covered with little brown and yellow lichens. It was neat, but yet one could see it was in want of repair, and looked like a poor lady in a faded gown and mended lace by the side of the fine shop-people in silk and satin. It was a winter day—a very still and bright one. The shadows of all the leafless trees made a network upon the brown gravel path. The old house seemed to be basking, warming itself in the sun. There were a great many twinkling windows, but not a creature to be seen except one little child on the white step of the deep doorway. There was a porch, and probably his nurse was there, but the little fellow was standing out in the sun, cracking a little whip he had, with his hair shining in the bright light, and his little face like an apple-blossom. He was shouting out some baby nonsense at the top of his voice. He did not care for us, nor for anyone. He was the monarch of all—quite alone in his kingdom, independent of everybody.

"Who do you think that is, Mary?" said Mrs Tufnell, taking my hand suddenly, as I looked out laughing and amused by him. Good heavens! I had never once thought. I fell back into my corner and began to cry, I cannot tell why. Of course I knew at once whom it must be.

And then *she* came, not in the least altered, kissing me just as if we had parted yesterday. But she was agitated, though she tried not to show it. She took the little boy and brought him to me, and thrust him into my arms without a word, and her lip quivered, and for some minutes she could not say anything. The meeting was hard altogether. When the thing that sundered you is too far off to be talked about, and when everybody counsels you to avoid explanations and go on again as if nothing had happened, it is very hard; you may succeed in uniting the old strands and twisting them together once more, but it is perhaps more likely that you will fail. We went into Mary's new home, and saw the lady who was the head of the school. It was holiday time—the Christmas holidays—and they were alone. This lady was middle-aged, older than Mary, but not so old as Mrs Tufnell. She was an unmarried woman, and I could at once understand what Mary had said, that her very name and her widow's cap told for something in the place. But what was most evident of all was that little Jack was the sovereign of Grove House. Whatever anybody might do or say, he was supreme. Miss Robinson was fond of his mother, and "appreciated" her, as she told us; but little Jack was the monarch, and did what he pleased.

Our visit was, as people say, quite successful. It went off perfectly well—we kissed when we met and when we parted—we had a great deal to say to each other of what had passed since we met—and there was little Jack to make acquaintance with, and a great many of his wonderful adventures to be told of. Mrs Tufnell came away with the thought that it had been a great success, and that henceforward nothing more was wanted—that Mary and I would be one again.

But Mary and I felt differently. I did, at least, and I am sure so did she. You cannot mend a rent so easily. Such a rent—a rent that had lasted more than five years—how can it be drawn together again by any hasty needle and thread like a thing done yesterday? We parted friends, with promises to meet again; but with hearts, oh! so much more apart from each other than they had been an hour before! An hour before we met I had all sorts of vague hopes in my mind—vague feelings that she would understand me, that I should understand her—vague yearnings towards the old union which was almost perfect. Did you ever see the great glass screen they have in some houses to shield you from the heat of the fire? You can see the cheerful blaze through it, but you feel nothing. Something of the kind was between Mary and me. We saw through it as well as ever, and seemed to enjoy the pleasant warmth; but no other sensation followed, only the chill of a disappointment. I felt that she was now nothing, nothing to me; and I — I cannot tell how I seemed to her. We had the old habit suddenly brought to life and put on again, but none of the old meaning. We were like mummers trying to make ourselves out to be heroines of the past, but knowing we were not and never could be what we appeared. I was very silent during our drive home. I did not know what to say to my dear old lady. She looked very fragile with her pretty rose-cheeks, lying back in the corner of the fly; she was fatigued, and in the daylight I suddenly woke up to see that she did look very fragile. I had not believed in it before. And how could I vex her by telling her of my disappointment? I could not do it; she was pleased and happy; she held my hand, and nodded to me and said: "Now you see you are not so much alone as you thought you were. Now you see you have friends who belong to you." How could I have had the heart to say otherwise—to say I had found out that we were separated for ever, Mary and I?

That evening, however, after tea, she began to talk to me very seriously. We were sitting over the fire—she on her favourite sofa, I on a low chair near her. The firelight kept dancing about, lighting up the room fitfully. It was a large room. We had some candles on the mantel-piece, which shone, reflected in the great mirror, as if from some dim, deep chamber opening off this one; but it was really the firelight that lighted the room. I had been singing to her, and I half thought she had been asleep, when suddenly she roused up all at once, and sat upright in her little prim way.

"I want to speak to you, Mary," she said; and then, after a pause—"You think I meant nothing but love and kindness when I took you to see Mrs Peveril to-day; but I am a scheming, wicked old woman, Mary. I had more than that in my mind."

I was a little, but only a little, startled by this: I knew her way. I looked up at her, smiling. "You are so designing," I said; "I might have known there was something underneath. You are going to ask them to spend the rest of their holidays here?"

"That if you like," she said brightly, encouraged,

THE TWO MARYS

I could see, by my tone; "but more than that, Mary; more than that."

I was not curious. I looked with an indolent amusement at the shining of the firelight and the reflection in the mirror of the flame of the candles, which shone out of its surface without seeming to move the dark ruddy gloom beyond. A glass is always an inscrutable, wonderful thing, like an opening into the unseen: it was especially so that night.

"Mary," Mrs Tufnell resumed, with a voice that faltered, I could not tell why; "do you remember when I first spoke to you of Mrs Peveril—when I was ill?—and what I said?"

"Yes," I answered, with sudden alarm, looking up at her. "You don't feel ill now?"

"No, but I have got a shake," she said. "When a woman at my time of life is ill, though it may seem to pass quite away, it always leaves a something. I shall never be as strong as I have been, my dear child. I feel I have got a shake. My life has come to be like the late leaves on the top of a tree. They may last through many gales, but the first gust may blow them off. I cannot feel sure for a day."

I went close up to her in my fright, and knelt down by the sofa, and put my arms round her. "Do not speak so," I said; "you could not leave me? What could I do without you? I am not an orphan as long as I have you. You cannot have the heart——"

THE TWO MARYS

"Oh, Mary! hush; don't overwhelm me. It was of that I wanted to speak. I shall live as long as I can, for your sake. But, dear, old people cannot stay always, however much they may be wanted. I have been thinking of it a great deal, and there is a proposal I have to make to you—with Mrs Peveril's consent, Mary. You must listen to all I have to say."

"Oh, you have consulted Mrs Peveril!" said I; and I got up, feeling my heart grow chill and sore, and went back to my seat to hear what was to be said to me. In the depths of my heart I must have been jealous of her still. It came all back upon me like a flood. My dear old lady gave me a grieved look, but she did not stop to explain. She went quickly on with what she had to say:—

"Grove House is a nice old-fashioned house, and cheap, and they have a good list of scholars; and Miss Robinson would be glad to retire, and would not ask very much for the furniture and things; and Mrs Peveril is so much liked by everybody. I have always set apart as much as I thought was right of my little property, intending it for you, Mary——"

"Don't!" I cried, in a voice so shrill and sharp that it startled even myself who spoke.

"It is not very much," she went on, "but it is all I can give away, and my whole heart has been set upon doing something for you with this money that would make you independent. My dear Mary,

THE TWO MARYS

I am half afraid you don't like the thought, you are so silent. I had thought of buying Grove House for Mrs Peveril and you."

"For Mrs Peveril and me!"

"Yes—don't you like the idea, Mary?—don't you like the idea? I thought it was something that would please you so much. You have always said you liked teaching, and it would be a living for you, dear, and a home when I am gone. I have so wished to make these arrangements for you, Mary——"

"Is it all settled?" I said.

"Nothing could be settled without your consent. All that I want is your good. I could not leave you, could I, at your age, without anyone to stand by you, without a home to go to, without a friend——"

Thus she apologised to me for those kind, tender plans of hers; and I sat like a clod, feeling that I could not reply. I was dull and heavy and miserable; not grateful, yet feeling how grateful I ought to be; understanding her, yet not owning even to myself that I understood her. It was not a very great destiny that was thus allotted to me, but that was not what I was thinking. My mind did not revolt against the idea of being the mistress of a school; which was a natural lot enough. To tell the truth, I cannot quite say what it was that gave me so miserable a feeling. Here was my life marked out for me; there was never

THE TWO MARYS

to be any change in it; no alteration for the brighter or better occurred to this dear old woman who loved me. She wanted to make sure I should have daily bread and a roof to shelter me, and some sort of companionship. How right she was! How good and how kind! and yet, oh, how dreary, how unutterably blank and hopeless seemed the prospect! I felt this with a dull fighting and struggle of the two things in me—wanting to please her by looking pleased, feeling how good she was, and how kind, how just, how suitable was the arrangement. I felt all this in a kind of way, and then I felt the struggle not to be wildly angry, not to burst out and ask her how she could think of condemning me so—for my life?

She was grieved and disappointed at the way I received her proposal, but she was so good that she took no notice, but kissed me, and said nothing should be done or thought of against my consent. For my part my heart was so heavy and dull that I could not even thank her for her kindness; but I hung about her when she went to bed, and held her fast in a speechless way that she understood, I think, though I said nothing. She cried; she looked at me with her kind old eyes full of tears. "Oh, Mary," she said, "don't break my heart! If I could live for ever and go on always taking care of you, don't you think I would do it, for your sake and your father's too? But I cannot. One must die when one's time comes, however much one may be wanted: and I must provide for that."

"Oh, why can't I provide for it?" I cried. "Why can't I die too? That would be the best way."

And then she was angry—half angry—as much as it was in her nature to be. And presently I found myself alone, and had to sit down and think it over, and make up my mind to it, as one has so often to do in this life. I had to teach myself to see how good it was. And I did. I made up my mind to it. What was there else in heaven or earth—as I could not die with my only friend, or compel her to live, what was there else that I could do?

CHAPTER IX

NEXT morning when I woke, the impression on my mind was, that Mrs Tufnell must have died in the night. I cannot tell why I thought so, but I woke with such a horror in my mind, that I threw a shawl over my shoulders and rushed to her door to ask how she was, before I could take breath. She was not up; but smiled at me from her bed, where she lay with all the pictures and the portraits of her friends about her, the centre of a silent company. "I am quite well— better than usual," she said; but I think she knew the meaning of my terror, and felt that after all that had been said it was natural I should be afraid. This perhaps threw just a little cloud upon her serenity too, during the morning, for however calmly one may think of dying, I suppose it must startle one to see that others are thinking of it. I suppose so—it seems natural. She was very grave, thoughtful, and somewhat silent during the forenoon; and when I went and sat down by her, and asked her to forgive me, and said I was ready to do whatever she thought best, she took me into her arms and cried and kissed me. "Oh, that it should be necessary to change!" she said. "I do not feel as if I could face the change—but, Mary, for your good——"

It was about noon as we thus sat talking it over. It comforted me to see that she liked it as little as I did; that she would rather have kept me with her to the last moment of her life. But then what should I have done?—this was what she thought of. We were talking it all over very seriously, with more pain than either of us would show. It was a chilly winter morning. The room was bright, to be sure, with a good fire burning, and all the comforts that so many poor people are without; but there was a chill that went to one's heart—the chill of the grave for her, which she thought near; and the chill of the outside world, from which she had sheltered me so long, for me. I remember the look of that morning—there was a black frost outside which bound all the dry street, and seemed to hold the naked trees in the square so fast that they dared not rustle, though an icy wind was blowing through them. There were traces still on the windows, notwithstanding the fire, of the frosty network of the night. The sun had begun to shine as it approached noon, but even the sun was white and cold, and seemed rather to point out how chilly the world was, than to warm it. After we had got through all our explanations and said all that was to be said, and arranged that Mary was to be invited to the Square with her child to spend a week of the holidays and arrange everything, we still kept sitting together holding each other's hands, not saying much. I could not pretend that I liked it even to please her, and she did not like it, though she thought it right; but all the same it was settled, and there was nothing more to say.

It was all settled by twelve o'clock, fixed and decided with that double certainty which is given by pain. If we had liked it we should not have felt half so sure. At half-past twelve the mid-day post came in, and I was still sitting by my dear old lady, holding her hand, feeling my heart sink lower and lower every moment, thinking how I should have to leave her when she wanted me most—when Mrs Tufnell's maid came in with the letters. She gave some to her mistress, and she gave one to me. I do not think I recognised the writing at first. But I got few letters, and it gave me a little thrill of agitation, I could not quite tell why. It was a foreign letter, with a number of unintelligible postmarks. I got up and went to the window, partly because my heart began to beat very loud, and partly to leave Mrs Tufnell at liberty to read her letters. I recollect looking out unconsciously and seeing the dried-up, dusty, frosty look of everything, the ice-wind sweeping the dust round the corners, the bare shivering trees—with a momentary thrill of sensation that my life was like that, dried-up, frost-bound, for ever and ever. And then, with my fingers trembling and my heart beating, and a consciousness of something coming, I could not tell what, I opened the envelope and found——This was what I found; without any preface or introduction — without anything to soften the difference between what was before my eyes and what was going to be.

There was no beginning to the letter; there were a good many blots in it, as if it had been written with a hand which was not very steady. There was not even a date until the end. He who had written it had been as much agitated as she who read it; and she who read it did so as in a dream, not knowing where she was standing, feeling the world and the white curtains and the frosty square to be going round and round with her, making a buzzing in her ears and a thumping against her breast.

What a plunge into a new world—into an old world—into a world not realised, not possible, and yet so strange in its fascination, so bewildering! Was it a dream—or could it be true?

"I have long wanted, and often tried, to write to you again. I do not know now whether I may or whether I ought. If this letter should come to another man's wife, if it should fall into your hands in such changed circumstances that you will scarcely remember the writer's name—and I cannot hide from myself that all this may be the case —then forgive me, Mary, and put it in the fire without further thought. It will not be for you, in your new life, but for someone else whom you will have forgotten, though I can never forget her. But if you are still little Mary Peveril as you used to be, oh, read it! and try to throw your thoughts back to the time when you knew me—when we used to meet. You were not much more than a child. How much I have thought of that time; how often and often I have gone over it in my thoughts I need not tell you. You were badly used, dear Mary. I was wrong—I will say it humbly on my knees if you like: having got your promise and your heart—for I did have that, if only for a little while—nothing could have justified me in appearing for one moment to place you otherwise than first in all I did or said. I will not excuse myself by saying how much startled I was by the sight of Miss Martindale, nor how anxious I was to know whether my mother had any share, or what share she had, in her disappearance from our house. I will say nothing about all that, but only that I was wrong, wrong without any excuse. Had I thought of what I was risking by my curiosity, I would have bitten my tongue out sooner than have asked a single question. Do you think, could you think, that I would have sacrificed you to the old foolish business which was over years before? I was an utter fool, I allow, but not such a fool as that. Therefore, Mary dear, dearest, whom I have always thought of, listen to me again; take me back again! I will beg your pardon a hundred and a thousand times. I will humbly do whatever penance you may appoint me; but listen to me now. You would not listen to me at first—and perhaps I was not so ready at first to acknowledge how wrong I was. I have had five long years to think of it, and I see it all. You were rightly angry, dear, and I was wrong; and if ever man repented, I have repented. Mary, Mary! take me back!

"I have been wandering about the world all this time, working and doing well enough. I can offer you something better now than the little cottage we once spoke of, though that would have been Paradise. I am leaving along with this letter, and hope to arrive in England almost as soon. I do not ask you to write—unless indeed you would, of your own sweet kindness—one word—to Chester Street? But even if you don't do that, I will go to Russell Square in the hope of finding you. Mary! don't break my heart. You liked me once. If I knew what to say that would move you, I would make this letter miles long; but I don't know what more to say, except that I love you better than ever, and no one but you; and that I am coming back to England for you, for you only—half hopeless, only determined to try once more. Perhaps by the time you have read this I may be at your door.

"Ever and ever yours,
"GEORGE DURHAM."

THE TWO MARYS

"Mary!" cried some one calling me; "Mary, what is the matter? Have you bad news, my dear? Mary! Good gracious, the child will faint! Mary, don't you hear me?"

"Oh, hush, hush!" I cried, not knowing what I said. "Hark! listen! is that him at the door?"

It was not him just then; and after a little while the curtains stopped going round, and the floor and the Square and everything about grew solid and steady, and I came to myself. To myself, yes— but not to the same self as had been sitting so sadly holding my old lady's hand. What a change all in a moment! If I had not been so happy, I should have been ashamed to think that a man's letter could all in a moment make such a change in a woman's life. It is demoralising to the last degree—it comes in the way of all the proper efforts of education and independent thought, and everything that is most necessary and elevating. If in a moment, without any virtue of yours, without any exertion of yours, you are to have your existence all altered for you—the greyness turned into brightness, the labour into ease, the poverty into wealth—how is it to be supposed that you can be trained aright? It is demoralising: but it is very pleasant. Oh, the change in one half-hour!

But I should find it very difficult to explain to anyone how it was that I behaved like a rational creature at this moment, and did not take a bad turn and torture him and myself with objections. It was not wisdom on my part; I think it was the absolute suddenness of the whole transaction. Had he left me more time to think, or prepared me for his reception, my pride and my delicacy would have come in, and probably I should have thrown away both his happiness and my own. But fortunately he arrived that very afternoon, before the first excitement was over, and hearing that Miss Peveril was at home, and that the servants had not been forbidden to admit him, walked upstairs when I was not thinking, and took possession of me as if there had been no doubt on the subject. Mrs Tufnell was begging me to write to him at the very moment. I had shown her my letter, and she was full of excitement about it. "Be an honest girl, Mary," she was saying: "a girl should not worry a man like that: you ought to be frank and open, and send him a word to meet him when he comes home. Say you are as fond of him as he is of you——"

"No, I could not—I could not," I was beginning to say; when suddenly something overshadowed us, and a big, ringing voice said behind me, "How could she? Let us be reasonable." Reasonable! After that there was no more to say.

But if it had not all passed like a dream; if he had not been so sudden; if he had taken more time and more care—the chances are, I know, that I should have behaved like a fool, and hesitated and questioned, and been proud and been foolish. As it was, I had to be honest and happy—there was no time for anything else.

This was of course the ending of the whole matter. I have often wondered whether, had my dear old lady been burdened with the anxiety of her charge of me, she would have died. As it is, she has not died. She lives with us often now, and we with her. On my wedding day she talked of departing in peace; but so far from departing in peace, she has been stronger ever since, and has a complexion any girl of twenty might envy. When I look back to Southampton Street and to Russell Square, where I was so unhappy, they all grow delightful and beautiful to me. It was very bad, no doubt (I suppose), while it lasted, but how I smile now at all my dolours! The delightful fact that they are over makes them pleasant. "That is how it will be, Mary," my dearest old lady says, "with all our sorrows, when we die and get safely out of them. We shall smile—I know it—and wonder how we could have made such a fuss over those momentary woes." This is a serious way of ending a story, which after all has turned out merely a love-story, a thing I never contemplated when I began to confide my early miseries to you. How miserable I was! and how it all makes me smile now!

THE TWO MARYS

As for Mary—the other Mary—we carried out that arrangement for her which had been proposed for me. We bought Grove House for her. I do not know what we could have done better. I never see that she is dull or weary of her life. What languors she may have she keeps from common view. Little Jack has grown a great boy, and she is very happy in him. But she does not give herself up to him, like so many mothers. "I must keep my own life," she said to me once, when I wanted her to give up, to live quietly at home and devote herself to my little brother alone. "He will go out into the world after a while," she went on; "he must, he has to make his way—and I, what should I do then? follow him or stay at home all alone?— No! I must keep my own life." And so she does. Happiness? I cannot tell if she has happiness: so many people get on without that —though some of us, I thank God humbly on my knees, have it without deserving it—without having done anything for it. Mary, I believe, never takes time to ask herself how about that. She said so once; she is not unhappy, and never will be; she has her life.

GROVE ROAD, HAMPSTEAD

CHAPTER I

"WHERE shall we go first? that is the only question. I know there are a hundred places to go to. Westminster and Whitehall, and the Tower, and St Paul's, and to see the pictures, and the river, and the Temple, and Cheapside. We cannot, of course," cried the eager girl, half regretfully, half pleased with the certainty of so much excitement, " see them all in one day."

"Considering that they are at different points of the compass, no," said the father, a serious man, who rarely relaxed even with his children. They were seated round a breakfast table in a London hotel—not one of the great caravansaries of the present day, but a small, grey, comfortable, quiet, very dear hotel in a little London street not far from Piccadilly. The houses opposite seemed almost within reach of their hands to the two girls, fresh and young and eager, who had for the first time that morning opened their eyes upon England. England! The thought made the blood dance in their veins. It was a little disenchanting, no doubt, to look out upon those grey houses opposite; but the fog through which the said houses loomed vaguely had an attraction of its own. A London fog: it was the right medium through which to see the metropolis of the world: they were almost as much interested in it as in Hyde Park or St Paul's. They were interested in everything; the very names of the streets made their hearts beat. They had arrived from Canada in the great steamboat the day before, had travelled up from Liverpool through a country veiled in the early and lingering dusk of a winter afternoon —for, though it was nominally spring, it was still winter—and entered London in the dark. When they opened their eyes this morning it had been, as they thought, upon a new world. They could hear the noise of wheels in Piccadilly, and that sound also went to their hearts. All England was before them. They had heard of it all their lives, and this arrival had been before them for months, a sensation keenly anticipated, and experienced now with a commotion of their whole being. Notwithstanding, it was a very ordinary table at which they sat, scarcely able to eat anything for sheer excitement. The room was somewhat dingy. The fog pressed upon the window like something palpable, the houses opposite looming grimly through it. There was very little in their external surroundings to justify the sublimated state of their feelings; but Grace and Milly Yorke wanted nothing to justify their feelings. These sentiments sustained themselves. They had never been out of Canada before, but England, as long as they could recollect, had been called "home" to them. They had said, "We are going home," when they communicated the great news to their friends. And now the moment had come to which they had looked forward for years.

Their father was not moved by the same ecstatic sentiments. He was not Canadian born, as they were. He had left England about thirty years before, and probably his return had recalled some feelings that were not altogether delightful. He was an angular, tall man, not unlike the commonly received type of an American, with a long face, somewhat sunken cheeks, a very resolute and determined mouth—altogether grey and rugged, like a gnarled tree. His eyes were deep-set and apt to get a fiery sparkle in them on occasions. He was a man of hot temper and inflexible obstinacy, not easy to deal with. But he was never ill-tempered to his children. The boys, indeed, were often more or less in conflict with their father; but to the girls he was always gentle and kind. Perhaps they knew better how to glide over all shoals and reefs, and find the safe channel to his favour. They and their mother knew very well what subjects it was best to avoid. They had put up danger signals on every side, and warned each other off this and that difficulty with a glance. They did this without intention, only half conscious of their own diplomacy. But so it was, that the girls were on the best of terms with their father, and to them he never said a hasty or unkind word. He sat very gravely between them, his countenance taking no reflection from the light in theirs. He was disposed rather to say, Confound the fog. He thought London just as dingy and disagreeable as it always had been; but he said nothing. The girls! The girls had their heads turned, poor children. He would not say anything to disturb their illusion. Let them entertain it as long as they could. But he had other things to think of. His mind was thronged with recollections. England was not to him a historical country, a place full of poetry, full of great events; but a very real world, with his own past in it, and many a thought and intent of which the girls knew nothing. He sat between them, scarcely hearing their eager chatter, but recalling with all the force of reality, as if they had happened yesterday, the circumstances which had attended his going away. He had not been very many years older than Grace, he recollected, with a sort of wondering half amusement; but how clear it was! Yesterday was not clearer—not so clear, indeed—for yesterday was nothing very important in his life; whereas that day——

"It is quite true what Mr Winthrop said. I never saw anything so poetical," said Grace;

GROVE ROAD, HAMPSTEAD

"such a wonderful dreamy vista!—don't you think so, papa? When you look out to the end of the street you can't tell what it is you see. The light is just like a dull topaz—wasn't that what Mr Winthrop said? and you can't tell what is beyond; it might be palaces or mountains, or one can't tell what. And to think it is England! and then that sort of roar of the carriages. It is not like the sea; it is like—— Oh, why should one try for similes?—it is like—just London, I suppose."

"Wait till you know a little more about London," said the father, "before you pronounce what it's like."

"One knows," said Grace, with a little solemnity. "One does not need to wait. I suppose London is like no other place in the world."

"Perhaps not," Yorke said with a half laugh; "but you will never know what it is if you should live a hundred years."

He spoke in one sense, they responded in another.

"I can believe that," said Grace, with the same gravity. "It is a mystery. We cannot know, but we can divine."

"God forbid!" her father said, and then he changed his tone. "Westminster is one way and St Paul's another," he said. "You can't go both ways at once. You had better make up your minds which you will have."

GROVE ROAD, HAMPSTEAD

And then a little argument ensued. The girls had read a great deal, and they had good memories. One of them espoused the cause of St Paul's and the other that of Westminster: the one going over the glorious inhabitants of the Abbey, demanding, with Milton—

> "What needs my Shakespeare for his honoured bones
> The labour of an age in pilèd stones?"

though I hope they knew that Shakespeare was not there—while the other launched herself upon Tennyson's ode—

> "Mighty Seaman, this is he,
> Was great by land as thou by sea."

The father remained quite silent in the midst of it all. It seemed, indeed, as if he had betrayed them into this fanciful controversy on purpose that he might be able to take refuge in his own thoughts. What was Westminster or St Paul's to him? His mind was busy with events which no poet had ever celebrated, which had never been put into history. Neither wife nor children knew of them — only some people at home, people who might be dead long ago, whom he had not heard of, and who had not heard of him for thirty years. He got the required leisure and quiet to think this all over while the others were busy with their poetry. They appealed to him, and he gave them a little nod and half smile, one of those smiles that are but for a moment, a gleam of enforced attention instantly falling back into the gravity of prevailing thought. The decision finally was for Westminster. As for these young people, they did not know the difference between St Paul's and the Abbey. They were both old, reverend, glorious structures to Grace and Milly; but what it might be that made the difference between them they did not know. One meant Poets' Corner, the other that about the mighty Seaman. They had never seen a Gothic cathedral in their lives.

And perhaps it is not ignorance so profound as this that is qualified to see and understand what is best. The girls read the names on the monuments with a kind of silent ecstasy of wonder. To think that they, two little girls from Canada, should actually be treading the storied pavement in Poets' Corner, and should be able to read with their own eyes the names upon those monuments, and see the Kings and Queens lying in marble, in solemn state, and touch with their little living modern fingers the chair in which the Confessor had sat! Could anything be more wonderful? They went through it all as if they were in a dream, looking at the monuments, reading all the names, thinking it was their own want of clear historical knowledge that made them at a loss about one here and there. But the Abbey itself was above their comprehension. They thought the Houses of Parliament finer, and were a little shocked that everything should be so grey and old. When you have seen nothing that is not new, all your life, it is difficult to understand the darkening of ages. But they spent the entire morning in one dream of pleasure, their hearts standing still as they came upon name after name, which they had heard of all their lives. There too was Whitehall, and that gloomy window, of which, perhaps, it is not true that from thence King Charles stepped to his execution; but they were not too critical; and they walked up the Mall to St James's Palace with a little thrill of easier admiration (which they thought rather vulgar in themselves, and were disposed to blush at) for the Lifeguardsmen on their horses. The little dingy old palace wounded their feelings somewhat, and brought down the bewildering splendour of imagination into very shabby limits; but they got over that. When they were not silent with awe, or with the shock of trying to reconcile to their own ideal something that fell short of it, they were talking all the way, calling upon each other to see this or that, reading out even the names of the streets to each other with many an " Oh, Milly!" and " Oh, Grace!" They were so absorbed in their sight-seeing that they never noticed the people who looked after them, the amused admiring looks with which the passers-by would contemplate their fresh faces. They were very fresh faces, delicate in colour, clear and animated, and so full of interest that their superabundant life brightened the foggy street. But fortunately the fog had lifted a little, and all the ghostly houses round the park, and the leafless trees, became more real under the mid-day radiance of a veiled sun doing his best to break through; and if they had thought the fog poetical before, you may imagine what they thought it now, with those rays streaming into it. It could not be real, they said to each other; by-and-by they would wake up and find themselves, let us say, in that other London which is on the farther side of the Atlantic. It could not be real; it was too wonderful to be true.

Meantime the father went on responding a little, but only a little, to the constant claim made upon his attention. He said " Yes " and " No," or even " Very pretty," " Very nice," " Very interesting " on occasion. For his part he did not care very much about the monuments. Sometimes his eye would wander away among the aisles, or through the lovely tracery and carved work of the roofs, to where the faint red sun caught a painted window, and threw a rosy oblique ladder of many colours across the grey. He understood the Abbey better than the girls did; but what he saw in the Abbey was, scenes of the past—the past, not of Shakespeare or the old Kings, but his own. He had been there in his youth, and he had been in other places which were recalled and suggested by this, and he remembered and mused in his heart. His companions were not surprised, because he was always a man of few words; though afterwards it gave them many thoughts, and the question, what he had been thinking of, what fancies might have been rising unconsciously in his mind, was often discussed by them; but at the present moment, as was natural, they did not realise that there was anything out of the way in his silence. They went back to their hotel late for their luncheon; they were tired in body, but not in their minds, which flowed over with wonder and pleasure. "Are you the least little bit disappointed?" said Milly to Grace. "No, not the least. Disappointed!" cried Grace with enthusiasm, though the next moment she was conscious of that little chill in her soul about St James's, and even felt that she had missed something in Westminster. This being the case with Grace, Milly cleared up in a moment from the slightest little cloud that had fallen upon her, and felt that neither was she disappointed, oh, not the least in the world! It was like walking with Shakespeare, they both said. And Mr Yorke gave a little nod across the table, and lifted his eyebrows at them. It was almost as much as he ever did when they were in full tide of enthusiasm. Papa was always quiet; though perhaps, indeed, he was more preoccupied than usual to-day. The winterly spring afternoon was beginning to close in a little before their meal was over. They were preparing, however, to go out again when their father called them to the window where he was sitting, looking more grave even than he was accustomed to look.

"I am going out," he said. "Can you manage for yourselves till dinner? I have something to do—out."

"Can't we go with you, papa?" they both said in a breath.

There was a kind of embarrassment on his face. "Not to-day, I think. After—perhaps: I have a call to make."

"Oh, it is about business!" said Milly, wondering, yet apologetic, looking at Grace.

"If it is not about business," said Grace promptly, "you ought to take us with you, papa. It is the right thing in England. In England girls don't go about by themselves; and then we want some friends, we want to know the people as well as the place."

A half smile went over his face. "You shall get the benefit of all the introductions," he said. "Don't be afraid; but you must not expect to be taken much notice of in London, just on the edge of the season, you know. People are very busy here; and then there are so many to be looked after—people of more pretensions than you. You must not expect too much ; but I am not going to deliver any of the letters. I am going—to see an —old friend."

"Oh, then, bring him here — will you please bring him here ? Do, papa, do! If it is an old friend, so much the more reason that we should know him. Is it a friend you had before you went to Canada ? Why has he never come to see us ? We have always wondered that you never had any old friends come to see you, papa."

Yorke did not make any direct reply. He said only, "What will you do with yourselves while I am away ?"

The two girls looked at each other somewhat blankly.

"We can't stay in here," cried Milly, while Grace drew herself up with youthful dignity.

"As for staying in every time you have any business to do or any calls to make," she said, with serious emphasis, " you must see that is impossible, papa. English girls may stop in-doors if they please, but we cannot. We are Canadian girls ; we are used to take care of ourselves. Milly and I can surely take care of each other wherever we go. It would be too humbling," she cried, " in the country of Shakespeare, to think two girls couldn't go out without—what was it, Milly ?— unpleasantness. I don't believe a word of it. Mrs Bidwell is only a vulgar Englishwoman. Unpleasantness ! I don't believe it ; and even if

I did believe it I shouldn't allow it to be true."

"Come," said her father, "you must not talk so of vulgar Englishwomen—you who are such enthusiasts for England. No, I don't see any harm in it. Come with me so far, I'll take you to where the shops are. Of course you would like to look into the shops."

They would have liked a great deal better to go with him upon this mysterious call, but he would not permit it, and accordingly they were taken to Regent Street, where he left them with a beautiful confidence. It might not be the best place in the world to leave young girls alone on a spring afternoon, no doubt; but what did they know of that? They were innocent, proud, modest girls, to whom no one had ever said a disrespectful word, and who were afraid of nobody. Nor did they get any new light upon the subject from that walk. The innocent do not even suspect the dangers which the knowing see all about them. Nobody molested Grace and Milly: they walked along in their armour of honest maidenhood, knowing no evil; and were as safe as in their own rooms. It was true, however, that their rapture waned a little, and a touch of local patriotism came over them.

"I don't think so very much of the shops," said Milly doubtfully.

Milly was often the first to start an opinion, but she never was quite sure whether she held it or not till she had the support of Grace's authority, which this time, as so often, was unhesitatingly given.

"I don't think anything of the shops," said Grace. "Of course one doesn't come to England to look at shops. Paris for that, I suppose; but it is England all the same."

"Oh yes," said Milly, "certainly it is England all the same. I wish the houses were a little bigger and cleaner-looking, and the streets broader. I wish there were some trees——"

"Trees! in the heart of London," said Grace with high contempt. "Trees are the things that show how new a place is. Where you have nothing else you have trees. But think how many people must have walked about here. If we only could see them all strolling up and down this pavement—people you would give your head to see."

"But Shakespeare—and people like that—could not have walked about Regent Street: it is not old enough."

"No; not Shakespeare, perhaps. I don't know —he might have walked about here, though it was not Regent Street then."

"I wonder," said Milly suddenly, "where papa can have gone. I never heard him talk of any old friends before; nor relations. By the way, isn't it very funny that we have no relations in England, Grace?"

"It is strange," said Grace thoughtfully.

It was not a subject which had occurred to them

GROVE ROAD, HAMPSTEAD

till now. Their father they were aware had been thirty years in Canada without ever going "home;" and he had no family correspondence, nobody belonging to him that they knew of except themselves. Their mother was a Canadian born, and she had relations in plenty; and cousins on their father's side had not seemed a necessity before. But as they thought of it, a little additional chill came into the air. England—so dear and delightful as it was, the home of all their traditions—they had begun to make acquaintance with. But to think that they had not a relation in England, nothing to justify their fond identification of themselves with this old country! The idea was somewhat alarming as it burst upon them. It increased the little shade of disappointment which had crept over them against their will, and sent them to their hotel, which was all that answered for home at this moment, with a little heaviness at their hearts.

CHAPTER II

MR YORKE went out in the quickly fading spring afternoon with an air of seriousness and resolution, which, indeed, had been upon his countenance all day; but which was not much like the expression of a holiday visitor. He had a long drive out to the northern outskirts of London, across those miles on miles of insignificant streets which are almost more imposing in their shabby dreariness than the more important portions of the greatest of cities. But though they wearied him with endless lines of shabbiness and monotony, the mind of the stranger was not sufficiently at liberty to make any reflection upon them. It was twilight before he reached, mounting upwards slowly for the last mile or so, the suburban heights to which he was bound. He dismissed his cab at the entrance to a leafy lane, lined on each side with detached houses, which were scarcely perceptible among the bare trees and thick hedges. To the servant who admitted him he gave a name which was certainly not that which he had borne an hour before in his hotel. The house which he entered just at the moment of twilight, before the lamps were lighted, was very warmly carpeted and curtained, and almost too warm in the air of its balmy soft interior. He waited for a moment in the hall, with an extraordinary gravity—the seriousness of painful restrained excitement on his face. Then a door opened suddenly, and a lady came out carrying a candle in her hand. The light shone pleasantly upon a fresh face and pretty eyes, undimmed by some fifty years of life; but those eyes were puckered up with a curious, anxious, alarmed gaze, looking into the darkness. She advanced hurriedly for two or three steps, then stopped short in front of the stranger, examining him not without some distress in her look. "Leonard Crosthwaite?" she said, "it is very many years since we have heard that name. Is it some distant cousin we know nothing about? or is it—— is it——"

"It is I, Mary. We have not seen each other for thirty years—but I should have known you anywhere, I think. Certainly, here, in the old house."

She held up her candle and gazed at him, then shook her head slowly. "It is so sudden," she said. "It is such a long time——"

"And you did not expect to see me, while I expected—hoped—to see you." Then he put out his hand. "Mary—you are not still Mary—not a Crosthwaite still, as in the old time? No—I can see that. You have married, and had children—like me."

This drew a faint little smile from her in spite of herself. "Yes, I have married. I have a son as tall as you. I am a widow. I—— Oh, but I don't know if I ought to enter into family particulars. How am I to know that you are—Leonard? You are—a little like him."

"Is there any reason why you should hesitate to own me?" he said, half sternly, yet with a smile.

This brought an overpowering flush of colour over her comely, matronly face; but the next moment she cried out with agitation, "Oh, no, no! How could you think so of me?—not for the world, not for the world! If every penny we had depended on it"—and here she stopped short, confused, and looked at him again.

"I will not meddle with your pennies, Mary, whatever you may mean by that. I have plenty. You need not fear for me. Ah!—Uncle Abraham, I suppose, is dead?—he must be dead long ago: and there is something—— The old people are all dead, I suppose?"

"It is not that," she said, faltering, which was no answer to his question; but he understood it well enough. He looked at her with increased seriousness, and she shrank before his eye.

"Yes: they are all dead——"

"Uncle Abraham and all——" He looked at her more and more keenly, with a slight smile on his face. "But he did not take his money with him, I suppose, as he used to threaten to do?"

To this the lady made no reply; and there was a pause, he standing somewhat sternly, with his eyes fixed upon her; she with her head drooping a little, drawn back a few steps, not looking at him. The door behind her was open, and after a minute, a voice called from it, "Mary, to whom are you talking?"

The stranger started visibly. He said, with a sudden catch in his voice, "Anna! Is she here?"

"Oh yes, Leonard, yes," said the lady. "She is here—so changed! so changed! I think it is because she has been unhappy."

"Unhappy!" he said softly. His tone had changed and softened; only to hear it the listener might be certain that there were tears in his eyes. "Unhappy! after thirty years."

The man was touched and flattered and compunctious all in one. There was no difficulty in interpreting the inflections in his voice. It was full of tenderness, of a mournful pleasure, and surprise as well—"while I have been making myself so comfortable," he added in an undertone.

"Oh, not in that way," the lady said, but in a whisper. "No, no," shaking her head, "not in that way."

His mood of tender complaisance was perhaps a

little subdued by this, but only a little. "If you think she would let me see her," he said—

At this moment she was called again—"Mary! there is a perfect gale blowing in at the door. Who have you there?"

The lady who was called Mary advanced to him confidentially. "She heard your name just as well as I did," she said, "but she pretends to take no notice; wait here till I go and speak to her. Oh, she is so changed!"

He caught her by the hand and detained her. "Nothing has happened? She must be old like all of us, I know——"

"She is as handsome as ever she was," said the other hastily. "I am coming, I am coming, Anna! It is a visitor—an old friend"—and she turned round with the quickness of a girl, leaving the stranger standing where she had found him, the candle on the hall table watching him like a little wakeful sentinel. A glow of warmth and light came from the door of the open room. He had not noticed it before; now it appeared to him like a glimpse into some sanctuary. He could see a beautiful Persian carpet, a softly-tinted wall hung with pictures; not that he noticed what these details were, but took them in vaguely as producing an effect of delicate brightness and luxury. Memory stole softly over the far-travelled visitor. His present life had departed from him altogether —he was living in the past, in his youth, thinking of the pretty caprices of the girl whom he had thought the most beautiful, the most delightful creature that God had made, in all her whims and fancies. She had always been like that; and through all those thirty years it had been constantly suggested to him, in the inmost recesses of his mind, when he saw anything that was graceful or pretty, "It is just like Anna—Anna would have liked that." He had felt inclined to say it to his wife a thousand times—his good wife, who never had heard of Anna, and would not have heard of her with any pleasure. And now, here was Anna close to him, enshrined in the warmth and surrounded by all the prettinesses she had loved. It made his heart beat to think that he was so near her, that he would see her presently—and even that she had been unhappy. At fifty-five men are not often sentimental, but the hardest would be softened by the thought of a beautiful woman who had been unhappy about him for thirty years. He stood quite patiently, and waited for admittance. The hesitation of the other, her evident unwillingness to consent to his identity, which he could see was mingled all the time with a conviction that he was the person he claimed to be, had irritated and filled him with suspicions; but all this flew away upon the breath of old, old, unchangeable feeling. Anna! he had never ceased to think that the very name was music all these years.

The sound of the voices within the room was low

at first, but afterwards grew louder. Then it was mingled with impatient tappings as of a stick on the floor, and Mary's voice—he could trace both voices, they were so different, even in the murmur of talk at the beginning—took an expostulatory tone.

"I assure you, Anna—"

"Assure me nothing. Let him come in, let him come in: and I will let him know what I think of him."

It was certainly her voice; but in all his recollection he had never heard this tone in it. He waited listening, half amused, half sad, beginning to wonder more and more. At last he yielded to a sudden impulse, and went straight forward to the half-opened door.

There he stood for a moment arrested, struck dumb. And they, too, struck by the sound of the man's foot, so different from their own velvet steps, turned round and looked at him. Was that Anna? His heart, which had been beating so high, stopped short, and seemed to drop, drop into some unknown depths. "Oh yes, I see," he said to himself. "I see, I see. She is as handsome as ever——" But was that Anna? He stood on the threshold of this room, which was sacred to her, holding his breath.

Then the strange old woman, who was Anna, beckoned to him imperiously with her hand.

"Come in, come in," she said, "whoever you are,

who are using a name—— Come in. I do not know if you are aware that Mr Leonard Crosthwaite, whose name you are assuming——" Here she stopped and fixed two great, brilliant, dark eyes upon him, opened to their full width, glowing like angry stars. She made a pause of about a minute long, which seemed to the two others like an hour. Then she dropped her voice with a careless inflection, as if after that gaze she disdained the risk she was running—"died," she added indifferently, but pausing on the word—"at least twenty years ago."

"He did not die, Anna, since I am here," said the stranger.

It was impossible to speak to her, even now, without some tenderness getting into his voice.

"Do not venture to speak to me, sir, by my Christian name. Do you know there is a punishment for impostors? Oh, you think perhaps you know just how far you can go without infringing the law. Perhaps you think, too, that we are alone here, and you can frighten us. But that is a mistake. There is a butler, a strong man, whom I can summon in a moment with this bell, and there is my nephew. Any attempt at bullying or extortion will be useless here."

"Oh, Anna!" her sister cried; then she clasped her hands, turning to the visitor—"I told you she was changed."

A series of different emotions passed over the

Canadian's face—he smiled, then laughed angrily, growing red and hot; but over these variations stole such a softening of regret as combined all in one sorrowful sense of change. He nodded his head gently in reply to what the other sister said.

"You are right," he said in a low tone; "as handsome as ever, but how different! Anna, Anna, though we have been separated so long —though you cast me off, and I thought had forgotten me — though I am married and a happy man—yet you have never been put out of your place in my heart all these years."

She looked at him with those keen eyes; though she kept up wonderfully her air of lofty scorn and indifference, it was possible to perceive a gleam of something else, a mixture of satisfaction and anger in her face. "It is part of the rôle, of course," she said, "to call me by my Christian name. But Leonard Crosthwaite, whatever he might be else, was a gentleman. So you will keep to your part better by acting like a gentleman in this point. That is one way of making an impostor look like him."

He restrained himself with an effort. "What am I to call you then?" he said, looking at her sister. "Has she never married? How wonderful that is! Miss Crosthwaite then: since you wish it, I will call you so."

A momentary shadow of humiliation went over

the proud face. She had chosen not to marry. She had always been beautiful, and she was not without fortune; but nobody whom she thought good enough had ever asked Anna Crosthwaite to marry him. And she did not like to remember this in presence of her old lover, whom she had loved once in her silly youth, though she forsook him: it was not, however, because of that love, or anything connected with it, that she received him thus now.

"I am Miss Crosthwaite," she said, "though you affect to be surprised. It is not all a woman thinks of to marry any fool that turns up, and to become the mother of fools. Go away to your son, Mary. That was your ambition: as it is your folly now, to believe in every deception, and allow yourself to be led by the nose. I think your *protégé* had better withdraw too, now that I have seen him. He has not a feature of poor Leonard Crosthwaite," she added, eyeing him steadfastly. "No one, I suppose, can doubt my capacity to judge. His complexion is different, his features are different. Go away, sir, and be thankful we don't turn you over at once to the police."

"Is this," he said, half-stifled with astonishment and indignation, "is this all you have to say to me—"

"It is all I have to say to you," she said; "and this is my room, where I am supposed to have some right to choose my visitors. Go! You can do anything you please; I, for one, am not afraid of you. You may go."

He burst out laughing at the extraordinary perversity of the scene. If he had not laughed he must have been furious—it was his only deliverance; and yet it may be supposed there was not much laughing in his heart.

"This is the most extraordinary reception to meet with," he said, "after coming so far, after staying away so long. If it is a jest, it is a bad jest, Anna. Suppose that it is hard upon us after all this long interval, to look upon each other with such changed eyes—still there is such a thing as justice. You know me as well as I know you. It is by instinct—it is because we cannot help it. For, heaven knows, you are as unlike the Anna I left as night is to day."

She did not reply. A hasty gleam of passion came out of her keen eyes. Then she put out her hand to the bell. "Simmons," she said, "will see this person to the door, Mary. I don't want to be hard upon any acquaintance of yours; you know a very strange set of people, I must say; but I will not be insulted. Simmons must see this person out of the house."

The other sister looked at him with a look of agonised entreaty, clasping her hands. He was touched by it, though his only answer to Anna was another outburst of harsh laughter. "I would not like to be in your Simmons' shoes," he said, "if he tries to see me anywhere that I do not choose to go. But I do not care to thrust myself on anybody. Good-bye, Anna; we shall meet ere long in different circumstances, never fear."

With that he went out hastily into the hall, where the sentinel candle was still burning. There he was met by a young man who looked at him surprised. There was so much resemblance in this new-comer to the lady called Mary that there could be no doubt who he was. The Canadian did not pause to inquire. He put his hand on the young man's arm—"Come out with me, or take me somewhere where I can talk to you. There is a mystery that wants clearing up, and you can help me. I am your mother's cousin, Leonard Crosthwaite. What! you have heard the name before?"

"Indeed, I have heard the name; but you were supposed to be dead long ago," the young man said.

"I am not dead—your mother will tell you—I am newly returned from Canada. Tell me what reason there is to wish me dead," he said peremptorily. "It will be no worse for you——"

"No reason at all, sir," said the young man promptly. "I do not know who you are, but there is nothing to conceal. You are welcome to hear it all for me."

Then he led the visitor into a small room at the other side of the hall, into which after a while the young man's mother stole softly, crying and greatly agitated. She was startled beyond measure to find the visitor with her son, to whom she was going for consolation. But they were not long in convincing her that it was better that all there was to tell should be told.

When Mr Yorke left the house it was very dark and cold, and the rain beginning to drizzle. Young Geoffrey Underwood would have gone with him, or, failing that, pressed all manner of wraps upon him, as his mother had pressed refreshments: but the Canadian smiled at the cold, and the dismal, continuous, but not violent rain. "I am used to worse cold than this," he said. He went out into the night, more grave than when he had entered, but with a fire in his eye and in his heart of which there had then been no sign. He walked slowly along making calculations, arranging his course of procedure as he went down the hill. The rain came down faster and faster, till it swept like a great sheet of water from the inky sky. It swept all the suburban streets both of passengers and vehicles; nothing was to be seen but the wavering dismal lamps, making distorted reflections on the wet pavement—not a cab, not a place of shelter. Mr Yorke was drenched to the bones and chilled to the very heart.

CHAPTER III

AN evening in a hotel is seldom cheerful, and this evening was very forlorn. Mr Yorke did not return, though the hour for which he had ordered dinner was past. The girls sat very dolefully one on each side of the table, and read the books which had been provided for their amusement on board ship. Everything had been so lively on board ship, there had been so much society, so many expedients to make the time pass pleasantly, that they had not required to have recourse to these works. It was very strange and dreadfully disenchanting on their first night in London to be compelled to take to this way of getting through the evening. They expected to have been dining, cheerfully chatting about all their impressions, or, perhaps, though it was the first night, to have been taken to a theatre, and seen Shakespeare, perhaps, on Shakespeare's native soil. Perhaps if they had attained this object of their desires they might not have found it much more satisfactory—but then that did not occur to their fresh minds. And instead of such delights, to find themselves seated in a common-place room with a lamp which smoked, and two dull novels, and the rain coming down in bucketfuls outside, was as dreary and disappointing a termination to the day as could well be supposed. The solemn waiter came in and laid the cloth, and the girls had to change their places. Grace went to the window and gazed out at the pouring rain and the street lamps twinkling feebly through it. Milly sat down vacantly in a big chair, too far off the lamp to continue her book.

"I beg your pardon, Miss," said the soft-voiced waiter: "will you have the dinner up, or wait till the gentleman comes?"

"O, Grace!" said Milly, startled, appealing to her sister.

"Of course, we will wait for papa," said Grace, turning round from the window.

When the man went away poor little Milly, overtired and depressed, fell a-crying. "Oh, how strange it is! Oh, how lonely it is!" she cried. "I feel as if there was nobody alive—nobody that knew us."

Grace's lip twitched and quivered a little too. "How silly!" she said; "this is how you always are—up to the skies one moment, and down to the depths the next. What does it matter if nobody knows us? Two of us can go through the world —with papa."

"But what has become of papa?" said Milly.

They did not know what to think. He was not a man to be out at night, nor, though he was so undemonstrative, was he a man to abandon his children to an evening in an inn by themselves. Could anything have happened to him? There flashed across the minds of both recollections of stories they had heard, of sudden disappearances, stories mixed up in a great confusion with the Morgue, of which they remembered the name and the dismal use, without clearly remembering where it was; and of people found in the river, and all kinds of terrible catastrophes. These were so much too terrible, however, that after a while Grace laughed.

"What are you laughing at? I don't feel at all like laughing," Milly said in an aggrieved tone.

"We are behaving as if something had happened," Grace said; "such nonsense! Papa has been detained, that's all. I hope he is not getting wet out in this rain."

"Oh, I hope he is not getting wet!" Milly said, rising up hastily and running to the window. Milly had a turn for taking care of everybody's health. She was pleased with the importance of being a little "delicate" herself.

"I don't see how he should," said Grace with another laugh, which was somewhat forced, "when there are cabs at every step. Of course, he has not made up his mind to get wet, or to get lost, or to have an accident, solely to make us uncomfortable the very first day, like a naughty child. The dinner will be spoiled; that is all that will happen."

"As if it mattered about the dinner!" said Milly with feminine indifference, coming back from the window. The rain was not quite so heavy, and their spirits began to rise.

"Here is papa's letter-case with all the introductions. Let us look them over and imagine what sort of people they will be. First of all and foremost," said Grace, "Lord Conway; that is *our* Minister. He was once at our house—don't you remember, Milly? years and years ago, when he was the Honourable Mr Something-or-other; at least I have heard mamma say so———"

"Mamma would be sure to say Something-or-other. Of course he will come directly and call———"

"And ask us to go and stay there," added Grace seriously, "which would be grander than a hotel; but then one would not be so free to go out and in. I think I will advise papa not to go, or to go only for two or three days, to see how noble people live. To be sure," she added, "if he is not married—I wonder if he is married?—he could not ask us; unless he has a mother, or sister, or something, to keep his house."

"He is sure to be married," said Milly, "if it is so long since he was in Canada—longer than we can recollect; and a Minister too: he must be quite old!"

GROVE ROAD, HAMPSTEAD

"On the contrary, the Minister for the Colonies is often quite young, I believe," said Grace. What she founded this opinion upon we are unable to state, but it was Grace's peculiarity that she liked to be wiser than her neighbours. "Put Lord Conway on one side. Now there is Sir John Didcot. He is married; there is not any doubt about that. Don't you remember *him*, Milly?—a fat man who had to do with railways. He was dreadfully rich. I should think very likely they live in the country, and would ask us for—Easter, or that sort of thing. Everybody in London goes out of town for Easter. There are several national solemnities of that kind, you know," said Grace half satirically, half complacently. "Easter, and the Derby-day, and the 12th of August, and a few more."

"What do people do on the 12th of August? But we shall be back home," said Milly, "before that, shan't we? How nice it will be to get back home. I shall make papa buy loads of presents—presents for everybody. I was thinking only to-day what Lenny would like, and old John."

"It is rather too soon to think of presents for home, considering we only arrived yesterday," said Grace: and then she, too, breathed a small sigh, thinking of the bright room at home with all the boys laughing and questioning, and the tables covered with the presents they would carry back, and the baby, the darling of the whole house, seated triumphant in the midst of them, the fairy distributor of all these riches. Though it had been such a great thing to come to England—though it was such an ecstasy to be in England—yet, after all, home was a different matter. She gave a glance round this inn parlour, and smothered another little sigh.

"I suppose we shall have to go to the Didcots," she said, "sooner or later. Oh, after that here is something delightful! Mr Rivers, the author—you know. Of course, he will ask all the best people to meet papa. That will be far the most interesting of all. Fancy, perhaps we shall see Tennyson!" Grace raised a pair of great brown eyes opened wide with awe and rapture. "I wonder how one ought to behave one's self to a great poet. I should like to go down on my knees and kiss his hand."

"Ladies never go down on their knees—except to the Queen," said Milly, rousing up. "I wonder if we shall be asked to Windsor Castle or Buckingham Palace, or any of those places! It would be nice to know the princesses, don't you think?"

"We ought to be," said Grace sedately, "for papa had so much to do for the Prince of Wales. Oh!" cried the loyal colonial maiden, clasping her hands, "do you think the Princess will ask us, Milly? He will tell her, of course, who we are. That beautiful, beautiful creature! I don't know which of the two would be most delightful—the

GROVE ROAD, HAMPSTEAD

Princess or Tennyson. One would have to call him *Lord* Tennyson, as if he were nobody, a common peer," she added with a plaintive tone; "but to the Princess one would say Madam, or Your Royal Highness."

"Cissy Nunn told me you only said Ma'am."

"Cissy Nunn had no manners," said Grace. "I like titles; they are so pretty. Everybody that is beautiful, or delightful, or has genius should have some beautiful title. Princess!—that is what I should like to call her; but I suppose you can only do that when you are intimate—and I am afraid, with so many people as she must have to see, *that's* not very likely," the girl said regretfully.

Thus they went on talking the greatest nonsense in the world without suspecting it. The Yorkes were persons of importance at home. Whenever a great personage from England appeared there, he was received with all the resources of their simple and graceful, but by no means magnificent, hospitality. The distinguished visitors accepted all these little attentions cheerfully. They were the best to be had in the place, and they were characteristic of it, and amused the wandering peers and lions as much as if their hosts had been lions also, or peers. But it need not be said that the Colonial Secretary was very unlikely to invite the Yorkes to make his house their home, though that was how they had treated him; and that even the most amiable of princesses would not feel herself bound to invite, nor her august spouse even to recollect the name of the good colonial people who had been altogether at his service. Nay, we doubt much if the author would have felt himself bound to assemble a literary party for the admiration of the Canadian family. The simplicity of the girls considered all these natural returns of their hospitality not only as natural, but inevitable, though some doubts on the subject of the Princess did cross their minds. Still they could not help thinking an invitation was at least possible. These anticipations kept them amused, and made them forget the passage of time. The bland waiter came up to the door, and looked in more than once. Finally he entered, and asked respectfully if they would not like to have dinner served? Then they looked at each other blankly, relapsing all at once into alarm and gloom.

"Perhaps it will be better to have it put upon the table," said Grace, faltering.

"I couldn't eat a morsel," said Milly energetically.

"Oh, hush!" said the elder sister, "most likely the people are angry having to wait so long."

And this argument was too strong to be resisted. They were still a little afraid of making people angry, and loved to please everybody they were brought in contact with. Then came the soup, cold, which they tried to swallow; then a terrible soaked rag of fish. But the next moment Mr Yorke himself walked in. He told the girls hastily that he had been caught in the rain—that he had been paying a visit in a suburb, where cabs were not to be got easily, and that he was so wet and it was so late that he would go to bed at once and have something brought to him to his room. This was a climax to the discomfort of the evening. They sent away the joint notwithstanding the almost tears of the waiter. "Oh, what do we care for dinner!" the girls cried. They had been warned when they left home that, above all things, they were to see that their father did not catch cold.

"Mamma will think it is our fault," said Milly, with quivering lips. Who had ever heard of papa going to bed unless he were very, very ill? Even Grace, though she had so much strength of mind, could scarcely keep from crying. "Oh, how I wish we had never left home!" she said. "Oh, if mamma were only here!" said Milly. Left to their own resources, they could think of nothing but a longing, useless appeal to the one authority. Mamma would know what should be done in such an emergency. She would understand at a glance the position of affairs, and whether he might safely be left alone, or what should be done for him. The girls knew that he was a very difficult patient, and that nobody but their mother could persuade him to attend to himself. It was a terrible problem for them so soon, before they had even awoke to the possibility of such an accident; for who ever thought of papa falling ill? it had been the thing against which no precaution had been taken. The girls had a little medicine chest full of Mrs Yorke's domestic preservatives, and had received the minutest directions respecting their own health — but papa! "Take care your father does not catch cold," she had said: but that was all. He had always been subject to bad colds. "But what could we have done?" Grace asked of herself unconsciously, hearing her mother's warnings in her ears. After a while she ventured to go to his room to see if anything could be done. Mr Yorke had not gone to bed; he was sitting by a fire which smoked a little, in his dressing-gown, with a steaming glass of brandy-and-water by his side. He did not send away the girls, who floated into his room with a doubtful air, keeping close together like a pair of doves; but he looked up with restrained impatience from some letters he was reading. "What is it?" he said. Oh, not crossly—not at all crossly! they said afterwards; but keeping from being cross with an effort. The letters he was reading were old letters. Some lying on the table before him did not seem even to have been opened. He threw his handkerchief over them as the girls came in. "What is it?" Clearly he had found something which was of more interest to him than anything they could do or say.

"I hope you have had something to eat, papa," said Grace.

"I don't want anything to eat. I am taking this by way of precaution," he said.

"But you ought to eat. There is some mutton; it is quite hot still. May I ring and ask the waiter?"

"Don't take any trouble about me. Don't you think I am old enough to look after myself?"

Grace did not know what to do. Her mother, as she felt certain, and as Milly immediately suggested when they left the room, would have asked no questions; she would have had a tray brought in quite noiselessly without saying a word, and made him eat something. "Why didn't you run, then, and ask for the tray if you knew that was the right thing?" Grace asked afterwards, aggrieved: but Milly had not the courage to take any initiative.

They stood for two or three moments more, looking at him with an anxiety that was altogether helpless.

"Is your cold in your head, papa? Is it in your chest? Have you got a cough? Do you feel any pain? Shall I bring you some lozenges?"

Poor Grace! she was cudgelling her brain to know what to do; but to ask questions was just the thing she was never to do. In the flurry and agitation of her feelings she forgot that.

"There is nothing the matter with me," said Mr Yorke. "I have got a little cold; that is all; not to-night; I felt it when we landed. Go to bed. You must be tired too."

"But, papa——" said Grace, gazing at him anxiously, helpless, with nothing to suggest, yet a scared consciousness that there was certainly something that she ought to do.

He had the air of a man interrupted in something much more interesting than their girlish talk. A little pucker of impatience gathered in his forehead; but he was too serious to smile, or to make a joke of it, as he often did. And there was a flush on his face, and he was very hoarse, looking exactly as he did when he caught one of his *worst* colds.

"Well," he said almost harshly, "have you anything particular to say? If not, you see I am busy. I should prefer to be left alone."

Grace's anxious eyes were surveying him from head to foot. Milly, behind, plucked at her sleeve, meaning to convey some suggestion which she could not put into words. They wanted to do something—anything: but neither of them had the least idea what. Milly, who thus tried to prick her sister into exertion, was still more destitute than Grace was of any perception what to do.

"Good-night then, papa," said Grace slowly. She stooped over him to kiss him; and, oh, how hot his head was! One of his worst colds! and nobody here who knew what ought to be done, or what the danger was.

"Good-night," he said quickly. He gave a little sigh of relief as they went away, and turned back

GROVE ROAD, HAMPSTEAD

to the papers which he had hastily concealed. The girls saw this and it did not console them. They went back much depressed to the sitting-room, which had never been very bright, and which now was doleful beyond description. And this was their first night in England! Hearing, however, a furtive sob from Milly, Grace turned round upon her quite suddenly, and "snapped her up."

"Well!" she cried, "after all, it is not anything so very dreadful; papa has a cold; he has often had a cold before. He is busy with something. I don't see why you should make a fuss about it. I dare say he had something to eat when he was out. An old friend would be sure to offer him something. Of course, he will be better to-morrow; and we had better take his advice and go to bed."

Now Milly began to cry in earnest. "We did not come to England all this long way," she said, half miserable, half indignant, "only to go to bed."

At which, though she was not much happier than Milly, Grace laughed. "Of course," she said, "you little goose, the first thing we do everywhere is always to go to bed. We must do that. You may live without going to the theatre," Grace added philosophically, with a little sigh, "without going into society—but not without going to bed."

Nevertheless it was forlorn to be able to think at nine o'clock of no other way of spending the evening. They occupied a little of the vacant time by ordering tea, for the spoiled dinner had not tempted them; and then sadly enough they put back the letters of introduction into the letter-case. It seemed less probable now somehow, they could not tell why, that the Princess would take any notice of them, or that Lord Conway would carry them off to his house. They put away those passports to society, through which they had seemed to have a momentary glimpse of everything that was splendid. As they did so a little piece of paper fell out. Milly took it up and read it first; then Grace came and looked over her shoulder. It was very inoffensive and unimportant in appearance—a simple address, 3 Grove Road, Hampstead, written in their father's hand. He had sent, they recollected, for the Directory and taken an address out of it that morning. Could this be where he had been visiting—the suburb in which he had not been able to get a cab? A slight tremor ran over them, a sense of mystery which could scarcely be called disagreeable. Who could it be who lived at 3 Grove Road, Hampstead? And why had he gone the very first day to call there? The girls held their breath. Visions of some old love, far too old to be anything but a memory, came into their minds. They were divided between a little jealousy on their mother's account and a romantic interest about the unknown.

"It is a lifetime since he left England," said Grace with emphasis. Their imaginations leaped into a whole romantic story. They put back the scribbled address into the letter-case with a sort of awe. They had never been so much interested in their father before.

"I wonder who she is," Milly said softly under her breath. "I wonder if we shall ever see her."

"Whoever she is," cried Grace, "and whether we see her or not, you must recollect—not a word, not a word to mamma!"

"As if I were such a goose!" cried Milly. "But she must be so old — so old! Mamma would not mind."

This discovery, or supposed discovery, relieved them from the nervous alarm and misery which was beginning to overpower them. After a while they even laughed softly under their breath. Papa's old, old love affair, though it was interesting and even touching, as a relic of the ancient ages, was yet more or less amusing too. They put back the scrap of paper along with all the big, imposing letters, which were so much more pretentious, but which it was very evident their father had not been nearly so much interested by. They liked him for going *there* first of all: and then they permitted themselves a little laugh.

"I dare say," said Grace, "they were quite young when they were parted. How strange it must be to meet after so many years! One reads of it in books sometimes. I wonder if he will take us to see her. I should think she would like to see us— if she is nice," she added with a little hesitation.

"She must be nice," said Milly, "or he would not have remembered all these years, and gone to see her the very first minute. I wonder if mamma would be angry, Grace? I wonder if *she* is married too?"

"Oh, no, no!" cried Grace, decidedly. "Men may do that, but not women. You may be sure she has lived all the time—oh, not making herself unhappy—but always faithful! She will be good; she will do all sorts of things for people; but marry —no! I *hope* he will take us to see her. It is like England. It is what I have always thought of England. People are so faithful here. Not changing about, not always looking for something new. I do hope he will take us to see her, Milly."

"I suppose mamma would have no objection," said Milly, her mind somewhat divided on the subject.

They exhausted this new theme, looking at it from every side. And at last, much more cheerful —having, indeed, to exercise restraint upon themselves not to chatter too much as they passed their father's door, and perhaps disturb him—they went to bed, no longer thinking it so dismal. This hypothesis, which was built upon so slight a foundation, was on the whole the most amusing and the most interesting suggestion that had ever yet entered their minds in respect to papa.

CHAPTER IV

ROBERT YORKE had gone to Canada about thirty years before the beginning of this history. He was then a robust young man of about twenty-five, a great athlete, and bringing from "home" all that science in cricket and other cognate sports which people out there are proud to think is the inheritance of every Englishman. He had begun in a very humble way, without introductions or recommendations of any sort—a thing which made the first steps of his course both slow and difficult; but besides being a gentleman, which is a thing never without effect, he was a young fellow of resolution and self-control, and there is no disadvantage in the world which will stand against those qualities. He made his way slowly, but very surely, always working upward. He was a man whom people could not fail to note wherever he went, a man who was loved and hated, or at least vehemently disliked: the mild approval of indifference never was his. Perhaps it might even be said that the majority of people disliked the man. He was not conciliatory. He was very silent, very reserved, so reserved that his wife even knew nothing about him, where he came from, who were his relations, or if he had any. On the other side of the Atlantic a man is permitted to be the son of his own actions. Where there are so many new people there are not the same researches into the antecedents of a candidate for social acceptance, as are common among us. He did not belong to a Canadian family, but was entirely a new man; and he was not enquired into. Any rash person who attempted to do so made little by his motion. Such anxious inquirers as ventured to put the question to him, whether he belonged to the Yorkes of Hardwicke, or any other great family of the name, were met with a stern and simple negative which made an end of them. "No," he would say, with a perfectly blank countenance, and remain silent, defying further inquiry. When a man is married, then is the moment for investigations; but though Yorke married into a very good family, a family which had been settled in Canada for at least three generations—which is something like coming in with the Conqueror—he would seem to have successfully resisted all attempts to make him give an account of himself. He said shortly that he had "no relations" to the inquiries of his parents-in-law. It is not to be denied that they disliked this at first; but finding that no better was to be made of it, they reflected that it was rather a recommendation to a husband in some cases, and permitted the marriage. Mrs Yorke was about ten years younger than her husband, still a pretty woman, as she had a good right to be, having had neither cares nor troubles to deepen the genial lines, or engrave a single wrinkle on her pleasant countenance. She had never been required to think of anything beyond the needs of her household. Her mind was as fresh as her face. Though she was a great authority to her children, and knew exactly what to do in household emergencies, and how to take care of them all when anything was the matter with them—and even how to manage her husband when he had one of his bad colds—she had never had any harder intercourse with life. All went smoothly with her in its bigger affairs. She had everything that heart could desire—according to her position in life.

That position was very different in Canada from what it would have been at home. Here, in this old island, we ordinary folks, who modestly call ourselves ladies and gentlemen without aspiring to rank or greatness, are quite aware that we are out of the way of Princes and Princesses, and Secretaries of State. When we go to London, even if we may have arranged a royal entry into our special burgh, or been "of use" to a wandering Prince, it never occurs to us that the Princess will have heard of our arrival in town, and will forthwith ask us to tea. But on the other side of the Atlantic things are different, and to be in the best society, to be in the way of meeting, and even entertaining all the illustrious wanderers of the earth, it is not necessary to be very rich or great. Your position in life does not depend upon money, but upon many things that are little taken into account in more formal society—upon energy and civic services, and even sometimes upon that faculty of keeping in the front of affairs which many people who have no other merit possess, and which tells everywhere, more or less. The Yorkes were not overwhelmingly rich. He had not made a colossal fortune; but, on the other hand, his expenses were moderate. And without living at all splendidly, or with any ostentation of wealth, it was recognised that they were to be reckoned among the best people. They lived that kind of life which to many people appears, or did once appear, an ideal existence—a life of domestic comfort, of homely wealth, and family companionship: in which Cowper's picture of the close-drawn curtains, the blazing fire, the hissing tea-urn was realised continually, with all the warm family adoration and mutual knowledge, and also, perhaps, something of the narrowness and sense of superior virtue which that ideal implies. The Yorkes living thus quite simply and domestically, parents and children together, had a position which people possessing six times their income, and living ten times as expensively, would not have had in England. They kept no more than one homely little carriage of all work, and were served indoors by maidservants; but, notwithstanding, they were among "the best people," and were not afraid to offer their simple hospitality, in happy ignorance of its want of splendour, to all the strangers who pleased them, and sometimes, among these, to very great people indeed.

While their children were young it had been several times proposed that Mr and Mrs Yorke should go "home" on a visit, to see England, and the ways of the old world. Mrs Yorke in particular, who had never been in England in her life, had been much excited by the idea of going "home;" but many things came in the way. Sometimes the drawback was on her side, in the shape of babies, or other natural impediments of a young mother's career; and sometimes on his, in claims of business. Indeed, it had been generally remarked by all the friends of the family that Yorke himself never showed any great inclination to go home. After it had all been settled over and over again that they were to go, it came to be a foregone conclusion with all observers that something would certainly come in the way to change all the plans. Yet nobody could say that Yorke was to blame; the accidents that detained and deterred them were perfectly natural, and so far as could be seen, quite unavoidable. After the two elder girls grew up matters became more pressing, for while Mrs Yorke, with her children always on her mind, very easily accepted any excuse for giving up an expedition which must have carried her away from them, Grace and Milly had no such reasons to hold them back, and clamoured for the tour in which they themselves were to have a share.

What it was which at last decided their father to this journey, nobody knew. He was no more explanatory upon this matter than upon so many others. All he did was to announce one evening, coming back from his business, that he thought if they could get ready to start by next mail he really would be able to go. There was reality, and there was meaning in his tone. This time nobody said, "You will see: nothing will come of it." From the very beginning everything was different this time. He went at once and inquired about berths in the steamers; he inquired after the outfits, the preparations which the ladies had to make, warning them that they could get all the new fashions in London—" or in Paris," he added, seeing the smile of scorn upon the girls' faces. But by this time Mrs Yorke had become more reluctant than ever to leave her little children, and encounter all the troubles of a long voyage. She had grown a little stout, not more than was becoming, all her friends said, though people who did not take any interest in her good looks were perhaps less flattering; and with this increased fulness there had come an increased disinclination to budge. She made a thousand excuses. Reginald was a little delicate. Lenny was just at that crisis in his education when, if he was not kept up to his work, something dreadful might happen. ("And mamma thinks she can keep him up to his work!" the girls said aside, with incredulous laughter; for, indeed, she was always the first to find out that he had a headache, and that health was of far more importance than any examination.) Then little Mary, the baby, had not yet got all her teeth. "And how a woman could find it in her heart to leave a baby teething—when everybody knows convulsions may come on at any moment," Mrs Yorke protested she did not know. The end was that two days before the day of sailing, she announced point-blank that it was impossible. She could not do it. Home! why this was home, where they had all been born. She was very glad that the girls should go, who had the energy: but she had not the energy; and the little ones wanted her. All the bystanders, breaking out into accustomed smiles, declared that they knew it from the beginning. When it was not one thing it was another. When it was not Robert Yorke who could not leave his office, it was Louisa who could not leave her nursery—everybody knew from the first mention of the plan that it never would be carried out.

But this conclusion, though so often justified, was not infallible. On hearing, in an outburst of despair from the girls, mamma's resolution, Mr Yorke stood stoutly to his colours. It was very unfortunate that mamma should feel so, but in that case he must go without her, he said; and he believed that he could take care of Grace and Milly, so as not to lose the passage money altogether. Mrs Yorke was very thankful to consent to the compromise. She was not of an anxious mind; everything had gone well in her family up to this time; there had been no losses, no accidents; there was no tradition of misfortune in the household, such as chills the hearts of some; and she saw them go with a cheerful countenance. The wind blew rather strong the first night, nothing to hurt, only a quarter of a gale; and she shuddered, and was thankful she was not with them. "Robert is an excellent sailor, and the girls are young. They were never at sea before; they will take pleasure in being a little ill as a new experience. But I cannot bear it, it puts me out altogether. I am thankful I am not with them," she said; and so settled herself quite quietly with her nursery tea-party to wait till the travellers should return; which would be "such an amusement."

This is how it happened that Mr Yorke and his daughters came to England without her. The girls lamented her withdrawal loudly; but Yorke himself said little. He made a half confidence to her the evening before they left. "To tell the truth," he said, "it is something I saw in the English papers that decided me, something about some property."

"What property?" said Mrs Yorke, to whom, as she had six children, the question of property was by no means uninteresting; but he only said, "It may come to nothing. I will tell you all about it when I come back." She had curiosity enough after he was gone to send to the office for the old newspapers, and to examine them carefully to see if she could find any clue to this mysterious speech; but she could not. And she was an easy-going soul, and found it not in the least impossible to wait for the information until he should come home.

Thus the father and daughters crossed the Atlantic, justifying her easy confidence in the invariable good fortune of the family by having a most prosperous voyage. And nothing could be more bright than the cheerful assault with which the two girls on that first morning took possession of London and all its associations. They had a delightful morning, but not a very cheerful night. As, however, the girls were both alive to the thought that a cold generally ("very often," said Milly; "almost always," cried Grace, more confidently still) goes off, when proper precautions are taken, in the night—they consoled themselves. To-morrow is always a new day.

CHAPTER V

THE girls knew nothing more till next morning. There was no reason why they should be alarmed. After all a cold is no such great matter. When they went to bed they went to sleep, as is natural at their age, and heard nothing more till they were up and dressed, having almost forgotten their father's illness altogether. Before, however, they were quite ready to leave their room, something occurred which startled them greatly. There was a knock at the door, in which of itself there was an alarming sound. Mystery and meaning were in it far beyond the sound of an ordinary knock. When one of them rushed to open it, a woman came in of imposing appearance. She did not speak to them at the door, as the servants of the hotel did, but came in even without being asked. Importance was in her look, in her rustling silk dress and lofty cap, in her soft and almost stately step.

"My dear young ladies," she said, "you must not be alarmed;" and with this came in, and with her hand behind her shut the door. Naturally the girls' imagination immediately leapt at things terrible—bad news from Canada, a summons home.

GROVE ROAD, HAMPSTEAD

"What is the matter? Is it a telegram?" they cried with one breath.

"Oh, no, it is no telegram; fortunately, the poor gentleman is in his own comfortable room, where he will be seen to as comfortably as if he were at home. He said you were not to be alarmed."

"We are thoroughly alarmed now," said Grace; "tell us the truth at once."

"Your poor papa, my dear young ladies, is very poorly," said their visitor. "I am the manageress of this hotel. He rang his bell in the night, and we sent for a doctor; everything has been done that could have been done. I made the mustard with my own hands for his poultice. We are always ready in our great way of business for everything that can be required. I had the *Foil de Rigolette* ready, but he preferred mustard. Everything was done that could be done."

The two girls instinctively had drawn together, and caught each other by the arm in mutual support. "Oh, tell us, tell us," they cried; "is papa——" and then their lips refused to fashion the other dreadful word that leapt to them. The manageress was satisfied with the effect she had produced. Instead of the fresh and cheerful girls to whom she had introduced herself, two woebegone and colourless ghosts stood before her trembling with dismay and terror.

Then she nodded her head encouragingly. "A little better—yes, a little better. We have made as much progress, the medical gentleman says, as can be expected in such a sharp attack. Mustard chest and back have eased the breathing, and though he does not wish it to be concealed from you that it is a very sharp attack——"

Milly dropped her sister's arm, and, sinking down upon a chair, fell a-weeping in mingled excitement and terror and relief. Grace stood still, holding by the table for support, very pale, and with trembling lips.

"You have not told us what it is. He had a bad cold."

"That is how it always begins," said the manageress; "but you will have the consolation of knowing that it has been taken in time, and that everything has been done. I was called up at once, and I have given him my best attention. I always say I am half a doctor myself. Yes, it is congestion of the lungs; but you must not be alarmed—indeed you must not be alarmed, my dear young ladies; there's no reason to suppose that he won't recover——"

"Recover!" they both cried together like a lamentable echo, turning towards her four beseeching eyes, as if she held in her hand the issues of fate.

"And do well—and do well," she said hastily. "That's what I meant. Go and take some breakfast, and fortify yourselves like good dears; and when the doctor comes, we'll see. You can ask him; and if the sight of you wouldn't agitate your poor papa——"

Why should it agitate him? Why should it not be the most natural thing in the world to see them by his bedside? That this should not have been his first thought was beyond measure extraordinary to the girls; but they yielded to the wonderful, appalling argument after a little. If it would agitate him, if it might hurt him, whatever it might cost them, they must stay away. There could not be any question about that. After a while they went, sick-hearted and miserable, into the sitting-room where their breakfast was laid, and where, the one persuading the other, they swallowed each a cup of tea. Then they sat down to wait the coming of the doctor. They had a long time to wait. It was a bright morning after the rain, and they sat at the window and watched all the comings and goings in the dingy London street. Opposite to them was a tall house with a balcony, filling up all the horizon; and the tradesmen's carts jostled up and down for an hour or two, and lugubrious organ-grinders stopped underneath, encouraged by the sight of the two faces, possible listeners, which appeared at their window. And thus the first of the morning passed, and hansom cabs began to rattle about, depositing, with loud clang and hum, now young men and now old, at the different doors; and the stream of passers-by quickened; and postmen and telegraph boys came and went with sharp rattles of knocking; and quick footsteps beating up and down the street. The girls were not always at the window: now one, now another would go to the door of the sick-room and listen to the sounds inside. And sometimes the door would be opened, and something asked for, which Grace or Milly, far more rapid than any waiter, would rush to get. "Just the same, just the same," was all the nurse could say to them. They began to feel as if they were entirely dependent upon this woman, and that in her hand was the decision of all.

When the doctor appeared at last he was so rapid and so hurried that it was all they could do to get him to pause to speak to them as he left the room. "No better; but I did not expect it," he said. "No worse: these things must take their course."

"But we are his daughters," cried Grace. "Is it possible that you will shut us out from his bedside? Whenever he has been ill, we have always nursed him. Oh, why must we be kept out now?"

"Always nursed him?" said the doctor; "that is well thought of. Step in here. Do you mean to say that he has had this before?"

"What is it?" said Grace. "He has had bad colds, very bad colds. Mamma was always anxious when he had one of his colds."

"And mamma told us above all things that we must not allow him to catch cold," cried Milly.

GROVE ROAD, HAMPSTEAD

"Oh, how badly we must have managed! but how could we know? and what could we do? And it was only the second night."

The doctor was quick-witted and sympathetic; but naturally he thought of his patient as a case, and not as a man. "Not to allow him to catch cold! that's easier said than done," he said with a half-smile, shaking his head. "I thought there must be delicacy of the chest to begin with; all that could not have been done in one day."

"No, no, there was no delicacy; he was always well and strong—always strong," the girls cried, emulating and supplementing each other. They poured upon him instantly a hundred examples of their father's robustness. He had never been ill in his life, except with a cold, and everybody has colds. He never took any special care. Mamma was anxious, but then mamma was always anxious about us all, though we are known to be the healthiest family! To all these eager explanations Doctor Brewer listened with that half-smile, shaking his head; but he was interested. From looking at this matter as only a case, he began to realise the human creatures involved in it, and to perceive that the man who was ill was the head of an anxious, probably dependent family, and that these two pale, frightened, eager girls, with their young beauty all obscured by this cloud of pale terror and confusion, were his children. He began to look at them with a certain tenderness of pity.

"You are very young," he said at last, when they gave him time to speak. "I think you had better telegraph at once for your mother."

"For mamma?" their faces were pale before, but this suggestion withdrew from them every tinge of colour.

"She is the best nurse he can have; she ought to be here to take care of you in any case. Give me her address, and I will telegraph. She ought to know at once."

"Doctor!" said Grace, separating herself from her sister, "oh, let *us* know at once. Is it so serious? is it dangerous? I am not very young, and I am the eldest, and have had a great deal of experience. Mamma could not be here for nearly a fortnight; and think what a thing it would be, the long voyage alone, and the fear of what she might find when she came, and no news—no news for ten days or more—for she might not have so good a passage as we had. And then she has never been used to travel, or do anything by herself. Oh, doctor, do you think—do you think that it is so serious as that?"

"Where is your mother?" he said.

"In Canada," they both cried in one breath.

Dr Brewer began to be more interested than was at all justifiable in what was after all only one case out of a hundred. "Poor children! poor children!" he said. They stood with their faces intent upon him, four great brown eyes, with the eyelids curved and puckered over them in deep arches of anxiety and terror, appealing as if to a god who could kill and make alive. He was overcome by this passionate trouble and suspense. He put out his hand (he had children of his own) and touched lightly with a soothing touch the nearest shoulder. "You must not be frightened," he said. "I see you are brave girls; you will do your duty. No; if she is so far away as that, we will not frighten your mother to-day—not to-day."

"You think he is very ill?" they said, searching his face as if it were full of secret folds and hieroglyphics which searching could find out.

"He has a sharp attack. Come, one of you shall go, one at a time, and be at hand if anything is wanted. I sent him a nurse last night, whom I happened to be able to lay my hand upon. She will want a rest occasionally. If you will obey orders exactly, and call her whenever you are at a loss—one at a time."

"Milly is not strong—not so very strong," cried Grace; "let it be me. I nursed them all when we had scarlet fever: and I never cry nor break down."

"Oh, Grace! I should not cry if I were with papa," cried Milly, with streaming eyes.

Dr Brewer almost cried too. He was tender-hearted, as so many doctors are, and then he had girls of his own. But he could not spend all his morning with these two pretty forlorn creatures, and their father, who was struggling for his life.

This went on for more than a week, during which there was to these poor girls neither night nor day, but all one confused languor and excitement and anxiety; the monotony of the sick-room, broken only by now and then a terrified consultation with nurse and doctor, or between themselves, as to what was to be done. During all this time they defended their mother from the telegram with which the doctor had threatened her. The more they thought of it the more impossible it seemed that she should be summoned upon such a journey at a moment's notice and kept, during all its course, in the terrible anxiety which was inevitable if once she knew what was hanging over them. After the first days Dr Brewer himself did not urge it. He said to himself that all would be settled one way or other before the poor woman could come: and that the girls, poor things! must bear it as they could if matters came to the worst.

Meanwhile, as the dreary days went on, the sick-room, in its stillness and monotony, became the scene of one of those hand-to-hand struggles with death in which there is all the terrible force of a tragedy to those who are aware of the conclusion which is drawing nigh; but it is seldom that the persons who are most interested are aware of this. And Grace and Milly were too young and inexperienced to realise more than that papa was no better from morning to morning, from night to night. There was always one of them in the room with the nurse, and occasionally Mr Yorke was well enough to talk to them. But either he did not realise the seriousness of his own position, or the torpor of approaching death, and the self-absorption of weakness and suffering had begun to steal over him. He liked Grace to do what was needful for him, but smiled at poor little Milly, bidding her run away and amuse herself. "You ought to be doing something. You ought to be taking advantage of your opportunities. Who knows if you will ever be in London again?" he said, once or twice, with that strange forgetfulness of all the circumstances which bewildered the girls; but either he had nothing important to say, or, in the languor of his illness, he deferred the saying of it, preferring to turn his face to the wall and escape from all consideration of what was coming. Once only this silence was broken; but not to much purpose. He had asked for something to drink; and as Grace raised him—she could do this now as easily as if he had been a child—he caught and was touched by the look of anxiety on her face.

"Poor little Grace!" he said, when he was laid back again upon his pillow, "this is a curious way of enjoying London." He had not much breath to talk, and had to pause between his words.

"Not at all, papa. Yes, it is dreadful for you to have to suffer, but for me quite natural, you being ill."

Then he gave a feeble laugh. " Your mother—will not suppose—that we are engaged like this."

" Milly has written to say you are not well."

" Not well—that was right—not to make her anxious." He laughed a little again. " But she will have to be told—some day: my poor Milly." This was his wife's name as well as his child's.

" Yes, papa, when you are quite well again. She will not mind then; but don't you think that it is best to say little till you are better? for she would be so anxious; and what would be the use of bringing her over, when you will be all right again before she could get here? "

" I shall be all right again," he said, pausing upon each word. The smile had gone off his face. He seemed to weigh the words, and drop them one by one. Was he asking himself whether that would ever be, or only lingering for want of breath? " Remind me," he said, " of the people I went to see: there is something I want—to tell you about. But I can't—be troubled now," and with that he turned once more, as he was so fond of doing, his face to the wall.

Thus the melancholy days went on. Grace had begun to feel something fatal in the air, but Milly had not yet gone farther than the fact that papa was very ill, and that it might be weeks before he was well again, when Dr Brewer came into their room after his nightly visit. They had been trying to eat something, which they simply acknowledged as a duty, but did not know how to get through. Their meals were the most dreadful moments of their day, the only things that marked its melancholy course. The doctor came in, not hurriedly, as he usually did. He drew a chair to the table and sat down beside them. "What are you having—tea? I never told you to take tea," he said.

"It is so easy to take," Milly pleaded, "far easier than anything else."

"In the meantime you must have some wine," he said, ringing the bell; "yes, yes, you must take it whether you like it or not. Now tell me a little about yourselves, as I have some time to myself to-night. My wife was talking of coming to see you. I have never heard anything about your friends in London. It is time to think of looking them up——"

"That means papa is better," said Milly. "I knew it from the first moment, as soon as I saw the doctor's kind face."

He turned his kind face away from them with a forced smile. He could not bear to meet their anxious eyes.

"But we have no friends—not to call friends," said Grace, who was not quite so sure as Milly, and yet was so glad to take Milly's opinion for this once. "We have letters to quantities of people, and some of them we have seen at home. There is Lord Conway," she said with a little hesitation—"he once stayed at our house. It is a long time ago, but we thought—oh, we did not want him to ask us, especially since papa has been ill. It would be dreadful to have a long illness in a stranger's house."

"Lord Conway!" Dr Brewer said, bewildered.

"But we don't know him, not as you know your friends," Grace made haste to add; "we don't know any one in that way. They are all people who have been in Canada, or the friends of people who have been in Canada."

The doctor shook his head. "Do you mean that you know nobody, my poor dear children? You have no *friends*—people who really are acquainted with you, who would take a little trouble for you, whom you could have recourse to——" Here he stopped, confused, feeling Grace's eye upon him. "I thought you might have—relations even, on this side of the water," he said.

"Whom we could have recourse to!" said Grace —"oh, doctor, tell us, tell us what you mean! Why should we want to have recourse to any one? That means more than ordinary words——"

"He means—to show us some civility—to show us England—now that papa is going to get better," said Milly, throwing back her head with a pretty movement of pleasure. But Dr Brewer did not raise his eyes. He could not face them, the one so anxious to divine his meaning, the other happy in her mistake. Milly was talkative and effusive in her joy. "Now we ought to telegraph to mamma," she cried. "She will have got the first letter saying how ill papa was. It will be delightful to relieve her mind all in a moment—to tell her he is getting well, almost as soon as she knew that he was ill. We must telegraph to-morrow."

Dr Brewer still did not meet Grace's anxious gaze, which would have read his face in a moment. "You are very young," he said, "to have had such a—responsibility upon you. You have been very brave hitherto, and you will not break down now. I am afraid, indeed, that I shall have to telegraph to your mother—very soon now."

It was his tone more than what he said which disturbed Milly in her happy confidence. She turned round suddenly and looked with an awful inquiry, not at him but at Grace. Grace for her part, trembling, had grasped Dr Brewer by the arm. "Doctor!" she said in a strange, stifled voice. She could not say any more.

He covered her soft little thin hand with his and patted it gently. "My poor dear children," he said, "my poor children! how can I tell you——" His voice was broken. It told all he had to say without the aid of any words. How could he put it into words? For a moment it seemed to the doctor as if the man's death must be his fault, and that they would have a right to upbraid him for letting their father die. He sat there with his head drooped and with his heart full of sympathetic anguish, not knowing what might happen next.

Milly gave a great cry. She had not feared all this time, and just now she had been happy and triumphant in the thought that danger was over. She cried out and threw herself suddenly on the ground at the doctor's feet. "Oh, no, no!" she cried. "Oh, don't let it be. Don't let it be! Doctor, think of us poor girls; think of mamma and all the children; doctor, doctor!" said Milly, her voice rising louder and louder in her despair.

Grace had not said anything. She stood, her face all quivering with anguish, her eyes fixed upon him. She seemed to take up the last quivering note of Milly's cry — "Is there no hope?" she said.

The doctor shook his head. He laid his hand tenderly upon poor Milly's hair—every line of his face was working. "Listen to me," he said, his voice trembling. "You have been very courageous, very good hitherto—and now there is one last effort before you. You at least will stand by him to the end. You will not make it worse, but better for him, Grace."

The girl tried to speak two or three times before the words would come. When she found utterance at last what she said was scarcely intelligible. It was, "And Milly too."

"It would be better, far better, that she should lie down and try to rest. I will give her something; but you—you must come with me, Grace."

"And Milly too," the girl said again, as if these were the only words she was capable of. She gathered up her sister from where she lay at the doctor's feet, and whispered to her, smoothing away her disordered hair. Milly was not able to stand. She leaned her weight upon her sister; her pretty hair fell about her face, all wild and distorted with crying. She wanted to get down again to the floor to kneel at the doctor's feet. "He could do something still if he were to try. Oh, Gracie, Gracie! think of us two miserable girls, and mamma, and all the children. He could do something if he were to try."

"Milly! we have got to stand by him—to keep up his heart——"

"I cannot stand—I cannot stand, I think I will die. Oh, doctor, doctor! do something, find out something! Couldn't you do something if you were to try?"

"Milly, am I to go alone—the last time—to papa?"

"Put our blood into him," cried Milly, holding up her small white wrists. "They do that sometimes. Take mine—oh, every drop!—and Grace's too. Doctor, doctor! you could do something if you were to try."

For weeks after, this cry rang in the good doctor's ears. They both caught at the idea; even Grace, who had command of herself. How easy it seemed!—to take the young blood out of their veins and pour it, like new life, into his. Sometimes it is done in stories—why not, why not, in actual life? Their voices ran into a kind of clamour, imploring him. It was long before the impression made by this scene left the doctor's mind and recollection. Nevertheless, that night both the girls stood by their father's bedside quietly enough, making no scene, watching eagerly for any last word he might have to say to them. But how few of the dying have any last words to say! He opened his eyes, and smiled vaguely twice or thrice, as though all had been quite happy and simple around him—he had gone out of the region in which anxieties dwell. Perhaps he did not remember that he was leaving them helpless among strangers—or if he knew, the ebb of the wave had caught him and he could feel nothing but the last floating out to sea, the sound of the waters, the tide of the new life.

Left to themselves in such circumstances, the poor girls had no alternative but to be crushed altogether, or to rise into heroic fortitude; and happily Grace had strength enough for that better part. She dressed herself, when the dreadful morning came, in the only black frock her wardrobe contained, with the composure of a creature braced by the worst that could happen, and knowing now that whatever might come, nothing so terrible could fall on her again. The shock, in-

GROVE ROAD, HAMPSTEAD

stead of prostrating her as it did her sister, seemed to rally all her forces, and clear and strengthen every faculty. She had scarcely slept, notwithstanding the calming dose which the doctor in his pity had insisted upon administering to both. It procured for poor little Milly some hours of feverish unconsciousness, but with Grace it acted on the mind, not the body, numbing the pain but giving an unnatural and vivid force to all her faculties. Her brain seemed to be beset by thoughts; and first among them was a yearning sympathy and pity for her mother. The sudden shock of a curtly worded telegram would be so novel, so terrible, to that happy woman, who never all her life had known what great sorrow was, that her young daughter shuddered at the thought.

As soon as she got up she began to write to her, while Milly still tossed and moaned in her unquiet sleep. Grace's letter was such as no poet, save one of the highest genius, could have written. It was love and not she that composed it. It was a history of all the last days, tender and distinct as a picture. Every word that she said led up to the terrible news at the end, imperceptibly, gradually, as it is the art of tragedy to do, so that the reader should perceive the inevitable and feel it coming without the horror of a sudden shock. When her sister woke she read this letter to her, and they wept over it together. It was almost as new to Milly as it would be to her mother, for she had not realised the slow constant progress of the days to this event, nor had Grace herself done so, till she had begun to put it down upon paper. When the doctor came in the morning the letter was all ready, put up and addressed; and then it was that Grace insisted no telegram should be sent.

"Mamma has never had any trouble all her life. He always did everything. Nothing dreadful has ever happened to us. The children have been ill, but they always got better. We never were afraid of anything. If this were flung at mamma like a shot—like a blow—it might kill her too."

"Yes, it might kill her too," Milly murmured, turning to the doctor her large strained eyes.

"But, my dear children, somebody must come to you at once; you can't be left here alone. Your mother will be strengthened to bear it as you are, and for your sake. Somebody must come to you at once."

"O Gracie!" murmured Milly, looking at her sister with beseeching eyes.

"Why?" said Grace steadily. "That is just what I cannot see. Nobody could wish mamma to come now. What good would it do? It would be dreadful for her;—and to him—to him!——"

Here, brave as she was, she had to stop, and could not say any more.

"Of course," said the doctor softly, "your father is beyond all need. He is safe now, whatever happens; but you—what can you do? Somebody must come at once to take care of you, to take you home."

Once more Milly's eyes travelled from Grace to the doctor, and back again. To have some one to take care of them sounded to Milly the only thing that was left on earth to desire.

"No one," said Grace, wondering at her own calm, "could be here for a fortnight; and the first days will be the worst. After that things will be easier. Don't you see, everything that can happen will have happened then; and why should some one—for it could not be mamma now, Milly; it would not be mamma : why should some one be disturbed and made uncomfortable, and forced to start at a moment's notice, only to take care of us? I can take care of Milly, and we can go home." Another pause till the tears were swallowed somehow. "It will be less hard, on the whole, to go home by ourselves, than with any one else."

The doctor was struck by this argument. He looked at them anxiously, fragile as they were, looking like shadows of girls after the long anxiety and strain of these ten days.

"Do you think," he said, doubtful, "that you are able for it?"

"Able!" said Grace with the petulance of grief. "What is there to be able for now? We have borne the worst. If it had been a week ago, and

I had known what was coming, I should have said, No, we were not able. But now!" the girl cried with a kind of disdain, "now we have suffered all that can be suffered, doctor. We can never lose our father again."

Here Milly broke out into hysterical cries.

"Oh, papa, papa! Oh, Grace! What shall we do? What shall we do?"

Grace took her sister into her arms standing by the bedside, while the other sat up, her hair hanging about her, her face distraught with a passion of grief over which she had no control. The tears rained from Grace's eyes, but she stood firm as a rock.

"We must bear it," she said; "we must bear it, Milly. We cannot have that to bear again. We will not make it harder for mamma."

This scene upset the kind doctor for the day; he could not give his attention to the other cases which awaited him for thinking of this heart-rending picture. And as for the nurse, whose services were imperatively demanded for another "case"—she could not bear to take leave of them at all, but stole away as if she had done them a wrong.

"How could any woman with a heart in her bosom leave them in their trouble?" she said, sobbing, to the doctor; "but I am not a woman, I am only a nurse——"

"And there is a life to be preserved," the doctor

said. The woman, after all, was only a woman, petulant and unreasonable.

"We are all fools and know nothing. We could not save this life," she said, "though there were no complications."

Dr Brewer, too, felt a little ashamed. What was the good of him? He had done everything that his science was capable of, but that had been nothing. Old Death, the oldest of practitioners and the most experienced, had laughed at him, and out of his very hands had taken the prey.

The girls never knew what happened till the funeral was over; and yet it troubled them in the midst of their distress that there was nobody to ask to it, no train of mourners to do honour to their father. They went themselves, following the lonely coffin, and the doctor, half ashamed, half astonished at his own emotion, went with them, to see the stranger buried. He had sent the introductory letter to the Colonial office, accompanied by a statement of the circumstances; but the Minister was up to his eyes in parliamentary work, and his aides knew nothing about Mr Robert Yorke of Quebec. The landlord, out of respect for what had happened in his own house—though at first he had been very angry that any one should have taken such a liberty as to die in his house at the beginning of the season—followed at a little distance. He came by himself in the second mourning coach which the undertakers felt to be necessary, and in which it was well there should be some one for the sake of respectability. Notwithstanding all that had been said and done, it did not seem to the girls that they had ever realised what had happened till they came back that dreary afternoon, and sat down hand in hand in their sitting-room, the door closed upon all things, the murk evening closing in, and nothing to look forward to now—nothing to think of but their own desolation. They "broke down;" what could they do else? But when there are two to break down, it is inevitable that one of the two must see the vanity of tears and make an effort to check them.

"We cannot go on like this," Grace said. "We will only kill ourselves too; that will not be any comfort for mamma. In the first place, we must find out whether there was anything that—papa wanted done while he was in England. Yes! I mean to talk of him," she said, "just as if he were in Canada, as if he were next door; he must not be banished from his own because he is dead. Mamma will never let him be forgotten and put aside. We must accustom ourselves to talk about him. Perhaps there was something he wanted done. Do you recollect, Milly? he went away by himself that night?"

"Oh, Grace," cried her sister, "whoever they are, I hate those people. They were the cause of it. He would never have caught cold but for——"

Hush," said Grace, "we must not hate anybody. I should like to go and ask about them; they must have been old—friends."

It was at this moment that the waiter came in—the waiter who had always been so kind to them. He came in with a countenance regulated to the occasion.

"Young ladies," he said, "here's a gentleman below inquiring for a party as has come from Canada. It's not a name as ever I heard before. Mr Crosthwaite, he's asking for. I said as I did not like to disturb you such a day; but if so be as you might have heard speak of the name—from Canada."

Grief is irritable, and Grace turned upon the questioner with quick resentment. "Oh, how can you come and ask *us?*" she cried. "Is there nobody in your house to be disturbed but my sister and me?"

"I beg your pardon, Miss," said the waiter, "I hope I'm not unfeeling. Nobody could have felt more—if it ain't disrespectful to say so—according to their station in life. If it hadn't a been that the manageress is that cantankerous about a death in the house I'd have followed the poor gentleman willingly to his last 'ome, and never grudged no trouble; but when a gentleman comes to me and asks for a party as arrived from Canada a fortnight ago——"

The two girls looked at each other. Was

this, perhaps, the clue for which they were looking? They felt that it was wrong and a breach of the decorum of their sorrow that they should see any one on this day: but if, perhaps, this might be the clue they sought. "Arrived from Canada—a fortnight ago?" it seemed years—but they gulped down that thought. "We did so, you know," said Grace, "but that is not our name. I know no one of that name. Did you say——?"

"I told him all as had happened, miss," said the sympathetic waiter who brought the message, "and the gentleman was very sorry. He's a feeling gentleman, whoever he is. He said, 'Poor young ladies!" as feeling as I could have done it myself; but he's very anxious about this name Crosthwaite, or whatever it is. I said you was very considerate, and that if you could help him I made sure I might ask you. He would have liked to speak to any one as was from Canada," the waiter said.

Again the girls looked at each other. Any one from Canada! Perhaps, though they did not know any Crosthwaites, they might know the gentleman who was inquiring for them; and even the sight of some one from home would be a kind of consolation. Grace, with a look, consulted Milly, who had no counsel to give, but only appealed back again to Grace with her beautiful eyes. Then the elder sister said, tremblingly, "We are not fit to see any one; but if he thinks it will help him you may let him come up-stairs." She said this with a sigh of what she felt to be extreme reluctance; but yet even the vaguest hope of an unknown friend and of some succour in their trouble gave a new turn to their thoughts.

In a few minutes the door opened again and the visitor came in. The girls were sitting together at one side of the table, two faint candles throwing a white light upon each white face. They looked small and young, almost childish, in their black dresses, and there was an anxious look upon the two little wan girlish countenances. The stranger came in with some diffidence. They could scarcely make out his face, but they saw at once that it was somebody unknown; and the look of expectation faded at once out of their eyes. They looked at each other with a piteous mutual disappointment.

"I beg your pardon," he said. "I fear this is an intrusion for which there is no excuse. I am looking for a gentleman who has been long in Canada—Robert Leonard Crosthwaite was his name: but I have some reason to suppose——"

"We never heard the name," said Grace. "We are very sorry. We came from Quebec. Canada is a large place. It might be in another part."

"He had been a very long time out of England. He came back only a few weeks ago. We were sure—we thought we were sure—that he came to this hotel."

The girls both shook their heads. "If there had been any other Canadian person here we must have heard. They would have come to us," said Grace, with a sob only half concealed.

"It is very important," said the young man. "There is property concerned, and the comfort of several people. Everybody thought he was dead. It will upset the arrangements of a family —and make those poor who were well off," he said in an undertone, to himself, rather than to them.

The girls looked at him with interest. There seemed a story involved, and that gave them a sensation that, if not pleasure, was, at least, relief from the pressure of their own continuously painful thoughts. Milly even ventured a little "Oh!" of wistful interest. Then he went on hastily—

"Pardon me: I ought not to disturb you. You can give me no clue? This gentleman must have arrived about the same time as I hear you did. I know—I know how painfully your time has been occupied. I am ashamed to trouble you: but do you not think you could give me a clue——"

"We never heard the name," said Grace. "We could write home and ask, but that would not be of much use. We are going back," she added with an explanatoriness which perhaps was not necessary, "as soon as ——" But here her little strength broke down, and she could not say any more.

"I beg your pardon, I beg a thousand pardons," the young man cried. "Forgive me for intruding upon you." And he turned with a respectful bow, and opened the door; but when he had done this he turned again and looked at them once more. "You will excuse me," he said in a voice which was full of emotion, "but I have a mother. If she could be of any use to you——"

Here the girls, being so weeping-ripe, again lost their self-control altogether. Milly began to sob audibly, throwing herself upon her sister's shoulder, and the tears dropped heavily one by one from Grace's eyes. She put one arm round poor Milly, and turned, with a tremulous smile through her tears, to the stranger.

"Thank you for being so kind," she said. "You are very kind; but we are not quite so miserable as perhaps you think. We have got our mother too. We are waiting till she tells us what to do."

He said nothing but "Oh!" and stood for a moment uncertain, not knowing what to say. But what could a stranger say? He was obliged to turn again and go away, after a great many fumblings with the door.

Next morning they began, sadly, the necessary work of putting away their father's papers and his little personal possessions. In his writing-book

GROVE ROAD, HAMPSTEAD

there was a letter half written to their mother, which they put aside carefully as a sacred thing, not looking, for love, at his last words. But on one of the pages of the blotting-book they found once more the address which had excited their curiosity before, "3 Grove Road, Hampstead," written obliquely across the page. It was repeated on a scrap of paper which marked his place in the book which they remembered he had been reading, and on which, besides, there were some jottings of dates and names which they did not understand. These were—"Left July '45——U. A. died '55———due with interest for 20 years ——." The word "interest" discouraged the girls; it must be something about business, they thought. This perpetually recurring address, however, bewildered them. They went on with their sad occupation without saying much to each other, but when they sat down to rest and to take the food which their youthful appetites began to demand, notwithstanding their trouble, Grace suddenly broke the silence.

"It must be some old friend, who lives there," she said.

Milly made no reply in words, but she looked up with instant response and comprehension.

"I think," said Grace, "we ought to go and see who it is. It might be a relation. It might be some one who would stand by us: we are so very lonely here. It might be some—lady. I think we should go—directly—as soon as you are ready, Milly."

"Oh, I am ready," Milly said, starting up. The new idea gave them a little spring and energy. They almost ran to put on their little crape bonnets and their out-door jackets—which had been made for them at the pleasure of the dressmaker, hastily summoned and allowed to work her will—and which were heavy and laden with crape. They were like monuments of woe, from head to foot, in these garments; their two little pale faces, so white and so small, looking out with increased pallor from their heavy black. Milly had a good deal of gold and a good deal of curl in her light brown hair, which shone out with double force from these gloomy surroundings, like a protest of nature. Grace's locks were darker and smoother. She was the least pretty of the two, but her eyes were larger and more expressive than those fawn eyes of Milly's, which at present wore but one look, that of startled wistfulness and pleading.— an entreaty to all the world to be pitiful. They went off upon their new mission, however, with a little consolation in the relief of the novelty, stealing quietly downstairs that nobody might come out upon them to ask questions or offer help.

CHAPTER VI

IT did not occur to the girls in their inexperience to make any attempt to find out who lived at No. 3, Grove Road. They got out of their cab at the door of the house with a flutter of anxious and excited feeling, but still without any thought that the stranger or strangers they were about to see were anonymous, and that their only warrant in thus invading an unknown house was the scrap of paper which they had brought with them as their credentials. The house was a kind of villa, such as abound in the suburbs, with shrubberies around it, and high hedges, and a green door, between two smooth green lines of privet. They stood for a moment and looked round them at the bare tree-tops rising all round against the chilly blue sky; and the unfrequented road all overgrown with grass; and the houses nearly hidden by these jealous hedges. The girls did not understand this jealous privacy of suburban life, and they shivered a little as they looked round, hearing nothing and seeing nothing. In the morning Grove Road was alive with tradesmen's carts, with nursery-maids and children setting out for their walk on the heath, but in the afternoon a

GROVE ROAD, HAMPSTEAD

dead silence fell upon it. The rooms in which the inmates lived were on the other side, and here nothing was visible except a blank range of windows over those green lines of hedge, broken only by the still more absolute enclosure of the shut door. They looked at each other, and thought of their father coming out here into the dark, into the rain on that fatal night. They understood now how impossible it would be for him to get either shelter or a carriage to bring him back.

"You would think there was spite in those dreadful doors," said Grace, "wouldn't you, Milly? As if it would give them pleasure to shut themselves tight and refuse all shelter; not a porch that any one could stand under. Oh, when we used to hear of the English liking to be private, we never thought of this!"

Milly looked at them mournfully too, and they both thought of the different scenes they had been used to, with that comparison which it is almost impossible for strangers not to make. Then Grace turned round with a sudden impulse and pulled the bell, which they could hear make a long but subdued tinkle just over the green door. But they had to wait still for some minutes before there was any response. The moment the deed was done, the bell rung and entrance demanded, Milly turned to her sister with her usual "Oh!" of appeal.

"Who will you ask for?" she said.

GROVE ROAD, HAMPSTEAD

It was a difficulty that never had occurred to them before; and in their sense of this extraordinary deficiency they had almost fled, shyness taking possession of them, and a sense of being altogether wrong and out of all respectable use and wont. But, on the other hand, it was shabby to run away, a trick not worthy of girls—a schoolboy crime. So they stood trembling, half with cold, half with terror, and by-and-by heard the opening of an inner door and steps approaching. If it had been a solemn butler who had opened to them, even at that moment they would have run away; but it was a pretty, smiling maid, with a white cap and white apron, over whose countenance there passed an indefinable sympathetic change as she saw first the two young faces, and then the deep crape of their dresses. They were cheered and encouraged by this mute sign, the freemasonry of youth and kindness.

"Is —— at home?" said Grace falteringly.

The maid was too intent upon the aspect of the young creatures before her to note that no name was uttered, but only a tremulous counterfeit of sound.

"Missis is not at home, miss," said the girl, with an air of sympathetic regret. Then she added, "But Miss Anna is, and Mr Geoffrey, if one of them would do."

The girls looked at each other again with a swift mutual consultation. "We should like to see Miss Anna, if you please," said Grace.

GROVE ROAD, HAMPSTEAD

And next moment they were within the house. They went along the shadowy green passage into the hall, and through another corridor to the drawing-room at the other side of the house, feeling as if they were in a dream. This, then, was an English home—the first they had ever penetrated into. It was an old house, not fresh and bright like those to which they were accustomed; a house full of old furniture, old hangings, old books. One or two doors were open, and they could not help glancing in as they passed, with a spring of youthful curiosity not yet quenched. When they got to the drawing-room they could scarcely restrain a cry of surprise. It had three long windows opening to a garden at the other side of the house. In front of them lay—all the world, as Grace thought—a great blue distance, in the centre of which rose a smoke, and a vision of distant towers and roofs—great London lying far below; and close at hand a slope of green lawn, with further slopes beyond of heath, and gorse, and dotted trees forming the foreground. This wonderful panorama quite unreasonably lightened their hearts. They had a long time to wait, but it was so full of curiosity and interest that it did not seem long. At length they became aware of the sound of a step coming slowly along the passages, a step accompanied by a little tap as of a stick on the floor. It kept them in tantalising expectation for a minute—then turned aside, and there was again a pause.

Finally the little maid came again to the door and led the way into another room.

It was a smaller room, with the same extended landscape before the window—a room very daintily furnished, lighted up with pretty china, pictures, everything full of delicate colour and glimmers of reflection; little mirrors hidden away in corners, shelves upon the dim walls with dainty vases and cups, everything delicate, everything bright. They took this in with one startled glance before their attention concentrated upon the occupant of the room—a lady who rose slowly, supporting herself with a stick, from a large easy-chair beside the fire. She rose with difficulty, yet there was a sort of slow stately grace in the very stiffness with which she moved. Was this Miss Anna? The hearts of Grace and Milly leaped into their throats: they were awed, and dared scarcely draw their breath. Ah, certainly this was England, the old country where queens and princesses were possible. They almost forgot themselves, and their trouble, and their sorrow, and all the strangeness of their circumstances, as they gazed upon this unexpected sight.

Miss Anna was a woman about sixty, with perfectly white hair, and keen, large, dark eyes. She was pale, but with a little evanescent colour, the colour of weakness, as if the slight movement she had made had set the blood in motion, and brought a faint rose tint to her cheeks; otherwise she was like ivory finely cut, her nose a little aquiline, her forehead softly shaded with the white, silvery lines of her hair. She was dressed in soft satin, clinging to her in long folds, which was not the fashion at the time, and, therefore, all the more impressive, and had on her head a sort of lace veil, half shrouding her hair and falling over her shoulders. Her dress had all the air of being studied and thought of, though the faint, yellowish tinge of the lace, and the dark sheen of the satin, wine-colour or plum-colour, were all the elements out of which this effect was produced. But the simple girls who stood before her had never seen anything like her, and the wonderful apparition took away their breath. She, on her part, looked at them keenly with her penetrating eyes—then she waved her hand towards two chairs set out in front of her throne.

"You asked for me," she said. "Sit down; I fear I have kept you waiting."

Grace and Milly were far too much excited to notice it—but, as a matter of fact, this stately lady was excited too, and the look with which she perused them, their faces, their mourning dresses, their whole appearance, was unquestionably anxious —though this would have seemed to them incredible, impossible. It was only when they sat down that they perceived some one behind at the other end of the room—a man leaning over a writing-table with his head turned away from them. Miss Anna sat full in the light between the window and the fire. She repeated, with a faint tremour of impatience, "You asked for me?"

"No," said Grace—she would have liked to say madame, or my lady, or something that would have shown her reverence; but was too shy, with all her self-possession, to venture out of the beaten way. She sat down timidly and folded her hands, and looked at her questioner with that wistful, propitiating look, a faint smile quivering about her lips, her eyes cast upwards with a shy but earnest appeal, which sits so prettily upon extreme youth. "No," she said, "indeed we did not even know your name. We are very unfortunate girls in great trouble, and we found your address among papa's papers."

"Who is your papa?"

Grace saw nothing but the old lady who gazed at her fixedly and riveted her eyes; but Milly, who had no responsibility of speech, saw more than her sister. She saw the man at the writing-table turn hastily round at the sound of Grace's voice, then rise and approach nearer. When he came into the light she recollected that it was he who had come to them at the hotel the day before.

"Ah," said Grace, her mouth all quivering; "papa is——. We came over from Canada——" Here, even she, absorbed in her story and the emotion it occasioned, made an involuntary pause, seeing the lady start and look over her head as if at some one behind with a curious look of alarm and trouble. Was it only sympathy? Grace paused while you might count ten, and then went on again—"only a fortnight since; and on Monday he died, and left us all alone, all alone in this strange place. We thought—we imagined that it was you he went to see the first night he was in England——'

Here she stopped again; the lady's mouth seemed to quiver too. "Many people come to see me," she said. "What was his name?"

"His name was Robert Yorke. We are his daughters; I am Grace, and this is Milly—we are the two eldest," said the girl, still with the same pathetic smile about her mouth, and a look which appealed unconsciously for help and pity.

Miss Anna eyed them all the time with eyes that seemed to pierce them through and through. "This is a very sad story," she said. There was a quiver in her voice which meant real suffering, not mere pity; but her words were not so tender as this emotion might have indicated; there was no effusiveness of kindness in them. "You are left, then, without friends, without resources? I feel for you very much; but I have a great many applicants——"

Grace started to her feet, pressing her hands together almost with violence. "Oh!" she said, "If you think we are coming to you for charity——"

"Aunt Anna," said the young man, coming forward, "these are the young ladies whom I saw yesterday; if they are so kind, in their own trouble, as to bring us some information, some clue——"

Miss Anna made him an almost imperceptible sign, in which an anxious desire to keep him silent was mingled with the utmost intolerance of impatience. The young man stopped short suddenly; and Milly, who was the spectator of all, taking no other part, saw vaguely this transaction carried on over their heads, and wondered, though she did not know what it could mean.

But Grace perceived nothing at all: for once her perceptions were dulled; the tears in her eyes blinded her, scalding as they were with indignation, and the quick passionate shame with which so young a creature is apt to feel and resent a humiliating judgment. She continued vehemently, "We are not asking anything—we have money enough; we are rich enough: if that is what you mean."

"I did not mean to be unkind," said the stately lady. "Sit down, do not be impatient. Geoffrey, I think we can dispense with your presence. These young ladies will be more at their ease with me alone."

He had pressed forward, in spite of her prohibition. He was a little like her, though not so handsome; but there was no mistaking the honest sympathy and feeling in his eyes. Both the girls turned to him with a conviction that here at least was a friend. A sort of faint half-smile of recognition passed between them. "Oh, is it you?" said Grace unawares. They seemed in this enchanted house, in this strange audience-chamber, to have encountered at last some one of their own species, some one who would stand by them. They looked at him with an anxious, unspoken entreaty not to go away; and he reassured them by the faintest movement of his head.

"I think," he said, "it will be better if I stay."

"I think otherwise," said Miss Anna; but she said no more to him, and made no further objection. "Sit down," she said, touching the chair from which Grace had risen, with her stick. "You must not be offended; I meant no harm. I should not have thought any worse of you had you come to me for help, and I don't think any better of you for being well off. I am sorry for you all the same. But tell me why you came to me. No, wait a little, you can tell me presently. In the meantime, Geoffrey, you can ring for tea."

He did it without a word, standing before the fire contemplating the group. The girls did not know what it all meant; but gradually it dawned upon them with a strange sensation that they were not the principals here, but that a veiled and hidden conflict was going on between the two strangers, who appeared to share this luxurious home, and who were somehow, they could not tell how, connected with themselves and their concerns. The innocent commonplace request to ring for the tea had, they felt, if they could but understand it, a much more serious meaning than appeared. Geoffrey obeyed, but they felt very grateful to him that he showed no intention of going away.

And then there was a curious pause.

CHAPTER VII

OF all innocent domestic entertainments there is none more innocent, not to say tame, than the recent institution which is now so universally popular, of afternoon tea. The virtuous dulness, the gentle talk, is seldom enlivened by any dramatic interest going on under the surface. Now and then, indeed, a mild love affair will give a little excitement to the circle round the tea-table: but this is the utmost stretch to which the imagination can reach as connected with that mild entertainment. And among all the pretty suburban houses, surrounding London with endless circles of comfort and brightness, there could not have been found a more attractive group than that which occupied Miss Anna's pretty sitting-room in Grove Road. But underneath this innocent seeming how many elements of tragedy were working! Miss Anna's motive was known to none of them; but, whatever it was, it was strong enough to make her exert herself in a way which startled her nephew and gave him the watchful, suspicious, gloomy air which entirely changed the character of his face. Grace and Milly for their part soon began to feel the strange fascination exercised over them to be intolerable, yet what with their shyness, and strangeness, and bewilderment, suddenly plunged into a scene so new to them, did not know how to break the spell—though Grace became every moment more sensible of the false position, and even felt it a reproach to her in her sorrow to be turned aside out of her serious course by the light and graceful current of Miss Anna's recollections and anecdotes. Geoffrey, who kept a sort of neutral place between them, was not really aware, save by the instinct which made him divine something wrong underneath the surface, of half the seriousness of the situation. It had not yet occurred to him to identify the dead father of the girls with the visitor who had caused so much commotion in the house some time before. He thought nothing more now than that they had generously come, though in grievous trouble, to convey some information respecting that stranger; and he saw clearly enough that the same motive which had induced his aunt to disown and dismiss the visitor then, was impelling her now to refuse to listen to anything about him.

"I have a great deal of fine Sèvres," Miss Anna said. "Many people tell me I should exhibit it. There are continual exhibitions nowadays to which people send their treasures. There is South Kensington, you know; there is always something of the kind going on there. What! you have not been at South Kensington? Oh, that is very great negligence on the part of your friends. You must really make them take you before you go away. Yes, I was very much urged to send my china there."

It was Milly who murmured the little response which civility demanded; for Grace's impatience was getting the better of her. She felt that she must speak, though the words were taken out of her mouth. But still the old lady went smoothly on.

"Now that I cannot walk I take a great deal of pleasure in having all my pretty things about me. If you ever should be in such a position—which I trust may never be the case—you will understand what a pleasure it is to have bright surroundings. What, going? It is really quite dark. You must let Geoffrey get a cab for you. Geoffrey, go, dear, and look for a cab."

Grace had got up with an irrestrainable impulse. She came forward a step with her hands tightly clasped. "It is not that we are going," she said. "It is that I must talk to you about the thing that brought us here. I—I—do not know your name —except Miss Anna, as the maid said. Oh, will you please for a moment listen to me? The last night my father was well, before he took his illness, he was, so far as we can tell, here. We found your address among his papers; and he went out and left us for a long time that afternoon saying he was going to see old friends. We cannot think of any other interpretation; we feel sure that he must have been here. If you are our dearest father's friend —anything to him—we should like—to know you," said Grace, once more unconsciously clasping her hands. "We do not want anything from—we only want to know you, if you were dear papa's friend."

There was another pause, for the fervour of strong emotion with which the girl spoke, her clasped hands and wet eyes, impressed even the vigilant woman who was prepared for everything. It required a moment's resolution even on her part before she could crush the hopes of the young forlorn creature who thus appealed to her. She made a pause, and drew a long breath. Then she said, "Who was your father? You forget that I know nothing about him——"

"Robert Leonard Yorke," said Grace. The familiar dear name almost overcame her courage, but she held herself up by main force with her hands clasped. "There is nobody better known where we come from—Robert Leonard Yorke, of Quebec——"

"My dear young lady," said Miss Anna—and she sank back in her chair with a certain relief—a relaxation of the strain with which she had kept herself up to be ready for any emergency, which was not lost upon her nephew at least—"you have made some mistake. I never heard the name in my life. I never knew any one, or, to my knowledge, saw any one of that name."

"A fortnight ago, on Tuesday: and it rained

very much in the evening," Grace said eagerly. "He told us he could not get a cab, it was so far out of town; and he got very wet."

"He caught cold—and it was that—it was that——" Milly added her contribution to what her sister said: but her voice broke, and she could not conclude her sentence.

Miss Anna sat and looked on politely attentive, but at the same time ostentatiously indifferent. "It is very sad," she said. "It is impossible to tell you how sorry I am; but I never heard of Mr Yorke in my life. Geoffrey, that is true, it is very difficult to get a cab; go and look for one. I cannot permit these young ladies to wander away alone in a strange place. Go, Geoff, go!"

She was very anxious to be rid of him; her voice took the imperious tone, which he had obeyed so often, but he did not seem disposed to obey now.

"A fortnight ago," he said, "on a dark afternoon, turning to rain?"

"Yes, yes! you remember—oh, do you remember?—and afterwards we saw you at the hotel." The two girls spoke both together, one saying the former part, the other the latter of the sentence, both turning upon him with the most anxious eyes, gazing, trying to penetrate into his inmost soul.

"Geoff, why do you stand there?" cried Miss Anna. She, too, became energetic, and more and more imperious. "Go, I tell you, and get a cab for them. Two strangers, and far from where they are

GROVE ROAD, HAMPSTEAD

living. You know what your mother will think of such visitors. Go, directly, as I tell you." She stamped as she spoke, first her stick and then her foot, impatiently on the floor.

"This cannot be settled so summarily," said Geoffrey; "there is more in it. It is not necessary that we should stay in your room, Aunt Anna, if you dislike it; but I wish these ladies to remain till my mother sees them——"

"Your mother, who always believes everything that is said to her! Let there be an end to this folly at once, Geoff; go and get a cab."

"Aunt Anna, there had better be no struggle between us—yet. What I ask is very simple—that they should see my mother."

"Do you want to see his mother?" she said, suddenly turning upon the astonished girls. "You have made acquaintance with him, I can see; but mothers have sharp eyes, and his mother thinks every girl she sees is in love with her fascinating son. Can't he see you at some other place? I warn you my sister will give you no pleasant reception if she finds you here."

"Grace, Grace, let us go away," cried Milly, rising to her feet, scarlet with shame; but Grace had other things to think of, and paid no attention to this assault.

"I don't want to be harsh," continued Miss Anna; "but if you are good girls it will be much better for you to go away at once. I don't

GROVE ROAD, HAMPSTEAD

say you are not good girls, far from it. I don't pretend to judge; but girls of your age should not be going about to strange houses without invitation, especially where there is a young man. It has a strange look—your people would not like it. I advise you as your friend to go away."

Here Milly clasped Grace by the arm, and drew her back a little; perhaps some passing communication from Geoffrey's eyes had made the younger sister the more keen-sighted of the two for once. Grace turned round a little, moved by her earnestness, and there was the usual consultation by looks between them; the result of which was that Grace's pale countenance became also suffused with colour; but she held her ground, though her sister drew her back.

"I do not think, if you were kind," she said, "that you would speak so to two girls like us. You would protect us rather from every evil thought. We came here because we have no friends, thinking that they must have been friends to whom papa went on his first day in England: thinking, perhaps, you were relations—somebody who would take a little interest in us. If it is not so, there can be no reason why we should stay."

Geoffrey put out his hand with an eager gesture. "Till my mother comes," he said.

"Young ladies," cried Miss Anna, "I will tell you what that boy means; he wants to make you out to be the children of a sort of madman who was here some time ago—an impostor: a fellow who gave himself out as—who represented himself to be—a man who has been dead for years. Would you like to have a slur put upon your father, who appears to have been a respectable person?" she added more calmly. She had yielded to an impulse of anger, and had flushed passionately. But at the last words she calmed down, and spoke with distinct and slow utterance, with a slight curl of contempt about her mouth.

"Grace, Grace," cried Milly, "let us go away!"

Grace's face varied every moment as one emotion after another swept over it. "I don't know what to do," she said piteously, "Milly": "But I think there is something to find out," she added —"I think there is something more!"

"If you wish to have your father's character taken away, and the cheat he attempted found out——" cried Miss Anna, with sudden fury. Then she stopped, seeing the mistake she had made. "I beg your pardon, I am sure," she went on, with fictitious amiability. "You are making me identify this respectable person from Canada, poor man, for whom I am very sorry—with a wretched impostor, a fellow that never came back, or made the slightest effort to support his ridiculous claim. Of course, if you like to stay till my sister comes back," she added, "I can have no objection. She is a silly, credulous woman; she will believe any story you like to tell her, so you may give the rein to your invention. But one caution I will give you: say nothing about her son. Make believe, at all events, that you know nothing about her son."

"Oh, Grace, why should we be insulted? What can it matter to us? Let us go away," Milly cried.

But if there was one thing better known among the young Yorkes than another, it was that Grace was obstinate. Nothing, the boys said, would make her give in, even when she was beaten. She turned round to Geoffrey, even while her sister was speaking.

"Sir," she said, "we don't know you, not even your name; but if you think your mother will understand better—if you think she will know anything about us, I would rather wait till she comes. We do not want money, or help, if that is what Miss Anna supposes; we want nothing except to know——"

"Then why in heaven's name do you insist on staying? against my will, who am the mistress of the house? I say I will not have you here. I will have no adventurers here. I do not believe there is a word of truth in your story. That man is not dead. Impostors never die. It is all a got-up affair from beginning to end. Look here!" cried Miss Anna, striking her stick on the floor, "as I don't want to have the whole story raked up in a court of justice, where you would not have a chance, not a leg to stand upon, you or your precious father—I'd rather come to terms with you, and let it go no further. How much will you take to give up your claims altogether? They are false, utterly false; but I don't want to be made a talk of. I would rather settle it and be done with it, if you will say how much you will take, and start by the next steamboat. There is a steamboat every week, every day perhaps, for anything I know."

The girls stood close together listening aghast, Milly thinking nothing less than that Miss Anna must be a mad woman, and that now her insanity was becoming visible. But to Grace's more active mind, this strange proposal conveyed an impression quite different. She looked at Geoffrey, whose turn it now seemed to be to blush. He had made an effort to interfere, and stop Miss Anna, but, failing in that, had drawn a step back, and stood with a painful flush on his face listening to her. As she ended, he stepped forward again.

"With this proposal," he said, "please to remark, neither I nor my mother have anything to do."

"There is something, then, upon which we have a claim," Grace cried; "and we are not mistaken after all!"

"Oh, Grace," cried Milly, "come away—come away! What does it matter to us? We don't understand this country, or its ways. Oh, how we used to think of England, how delightful it was to be! but now it is dreadful. If you went to the poorest house in Canada," cried the girl, "and said, We are in trouble, we are all alone, our father is dead, they would take you in, they would be kind to you; but here they say we are impostors, and offer us money. Oh, Grace, Grace, come away!"

With her eyes sparkling through her tears, her soft cheeks flushed with resentment and shame, her hands clasping her sister's arm, whom she endeavoured to draw away, Milly turned towards the door. It was not often she took the initiative, or even gave utterance to so many words; but Milly was not quick enough to divine any secret meaning, or to see anything but offence and insult in what had been said. Her only thought was to escape—all the more as she had felt a secret confidence that they had fallen among friends on seeing Geoffrey; and the disappointment made her revulsion of feeling more complete.

The door opened behind as she spoke, and another lady came in. The newcomer had her bonnet on, and brought with her a waft of fresh air from out of doors. She was not beautiful, like Miss Anna, but she had the same white hair and dark eyes—eyes not so penetrating, but kinder. She came in with an untroubled air, as a woman comes into her own house, expecting nothing but the ordinary domestic calm. She stopped short, however, when she saw the visitors, and uttered a little exclamation, "Oh!" somewhat tremulous, like Milly's own. She was a shy woman for one thing, and for another, having been so lately excited by an unusual visitor, she felt slightly nervous of every new figure. "I did not know you had visitors, Anna," she said.

"These are not my visitors," said Miss Anna; "if they are anybody's visitors, they are your son's."

Then the friendly face before them clouded over. She cast one reproachful look at Geoffrey, and turned her back upon the two dark figures in their depth of crape. This was her weakness, but it was a weakness which was full of compunctions. Her son was all she had in the world; and though she would say now and then that to see him married was the height of her ambition, yet this good mother feared and almost hated every feminine creature under thirty, and turned her back upon the whole race lest Geoffrey's future wife might be found among them. When she had done this, however, her heart always melted, as now. She was, in reality, one of the most womanly of women, and liked nothing so well as feminine companions when she could put confidence in them that they would not take her son from her. The two faces, however, upon which she cast a remorseful glance now, after she had turned her back upon them, were of the most dangerous type. They were the faces of two predatory creatures against whom she felt she had no means of defence. Either of them was capable under her very eyes of sweeping

GROVE ROAD, HAMPSTEAD

Geoff away from her for ever and ever. Never did hen look upon fox with more dismay; but Mrs Underwood was not a consistent or firm woman. She looked and trembled; but then looked again, and was touched in spite of herself. They were very young; they were in deep mourning; and *they were not paying the slightest attention to Geoffrey.* Perhaps that last was the most moving circumstance of all.

"Visitors of my son's? That means, I suppose," said Mrs Underwood, with a little gasp, yet a heroic effort, "Visitors to me?"

"I am glad you think so, Mary. It is no concern of mine," said Miss Anna, turning pointedly away.

And then politeness compelled Mrs Underwood to offer civilities she had very little mind to. "Won't you sit down?" she said. "Geoff, you will perhaps introduce me to your friends."

She sighed; there was something half-ludicrous in the pathos of her tone.

"I hope we may be friends hereafter," said Geoffrey; "but at present there is something to be settled which is more than friendship. Mother, you remember your cousin, Leonard Crosthwaite, and his sudden visit here a fortnight ago?"

"Leonard Crosthwaite?" she said the name trembling, and turned involuntarily with a frightened look to where her sister sat.

"He means," said Miss Anna, without turning

her head, "the impostor, or madman, who assumed the name of—our relation who died twenty years ago."

"Mother, listen," said Geoffrey. "It is a terrible story, so far as I can make it out. He went from you, to die: and these are his daughters."

Mrs Underwood turned from one to another as her son spoke, now reading his face, now Miss Anna's, now throwing an anxious glance at the sisters who stood together in the centre of the room, not knowing what new turn their affairs might be about to take.

At this an exclamation burst from all three at once. The girls said, "No, no!" while Mrs Underwood cried out, "Leonard's daughters!" "No, no, no, no!" the others said.

"So far as I can see," repeated the young man, "he is dead, and cannot tell us how it stands. These are the young ladies whom I found at the hotel to which I went in search of him—his hotel, the address he gave you. And their father came out on a wintry afternoon a fortnight ago, a Tuesday, to visit friends—old friends of whom he told them nothing. He went home drenched—you remember how it rained, mother?—and took to his bed. Now that he is dead, they found our address among his papers. This is the story, and what can you want more? It seems to me that it is clear enough!"

"But," said Grace, "there is one great mistake

you make. Our name, it is not Crosthwaite—oh, nothing like it ; we never heard that name before. Papa was not a man to go by a false name. Oh, no, no ; he was true in everything. There must still be some mistake."

Miss Anna, who had turned her chair away, turned round again at this. " I told you," she said ; " this young fellow wants to prove you to be the daughters of an impostor or a madman. Of course, your father was not a man to go by a false name. Nobody would do that who was, as you say, a respectable person, a man thought well of in his own place. You know better than to think so. Of course: that is exactly what I said."

But this support sent Grace instantly into opposition. She paused to consider, when she found herself suddenly embarrassed by this unexpected backing up. Miss Anna's eyes fixed upon her seemed to have a baneful influence, and oppressed her soul.

" Does it make any difference to you," she said, with the trenchant simplicity of ignorance, " what was my father's name ? "

The question was so entirely unexpected that each of the three showed its effect in a different, yet characteristic way. Miss Anna, listening with the complacency and satisfaction with which Grace's denial of the name had filled her, received this stray shot full in her breast, and without any preparation. She wavered, drew back, contracted her features involuntarily in the effort to preserve her perfect calm. Mrs Underwood gasped as if some one had seized her by the throat. As for Geoffrey, he was the only one who replied.

"If," he said, "you are Leonard Crosthwaite's daughters, as I believe, it will make a great deal of difference to us all."

"The question was addressed to me," said Miss Anna, with a slight trembling that ran over all her person; "and it is for me to answer it. Young lady, whoever you are, if you are Leonard Crosthwaite's daughter, which I don't believe for a moment—I have no doubt your father was a much more respectable man: but if you are, and can prove it, you will be able to give rise to a great lawsuit, which will be fought out on both sides for years; which will cost you every penny you have, if you have anything, and ruin everybody belonging to you: besides bringing out a great many things about the family you claim to belong to, which we would all much rather keep to ourselves; and in all likelihood it would be a failure at the end. That is the true state of the case, whatever that boy may tell you—or anyone else," she added after a moment, with a glance at her sister, "or any one else. This world is full of fools."

"Oh, Grace, come—come away!" cried Milly in her sister's ear.

But Grace was less easily moved. She was bewildered, and confused, and alarmed. It seemed to her that the rights of her family were in her hand, and her mind leaped to great things—far greater than this simple house and its riches. Perhaps Lenny—yes, certainly, she remembered now, though it had not occurred to her before, her father had Leonard in his name, and her boy-brother was also Leonard—might be the heir of some great property, and only she to defend his rights. Grace stood and looked at them all with a swelling of her breast, yet a dazzled dimness in her eyes, as if she were about to faint. She never had done such a thing in her life; but then she never had been in such an extraordinary strait, and with nobody to advise her. No wonder the light which she wanted so much within to clear up the way before her, should seem to fail without.

"I can't see my way," she said faintly. "I cannot tell what to do. Yes, Milly, we will go away; but for all that, it is not finished," she said, turning to Miss Anna with a gleam of dim defiance in her eyes.

CHAPTER VIII

THE girls were now as eager to go away as they had been to come; they would scarcely wait for the cab which was sent for, and they paid very little attention to the anxious civilities of Mrs Underwood and Geoffrey, who conducted them to the door and put them into the carriage, making every kind of wistful endeavour to obliterate the impression made upon their minds by the other member of the family. Grace and Milly were in too great haste to consult each other, to compare notes, and to realise this strange new complication in their lives, to have their ears open to Mrs Underwood's apologies.

"You must not mind Anna," she said in an undertone, as she led them into the hall, with its dark oaken furniture and scanty light, out of the warm and softened brightness of Miss Anna's room. "She has always been used to having her own way; she cannot bear to be contradicted. When she takes anything into her head it is so difficult to convince her; oh, she is a great deal cleverer than I am, that is true; but she will not be convinced when she has taken a thing into her head."

GROVE ROAD, HAMPSTEAD

This little explanatory stream of talk seemed to flow round them as they went to the door, but they paid very little attention to it. They scarcely heard Mrs Underwood's promise to go and see them at their hotel next day; and they submitted with a little surprise rather than accepted with any pleasure her offer of kindness, when she took each in succession by the hand and kissed her, with a mixture of nervous timidity and affection. "If it is so, we are relations," she said almost under her breath; "and if it is not so, my poor dears, my poor children, my heart bleeds for you all the same." The water trembling in her eyes and the quaver of her voice showed the good woman's sincerity; but the girls were scarcely moved by it, so full were their minds of this discovery, which they did not understand. As for Geoffrey, he said nothing at all; he shut the door of the cab and lingered for a moment looking at them wistfully, but that was all. There was in his face a pained consciousness of the difference between his own position and theirs. He, with his home behind him, and all the long-established household gods which had protected him all his life; while the other two, so much younger, feebler, and less able to shift for themselves, had nothing but the cold foreign shelter of a hotel to go back upon. He stood bareheaded in the rain, which, to complete the resemblance with their father's visit to this place, began to drizzle down continuously out of the dim persistent skies; and his face was the last thing they saw, gazing compassionately after them as they disappeared into the darkness. They were too much preoccupied even to notice this—at least Grace was too much preoccupied. Milly for her part saw him very well, but said nothing. Her mind too was full of other thoughts—yet not so full but that she could remark this quietly to herself.

But though they thus left Grove Road in great excitement they were not disappointed. If they had found themselves simply mistaken, and that nothing was known there of their father or his visit, they would have fallen from an eminence of hope, which in present circumstances they had by no means lost. Had they been received with kind indulgence as strangers, rousing no hostile or any other kind of feeling, but simply a little surprise, they would have been cruelly disappointed; but the excitement of seeing themselves regarded with alarm as dangerous intruders, so important as to be perilous to family peace, flattered them in the most subtle way. As they went slowly down the hill, jolting over the stones, their hearts were fluttered by a sense of dignity which they had never felt before. They laid their girlish heads together as they had been longing to do since ever they set foot in that strange enchanted place. What could it be? what solemn inheritance, what great fortune, to justify the panic which they had seen by movements beneath all the glitter and bravado of Miss Anna's words? Between that exciting and wonderful idea and the associations with their father of which the darkling road seemed full, their minds were transported altogether out of their own trouble and raised into an atmosphere of high interest and responsibility. It would depend, they thought, upon how they now behaved whether their whole position might be changed. They were well off enough; there was no want in their house, nor had they any reason to suppose that their father's death would leave them destitute. But there was a great difference between that state of ordinary and commonplace comfort, and this dazzling probability. It might have been a vacant principality, almost a throne, from the way in which Grace and Milly contemplated it. They felt as if their former life had been stopped, and that something new, altogether unrealised and unrealisable, awaited them in the future. "If we only knew what to do; if we could only decide on what is best," Grace said. That was the difficulty now. This morning there had seemed nothing before them but a patient, melancholy waiting for their mother's sad letter, and the news of her arrangements for their return to her; now they thought no longer of the voyage home or of anything connected with it, but of what to do and say as representatives of their father, and heads, so to speak, of the family, working on their behalf. "It will change everything," Grace said again thoughtfully. "Instead of all of us being alike, Lenny— Lenny will be the heir. That is one thing that gives a likelihood to it," she added, sinking her voice as if the cab-driver might perhaps hear and report the matter. "His name, Milly! I never thought of it till a few minutes ago. Lenny; of course he is Leonard; and when you think of it, papa had Leonard in his name too."

"I thought of it directly," said Milly, with a little satisfaction.

Grace, in her excitement, threw her arms round her sister. "It is you who ought to be the first of us two," said Grace admiringly. "It is true that I am the eldest—but so many things occur to you that never come into my head."

"It is because I have the time to think while you are talking," Milly said with modesty; but she was not displeased with this testimony to her superior insight. She added, with a little awe: "Gracie, I wonder if *that*—is our real name?"

This was a question that took away the breath of both. They looked at each other almost with an inclination to laugh, then stopped short and mutually contemplated the impulse with horror. "It is dreadful," said Milly, "isn't it, to have a false name?"

"I don't know," said Grace, who had been so indignant an hour ago at the suggestion; "it cannot be so very dreadful if papa did it. He must have had his reasons for taking another name. There are reasons that account for everything." Her momentary humility had disappeared by this time, and she felt equal to explaining all mysteries to her sister in her usual way. "He must have been wronged somehow when he left home. I suspect that Miss Anna, Milly; I am sure she is at the bottom of everything. She must have told lies of him, or invented stories; and then perhaps he was disinherited, and the money given to her. It would not be money; it would be lands or an estate—perhaps a fine old house." Then they paused and looked at each other for a moment. "If that was how it was, and we got it back, mamma would certainly have to come home *then*."

"But it could not be for all of us; it would only be for Lenny," said Milly doubtfully.

"Lenny is only fifteen; he would not be of age for ever so long. And then it is always stipulated," said Grace, "that when people have estates, what is called a great stake in the country, they should be educated in the country and made to understand it." Insensibly she drew herself up, holding her head higher at the thought—"Mamma would not like it; but she would do what was best for Lenny——"

"Then I suppose—" Milly said, and now in spite of herself the smallest little laugh, instantly repented of, burst from her. She looked at her sister in great alarm, with a portentously serious countenance. "I suppose," she repeated, as if, instead of something ridiculous, this had been the most solemn suggestion in the world, "that ¡Lenny —will be the one of us that will be important now."

So full was Grace of the seriousness of this thought, that she replied, without taking any notice of that guilty laugh, only by an inclination of her head : " We will have to learn all about the English laws, and how things are managed, for Lenny's sake," she said seriously. " He will be a magistrate, you know, and most likely in Parliament ; and he will be rather behind by losing so much time in Canada. We will have to coach him up."

"Oh but, Gracie, I don't know things myself ; I never was able to do that."

"I must begin directly," said Grace with a little sigh—the sigh of the self-devoted. "It was such a business—don't you remember, Milly ?—to coach him for school ; and England—England is a great deal more difficult. I think I must begin Greek directly, and law—or he will never know his lessons. I hope mamma will see that it is her duty, Milly, to come at once," she added still more seriously. Milly for one second was inclined to laugh again at the portentous and preposterous importance of her young brother, but then she recollected herself, and the tears filled her eyes.

"Oh, poor mamma !" she cried, "poor mamma ! to come now !"

GROVE ROAD, HAMPSTEAD

This turned once more the current of their thoughts. But when they got back to their hotel the argument was resumed: for it soon became an argument maintained with great heat on one side, with an unimaginable gentle obstinacy on the other. Milly, who never went against her sister's will, was for once in opposition, and though she was not strong enough to subdue Grace, she did not yield to her.

They had begun languidly and mournfully to arrange their father's papers in the morning. Now Grace betook herself to this pursuit with passion. She found nothing: some fragments of torn letters, torn up into very small pieces, on one of which the name of "Anna" occurred, lay in the bottom of his dressing bag; but Grace was not sufficiently skilled in the art of detection to join them together as a more experienced investigator might have done. And it revolted her to pry into what the dead man had thus wished to conceal. In all his other stores there was not a word which even suggested any information. He had scrawled, "3 Grove Road," on a page of his blotting-paper, and twice over in other places, as if afraid of forgetting it. When she came to a little diary he had kept she paused with a sensation of awe. She had seen it a hundred times—had seen it lying open, and knew that no special sanctity was attributed to it. It was nothing but a little record of events and engagements; but when the hand is still that has scribbled these careless memoranda, how strangely their character changes! She took it to where Milly sat, and placed herself on the sofa beside her. "I cannot read this by myself," she said.

"Oh, why should we read it at all, Grace? If papa had wanted us to know he would have told us."

"Hush! even papa shall not make me suffer injustice!" cried the excited girl. But when the little book was opened it gave but the scantiest information. There was one entry since the landing in England, and no more; and this was all it contained:—

"Same name in directory, at old address; to go first thing and inquire."

Grace gave a little cry when she read this; it seemed to her to tell all she wanted—and yet it told nothing. "It is quite clear," she cried in her mistaken little triumph. Milly looked at it too with all the feeling that it was an important revelation. Then they cried a little over the foolish little events of the voyage, all set down there, with that strange unconsciousness of what was coming, which makes death so doubly terrible to the survivors. If he had but known, surely he would have put something in that little record to console, to elevate, to calm the survivors, to whom his every word was so soon to be sacred! But he did not know, and put down nothing except "Wind so-and-so; a little fog in the morning. Captain's birthday; champagne at dinner," and such other trifles.

GROVE ROAD, HAMPSTEAD

They folded it carefully away in paper and sealed it, with an ache at their hearts. Oh, if he had but known! and so told them something, left them some information, if it had only been a task to do! "But there is something to do!" Grace cried; "this that he began; and I will never, never give it up till Lenny has his rights! He is papa's heir."

CHAPTER IX

THESE vague gropings after an unknown fact were very different from the discussions which took place in Grove Road when the girls were gone. Mrs Underwood and her son lingered together for a moment in the hall. She took hold of Geoffrey's arm with both her hands, and leaned for a moment upon his shoulder and shed a few tears of agitation and distress.

"You must not be frightened, mother. We can get on together, whatever happens," he said in her ear.

"Oh, Geoff, how can I help being frightened? I would not wrong anybody—not by the value of a straw."

"I am sure you would not, mother. I know you would not."

"But what a difference it will make—oh, what a difference!" cried poor Mrs Underwood.

She cried for a momemt on her son's shoulder. Was it to be expected that she could give up the greater part of her living without a sigh?

"And then Anna," she said, "Anna!" in a tone of mingled fright and pain.

It would seem almost as if her sister had

divined, for she could not hear, this reference to herself; for she called sharply in a keen voice which penetrated through the closed door. Mrs Underwood started immediately, dropping her son's arm.

"Must you always fly the moment she calls, as if you were her maid?" said Geoff indignantly.

His mother put up her hand to his mouth.

"I have always done it: and could I stop it now when perhaps she is going to lose everything? Oh, hush! hush! I am coming, I am coming, Anna," she cried.

"She will never lose you, mother," he said, detaining her. "I can see already what will happen. You will make yourself her slave, and give up every comfort in your life."

"What can I do? What can I do? I have you, but she has nobody. I am coming, Anna, I am coming," she said.

Miss Anna still sat in her easy chair, with the tea-table before her. Her forehead was slightly contracted, her lips parted with a quickened breath; but these faint indications were all that showed any agitation in her. She addressed her sister when she appeared in a sharper tone than usual. "You two have been having a little consultation," she said. "Oh, quite right; quite right. Two heads are better than one. It might be considered a little ungenerous, perhaps, to the other who has no one to consult with—but I am used to it.

I know what a single woman has to expect in life."

"Oh, Anna!" her sister said, with a faint remonstrance, "when you know that you are always our first thought."

"Your first thought! I did not know I was of so much importance," said Miss Anna with a laugh. "One would scarcely think it to see how little attention you pay to me—either you or Geoff. But I must not complain: for it is your money as well as mine that he is so anxious to make a present of to the new claimants. And I can see very well what his motive is—very well. Oh, I know men and their motives, though I have never married. I can see through them well enough."

"My motive! what motive can I have but justice?" the young man said.

"Oh, Geoffrey! hush, my dear. When you know it is your aunt's way. Why should there be any quarrelling, to make everything worse?"

"Yes, it is his aunt's way. I am not the sort of fool that accepts everything," said Miss Anna. "I can read him like a book. He has had to have his living doled out to him through you and me, and now he sees a way of getting the better of us—of turning the tables upon us. Oh, it is clear enough. Two girls—two silly creatures that will believe every word he says; but take my advice, Geoffrey, and choose the little one. She is the one that you can turn round your little finger; the other has a will of her own. Though it is against my own interest, you see, I can still give you good advice."

Geoffrey made no reply to this speech. His mother fluttered between him and Miss Anna with her hands spread out like the wings of a protecting bird, ready to burst in and forestall him had he attempted to reply; but he did not speak for some minutes. Then he said coldly, "We must not quarrel, as my mother says. We are all threatened with a great danger. For anything we can tell, the girls you are talking of so lightly can take the greater part of our living from us. The question not only is, have they a real claim? but can they establish it? and how far are we ready to go in the way of resistance? Rather, how far are *you* ready to go? Will moral certainty be enough for you, or do you demand legal proof?"

"Moral fiddlestick!" said Miss Anna. "Morals have nothing to do with it. We were always as near in blood as Leonard was; we had as good a right as he had; indeed, we had a better right, being girls, to be provided for. Uncle Abraham thought of the name when he chose his nephew instead of his nieces. And that showed his folly —for the nephew seems to have thrown off the name the moment he left the country: and of all the claimants there is only one Crosthwaite, and that is me. I do not care a brass farthing for your moral certainty. All it means is, that you have made up your mind to stand by your opinion through thick and thin. It is your opinion that the man who came here the other night was Leonard. Well! you think so, and he said so—but that is no proof."

"Oh, Anna!" cried her sister, "speak of him kindly. Poor Leonard! when you have just heard that he is dead——"

"What is his dying to me?" she cried, with a glance of fury. "That's the man that was held up to us all as the image of faithfulness. Not one of you but has told me if I had not treated him so badly, this and that would not have happened; and the hound had changed his name, and married, and been happy all the time!" Then she stopped and looked at Geoffrey with a contemptuous laugh. "Mind you, I don't acknowledge that he was Leonard Crosthwaite. It suits my purpose a great deal better to believe that he was the pink of fidelity, and died of a broken heart."

"Very few people, they say," said Mrs Underwood, in a reluctant voice, "die of broken hearts."

Miss Anna's bright eyes seemed to give out gleams of malice and scorn and indignant ridicule. "But I believe in them," she said. "I am romantic, not prosaic like you. When you know it's for your sake, then, naturally, you believe in it." She stopped to laugh, her bosom panting with a mixture of contempt and fury. "If Leonard did not die for me as he promised he would, he was a poor creature. Heirs! what had he to do with heirs? If he did not die he was a traitor and a liar. Geoff, there is no poetry in you; you are a commonplace being; that is why you are capable of believing that Leonard Crosthwaite lived, and throve, and married, and had heirs. I do not believe a word of it," she said. And again she laughed. After all, there was something behind the self-interest that determined her resistance— something which the more honourable people who gazed at her with so much wonder and alarm did not understand. Her laugh was not of merriment but of that last scorn of humanity which is despair. It made her furious, it transported her beyond all limits of nature. She had believed in this one man as true and faithful beyond all question; and he had been the greatest deceiver of all. This put such fierce scorn into her breast that she could not contain herself. The more selfish a nature is the more is it lacerated by desertion. This was a woman who had put herself above others all her life, and had been punished by the gradual failure of all whose worship she had once believed in. It was the final blow to her self-esteem, and she resented it with wild wrath and frantic ridicule of the traitor. But nobody knew the tragic element in it, or that her belief in the possibility of honour and truth went with this discovery. She appeared to the others like an unscrupulous woman, firmly determined to hold by her inheritance against all claimants—which she was: but also something more.

"All that is beyond the question," said Geoffrey; "it is very possible that legal proof may be hard to get. We might fight it out at law for years; we might ruin them and ourselves too in the effort to make it quite clear. The question is for you, mother, as well as Aunt Anna. If you are sure these are the heirs, though they cannot prove it in law, what will you do?"

Poor Mrs Underwood was taken entirely without preparation. She turned to her son with a gasp, clasping her hands together in dismay. She was a woman who had always been told what to do by somebody—her husband, her sister, her son, had managed her mind for her. When she knew what was expected of her she did it faithfully, holding by her *consigne* whatever happened. She had kept steadily to her orders under the most trying circumstances already: struggling against the glimmerings of right judgment in her own breast, even while silenced by Anna's casuistry. Since Geoffrey grew up her course had been easier, though even with his support her sister's older influence was sometimes too much for her. But now to be asked instead of being told—to have a decision demanded from her instead of made for her, took away her breath.

"Oh, Geoff," she said, "my dear! how can you expect me to understand anything about the law? I should like to be kind to the girls, poor things.

GROVE ROAD, HAMPSTEAD

Of course I should like to be kind to them. I would not ruin them, poor fatherless children, for all the world. How could you think such a thing of me?"

"That is not what I am asking you, mother. If you are sure they ought to have the money, though they cannot prove it legally, what will you do?"

Mrs Underwood turned a frightened look towards her sister, who laughed; then her eyes returned to the face of her son, which was very serious, and gave her no guidance. "Do?" she murmured faintly, "I will do — whatever is thought right, Geoff."

"But what do *you* think right, mother?"

Geoffrey felt that if he had not put a powerful control upon himself, he might have turned round upon the laughing spectator behind him and taken her by the throat.

"Poor Geoff!" said Miss Anna; "between his mother, who cannot understand, and I who understand better than a woman ought, he is in a hard case. You had better have it out with me. What shall we do in case there is no legal proof? You know very well there is but one thing to do. Keep ourselves on our guard and refuse any concession. What else? Fancy is one thing, but property is another. You can't go chucking that about like a ball. It must stay in the hands it is in, until others have proved a right to it. You who were brought up for the bar, and you need me to tell you that?"

"This is how the case stands, mother," said Geoffrey. "The money which is the greater part of our living was left to your cousin, Leonard Crosthwaite, and only to you failing him and his heirs. You thought he was dead, without heirs, and you have enjoyed it all this time with an easy mind. But a fortnight ago Leonard Crosthwaite appeared. You did not know him at first, but before he went away you were convinced it was he. Is not this all true?"

"She fancied it was he, being a silly woman who believes everybody's story, and never knew a lie from the truth all her days."

'And you, Aunt Anna," said Geoffrey, turning upon her with quick impatience, "did you always know the truth from a lie?"

"I have had no practice to speak of," she answered; "lies have been told me ever since I can remember. The other is a great deal more uncommon. Don't puzzle your mother with sophistries. Tell her what you want, that is the shortest way."

"Indeed, dear," said Mrs Underwood, with deprecating looks, "your Aunt Anna is right; it would be better just to tell me what I am to do. I would have done anything for poor Leonard. Poor fellow! to die among strangers, far from his poor wife and everybody that knew him! My heart bleeds for *her*, Geoff. If they had sent for me I would have gone in a moment to nurse him and take care of him. You don't suppose I would have been so cruel as to let him die by himself if I had known? And now these poor girls. Oh, what a change for them! to come here for pleasure, and to have all their amusement, poor things, turned into misery and sorrow!" Here the kind woman's voice was choked with tears.

"Mother! mother!" said Geoffrey, "you are the best woman in the world: but I think you will drive me out of my senses all the same."

Mrs Underwood dried her eyes after a moment and looked up in his face with a tremulous little smile. "That is what your poor father used to say," she replied with great simplicity. "I am not one to see the rights of everything at a glance like Anna; but if you will explain to me what it is best to do, you will see I will always do it, Geoff. You may trust me for that."

What was Geoffrey to do? He did his best to shut his ears to Miss Anna's laugh and her remark, "You perceive it is always a great deal better to talk things over with me." It was quite true, though he never would own it: and to discuss this matter with her was impossible to him. He stood for a little while by the fire, staring into the mirror, where his own troubled countenance appeared in the centre of all the little carved shelves covered with china, which were reflected on every side. He felt himself, as he had done so many times before, altogether out of place in the house, where he was sometimes the master and sometimes of less account than the dog. So far Geoffrey was always the master. His tastes, his comforts, and even his convenience were the subjects of endless study. But between his mother's incapacity for any mental exertion, and his aunt's too keen and casuistical intelligence, it often happened that Geoffrey was driven to the end of his patience, and felt himself no better than a puppet between them, vainly struggling against Miss Anna's false logic and his mother's shifty feebleness. At these moments a sort of sickness of despair came over the young man. He thought with longing of any wild scene of emigrant life, any diggings, or sheep-walks, into which he could escape, to encounter the grosser elements of life, and be free of this feminine atmosphere. To plant him here between these two ladies seemed a freak of fate which was unaccountable. Their motives, their ideas, were all different from his. Geoffrey stood for a few minutes staring at himself, thinking what a gloomy ruffian he looked, and how much out of keeping with all those dainty surroundings; then he went hastily out, notwithstanding the appeal of both ladies to him. "You are not going out in the rain, Geoff?" cried his mother; while Miss Anna bade him recollect that it was past six o'clock. Geoffrey paid no attention to either. It would be almost a satisfaction, he felt, to make her wait for her dinner. Not his mother, who cared as little for her dinner

GROVE ROAD, HAMPSTEAD

as any woman could do, but Miss Anna, who was *gourmande*, and could not bear to wait. He was glad, too, of the sting of the rain, blown in his face as he stepped out from all the comfort and warmth of the too warm, luxurious house. The chill air and the darkness refreshed him—they were such a contradiction to all the conditions of his life.

He went out upon the borders of the heath, and looked down through the rain upon the distant lights, the smoke of great London lying spread out before him. Though he had been bred among women, and luxuriously cared for all his life, he was not without some knowledge of what existence was outside. And now, when he set himself to think of it, the prospect gave him a shiver. It was almost as discouraging, as dismal as the wet world upon which he looked. He had been called to the bar a few years before, and he had got one or two briefs, which had been a matter of much pride and amusement to the household. But this was a very different thing from living by his work. He tried to realise what the consequences would be of giving up the fortune of which he was aware he had thought lightly enough. If it was all he could do to put up with that feminine atmosphere now, in the midst of abundant space and the many pleasant engagements which relieved him from its monotony, what would it be when he was shut up with it in a few small rooms—when his only relaxation would be home, and his home still, in its scantiness and impoverishment, the domain of Aunt Anna? There flashed before him a vision of one small sitting-room, with her chair in the chief place, her work occupying the table, her nerves affected by every sound, her quick ears catching every word that was said. Geoffrey felt himself able for other kinds of privation, for hard work if need was, for the resignation of most things that were pleasant in life — but when he thought of this his heart failed him. And there was no help for it. Anna had been the tyrant of her sister's life as long as she remembered, and to withdraw from her now when she was poor would be impossible. To suffer is always possible; there is nothing in life so likely, so universally put up with — but to abandon those who have shared our lives is not a thing that can be done. It is a bond which the worst recognise, which it does not even require heroic virtue to be faithful to. To do it may be heroic, but not to do it is miserable. In prosperity Aunt Anna might by possibility—though by so distant a possibility that Geoffrey hitherto had always felt it hopeless—have been shaken off; but in trouble or poverty she would be the absolute sovereign of his life, and his mother would be her slave. As the young man stood with the rain beating in his face, seeing by times, as the blast permitted, the glimmer of the distant lights through the wet mist, he perceived and consented to this with a sort of desperation. He must work for them both, he must hold by them both. He could never emancipate himself till he or they should die.

If, after this terrible realisation of what was before him, he looked upon the loss of the money with less composure, could any one be surprised? When he got home he went into his study, the room which was sacred to him, where he was free from all intrusion, where, however oppressive the domestic atmosphere might be, he could always escape from it, and feed himself alone. No such refuge would be his were he poor. He would have to sit and do his work at the same table where Aunt Anna spread out her beads and her wools, and worked her impossible, useless fancy work. Was it a duty, after all, to throw all his comfort, all that made life tolerable, at the feet of these two strangers? Geoffrey's heart was rent in two. His way was no longer clear before him, but covered with doubt and darkness and bewildering clouds.

With all this there was a something unsaid which had glanced across his mind many times in the course of the afternoon—a compromise, a way out of the worst of the trouble, a new life—but he did not dare to think of that. He pushed it away forcibly from the surface of his thoughts.

CHAPTER X

"IT is pouring rain," said Mrs Underwood, "and he will get his death of cold. Oh, how can boys be so incautious; and just when he has heard what comes of it! Poor Leonard! I have not had time to think of him yet, with all you have been saying; but when one thinks how well one knew him once, and that he was our own flesh and blood! And Geoff doing the same thing, the very same thing, in spite of such a warning!"

"You are insufferable," cried Miss Anna; "hold your tongue, for Heaven's sake. Do you think the man died, whoever he was, only to give a warning to your son?"

"I think nothing of the kind, Anna. Poor Leonard, there never could be anybody more sorry: and his poor wife, I am sure my heart bleeds for her: but Geoff ought to take example by him, all the same."

"His wife?" Miss Anna said; and she laughed: "the wife of the man who left England thirty years ago with a broken heart. It has been on my mind ever since that I might have been kinder to him. I thought at first I had killed him." She laughed again. "I might have saved myself the trouble.

GROVE ROAD, HAMPSTEAD

He is dead now of a wet night—a great deal more deadly a thing than a love rejected; and here are you maundering about his poor wife. His poor wife! I have no doubt she'll marry again before the year's out. It's the way of the world."

"It is not the way of all the world, Anna," said Mrs Underwood. She would not make a direct claim of superiority on account of her faithfulness, but she drew up her head a little and sighed, with a look of conscious merit; at which Miss Anna laughed the more.

"That is true," she said, "you've never married, Mary, nor wished to, I believe. You are a superior creature. I ought to have made an exception for you."

"Not so superior as you think, Anna," said the simple woman; "there is many and many another like me, that would not, could not—oh, no, no, for nothing in the world! Yes; I thought too that he never would have got over it, he was so devoted to you; but he was young; if you will remember, he was two years younger than——"

"Have done with these absurd recollections, Mary," said her sister angrily; "I want to hear no more of him. He's safely out of the way now at last; and there's his—there's these girls to deal with. If I had only been by myself and had all my wits about me I should soon have settled these girls; but I never have it in my power to act for myself. There was Geoff standing by with those glaring eyes of his—not that I am afraid of his eyes. They don't know a single thing, these girls. If I had taken my own way I should have asked them here, and made much of them."

"Oh, Anna, dear! I always said you had such a good heart!"

Miss Anna paused to look at her sister with contemptuous toleration. "Was any one talking of my good heart?" she said. "But, never mind, I should have taken them in—in every sense of the word. I would have been Aunt Anna to them. I would have packed them off to their mother with my love and a little present. To have to do with fools blunts the sharpest intellect. That is what I ought to have done. And it was all they wanted. To find their English relations, to get up a little sentiment; that was all they wanted; they have money enough; and they did not know a thing, not a thing! To think I should have missed my opportunity like that! A bit of china that would have got smashed on the voyage out, and our love; they would have written us gushing letters and talked of our kindness all their lives."

Mrs Underwood, good woman, was puzzled. She did not understand what this meant. "If they had known you, Anna, I am sure they would have — loved you," she said, faltering a little. This was not always the result of more intimate knowledge in Miss Anna's case, but her sister had a robust faith. Miss Anna cast a contemptuous glance upon her, but it was not worth her while to argue.

"If it had not been for your son I would have done it," she said; "what could have been more easy? If Geoff had been out in the world, as I always said he ought to have been, in chambers of his own, not tied to our apron-strings, out of my way——"

"Anna! you never said such a thing before! You have always said you liked to have him at home."

"I like a man in the house," said Miss Anna; "I don't deny it. There is an advantage in having a man in the house, if he would hold his tongue and do what he is told; but as you have never known how to hold your own tongue about anything, Geoff understands all our affairs. What is the use of talking? I could have done it, but the opportunity is over. Now there is that little spitfire with her imagination all aflame. I should not wonder if she thought there was a dukedom dormant in the family, and a romantic vast estate that we are keeping from her; and Geoff with his ridiculous ideas and all that false nonsense about honour——"

"Geoff has no ridiculous ideas," said his mother, flushed and tearful; "there is nothing false about Geoff. He is honour itself, and sense and judgment; and he is as true as the day—and——"

"Everything that is perfect, we all know."

GROVE ROAD, HAMPSTEAD

"I did not say that; he has his little faults, like all of us. He is a little hasty; he is perhaps too generous; but as for interfering with any kind thing you meant to do, Anna, you are mistaken, quite mistaken, my dear. Let me go and see them to-morrow; poor things, poor things! of course one wants to be kind to them. And to think that Geoff would have had any objection! For that matter," the mother said, faltering a little, "he has always so many invitations; people are always asking him; he might go away upon a visit while they are here."

"That is an idea," said Miss Anna; "but no, things have gone too far now; besides," she said with conscious malice, "that would balk me in one of my plans. If the worst comes to the worst we might marry him—to the youngest of them."

Mrs Underwood sat bolt upright in her chair; the colour went out of her comely cheeks; her very voice failed her. "Ma—arry him!" she said with a gasp.

"They are both pretty," said Miss Anna; "and especially the little one—the younger one. I saw him cast many a glance at her. Oh, I notice that sort of thing always. Though I never married like you, I was not without my experiences. And I think I know. It would not have wanted much on his side; and that would have saved your share of the money, which would always be something if the worst came to the worst."

Geoff's mother had become incapable of speech as this dreadful prospect was placed before her. She made a little movement with her hand, as if to clear it away.

"Geoff is thinking of nothing of the kind, Anna. Geoff—has his heart entirely in his home. He is just as simple-minded and as—pure-hearted as when he was a boy."

"Dear me!" said Miss Anna, "I thought it was the height of purity and simplicity to marry early; I have always been told so. Some French young men, who you know are the types of everything that is improper, can't be got to marry. But Geoff, being the best of good boys, of course will want to marry as soon as possible; and here is a capital chance for him. That was my plan, Mary —if the worst comes to the worst. If you have a better, of course I have nothing to say."

Mrs Underwood sat all limp and downfallen, every line of her showing the droop of dismay and depression which her sister's words, spoken in mere mischief—for the idea of Milly, though it had glanced across her mind, had gone no farther —had produced. "I——" she faltered, "Anna— I have got no plan. How should I have any plan? If they have a right to—the money, we shall have to give it up to them. And we will have to give up our pretty house, and live in—the poorest way. He says, Never mind, dear boy. He will work for us, he will never forsake us, Anna! Now you will see what my Geoff is made of. He has the best heart; but it will be a dreadful change, a dreadful change for him—he that has been used to have everything he wanted all his life."

"And you will rather let him fall into poverty, and be compelled to work, and have us two old women hanging upon him and cramping him— than save his share of the money for him and get him a nice young wife? That's what mothers are! I have always said, when they made such a fuss about their children, it was themselves they were thinking of. Now, what concerns me," said Miss Anna with only the malicious gleam in her eyes to contradict her dignified assumption of superior virtue, "what concerns me is Geoff's real advantage, not the selfish wish of keeping him for ever at my side."

Mrs Underwood's countenance fell more and more. She looked haggard in the sudden severity of the conflict set up within her. "I—thinking of myself?" she said, almost weeping. But the accusation was too terrible to be met with mere tears, which are fit only for lesser matters. She gazed at her sister with large round eyes full of wretchedness. No crime in the world was so dreadful to her as this of thinking of one's self; it is the thing of all others which cuts a virtuous Englishwoman to the heart. "For Geoff's good, you know, you know, Anna," she cried, "I would submit to anything. I would go to the stake; I would give myself to be cut in pieces."

"Nobody is the least likely to cut you in pieces, my dear," said Miss Anna coolly. "The stake is not an English institution. It is easy to promise things that never will be asked from you. The question is, will you let Geoff be happy, poor boy, in his own way?"

"Happy!" the poor lady cried in a lamentable voice; but then her voice failed her, though a dozen questions rose and fluttered through her mind. Could Geoff be happy in abandoning his mother? Would he give her up for a bit of a girl who never could love him half so well? Was it possible that there was anything wanting to his happiness now, watched over and cared for as he was? She sat gazing aghast into the vacant air before her, suddenly brought face to face with a question which was far more serious even than the loss of the money. If the money was to be lost, Mrs Underwood felt in herself the power of enduring everything. To be housemaid and valet to Geoff would be, in its way, a kind of blessedness; it would knit the domestic ties closer. She would have more of her boy if they lived in a smaller space, in a poorer way; and with that happiness before her, what did she care for poverty? But her sister's suggestion brought in an entirely different circle of ideas. She saw herself dropping apart from Geoff's life altogether. He, happy with his young wife : she, set aside from his existence : and she looked at that visionary picture aghast. To be cut in pieces was one thing, to stand aside and let him go away from her was another. Was it all selfishness, as Anna said ?

"I see I have startled you," said Miss Anna; "but it is too late for anything now ; that eldest girl is not to be taken in. She will fight it out ; she will drag us through the mire. Never mind, it was Geoff's fault, and Geoff will have to bear the brunt. But you will be able to keep him to yourself, and that will be a consolation," she added with a sneer. "Never mind what he has to put up with as long as you can keep him to yourself : that is everything to you, I know. And there's the dressing bell, Mary. We must have our dinner, whatever happens," Miss Anna said.

But Mrs Underwood, poor lady, did not have much dinner that day. She came down to the meal in her pretty cap, but it was a haggard countenance that showed beneath the lace. She could not talk nor eat, but sat mute at the head of the table choked with natural tears. To Geoffrey, who had come in hungry and full of thought from his wet walk, there seemed nothing wonderful in his mother's woebegone condition ; it chimed in with the tone of his own thoughts. To some certain extent she would feel for him, she would sympathise with him, though even she could never know the whole extent of the sacrifice he would be called upon to make. The dinner was a very silent one. Miss Anna tried a few sallies of her malicious observation, but in vain. The others were too much depressed to take any notice, even to resent them. The old butler made his solemn rounds about the table with a gradual increase of curiosity at every step. Whatever was the matter? the worthy servant asked himself. He was a north-countryman, and knew a little about the family history; but an unfortunate chance had taken him out at the moment when the strange visitor arrived who had caused so much commotion in the house a fortnight since. The twilight hour, when it was too late for visitors (as he chose to think) was Simmons' hour for taking a little walk, sometimes to the post, sometimes to the fishmonger's, who had a way of forgetting. He had missed the young ladies too, of whom the housemaid had told such stories downstairs. But he saw there was "summat up," and he bent the whole powers of his mind, as was to be expected, to make out what it was. When Miss Anna's speeches met with no response she turned to Simmons, as she had a habit of doing when she was in want of amusement. "Did you hear any news when you were out for your walk?" she said. "If it were not for Simmons I should know nothing about my fellow-creatures. You never bring in a word of gossip from year's end to year's end, Geoff; and what is the use of a man with a club to go to every day if he never brings one any news? Simmons, you are a person with a better sense of your responsibilities. Tell me something that is going on outside. What's the last news in Grove Road?"

"There is no news, Miss Anna, as I am aware of," said Simmons, coughing a little behind his hand by way of prelude. "There is nothink that is of any consequence;" and then he began to tell of the gentleman at No. 5, whose conduct troubled the entire neighbourhood. Miss Anna had an eager interest in everything that was going on. She asked about the gentleman at No. 5 as if she had no greater interest in life. Her beautiful eyes sparkled and shone with eagerness. All the details about him were acceptable to her. A spectator would have vowed that she never had known a personal anxiety in her life.

Geoff sat late that night thinking over all that had happened and was going to happen. He had begun to ask himself what he could do to make a little money, and the answer had not been a satisfactory one. It is very common in novels, and even in society, to represent every young man who is without occupation as doing literary work and finding it always ready to his hand. And, naturally, Geoff thought of that among other things. But he did not know what to write about, nor to whom to take his productions if they were written. He knew what he had learned at school and at Oxford, but he did not know very much else.

GROVE ROAD, HAMPSTEAD

Classics and philosophy are very excellent things, but it is hard to make money of them immediately, save by being a professor or a schoolmaster, which were occupations Geoff did not incline to and was not fitted for. He did not understand much about politics; he was not deeply read in general literature; he had no imagination of the creative sort. In short, like a great many others, though he had all the will in the world to embrace the profession of literature, which seems such an easy one, he did not know how to do it; and to hope to support his mother and her sister upon the few briefs which he was likely to get was ridiculous. As well attempt to support them by sweeping chimneys. He reflected with a doleful smile that even that required, if not special aptitude, at least special training, of which he had none. He was thinking of this drearily enough long after the rest of the household had, as he supposed, gone to bed, and all was still.

Suddenly his door creaked a little, softly opened, and his mother stole in. She was dressed in an old-fashioned dressing-gown, of what was then called a shawl pattern, with a muslin cap on her head tied round with a broad black ribbon. She had been going to bed, but had not been able to go to bed without a little reconciliation and kind good-night to her boy. "Did we quarrel, mother? I did not know it," he said.

"Oh, quarrel, Geoff! we never quarrelled in our

lives. You have always been the best of sons, and I hope I have always appreciated you. I couldn't go to bed, my darling boy, if there was the least little thing between me and you."

"But there is nothing, mother," he said, caressing the hand she had laid upon his.

"Yes, there is something; I could not rest for thinking of it. Oh, is it true, my darling, is it true that you want to be—married? If you had that in your mind I would never stand in your way, you may be sure never, whatever it might cost me. What is my happiness but in seeing yours, my boy? I would never say a word. I would give up and go away; oh, not far, to vex you, only far enough not to be spying upon you and her; to leave you free, if you are sure it is really, really for your happiness, my own boy."

"Mother!" cried Geoff, staring at her, "I think you must have taken leave of your senses. I—marry? at such a moment at this?"

"Anna thinks it would be the only thing to do. She thinks, Geoff, she says, it is—the youngest of the two."

Here Geoff, unable to quench entirely the traitor in him, blushed like a girl, growing red up to his hair under his mother's jealous eyes. "This is mere folly," he said, trying to laugh. "Why, I have only seen her twice."

"Sometimes that is enough," Mrs Underwood said mournfully. "Things look so different at my time of life and yours. I dare say you think it is very fine to fall in love at first sight; but oh, when you think of it—on one side those that have loved you and cherished you all your life, on the other somebody you know nothing about—that you have only seen twice!"

"My dear mother," the young man said. He made this beginning as if he intended to follow it up with a warm disclaimer and protestation of his own superiority to any such youthful delusion. But when he had said these words he stopped short suddenly and said no more.

His mother had her eyes fixed upon him, anxiously expecting to hear something in his defence; but when he thus broke down, and it appeared that he had no plea at all, no justification to offer, her heart sank within her. She stood by him for a minute waiting, and then she put her hand tremblingly upon his shoulder. "Have you nothing to say to me, Geoff?"

"I don't know what you would like me to say, mother," he replied somewhat impatiently. "What you are speaking of is preposterous. What might have happened in happier circumstances I can't tell—but that I should think of marrying anybody just now, and above all one of the people whose fortune we have taken from them——"

"Geoff! we never meant to take anybody's money. We never dreamt that it was not our own; we don't know even yet," said his mother, faltering.

GROVE ROAD, HAMPSTEAD

"No; we don't know even yet; and perhaps I am wrong in urging you to a decision. Perhaps we ought to wait and see what evidence there is. It is a hard thing to contemplate, anyhow, mother."

"Oh, my dear! very hard, very hard! and if it separates you from me!"

"I do not see how it can do that in any case," he said coldly. It chilled him to think that her chief terror in the matter was lest there should be any opening of happiness to him in it. It was preposterous, as he had said; but still, was that the chief thing she feared—that he should have a life of his own, that he should be happy? It made him recoil a little from her. "Go to bed, mother; there is nothing that need disturb your rest, at least for to-night."

She would have stayed and questioned and groped into every corner of his heart, if she could, and protested that it was for him, not herself, that she feared anything; but Geoff was not so tractable as usual to-night. He opened the door for her, and kissed her and bade her good-night with something like a dismissal. Then Mrs Underwood perceived by a logic peculiar to herself that Anna was right, and that her worst fears were true.

CHAPTER XI

DR BREWER came in upon the girls that same evening somewhat abruptly. He was a busy man, with little time to spare, and he thought his sudden arrival like a gale of wind was a good thing for them in the languor of their grief; but there was no languor about them as he found them. The table was covered with papers, dispatch boxes, and writing materials. Grace had turned out all the contents of her father's boxes, and was gathering together and examining every scrap of written paper, while Milly, with a pen in her hand, obediently wrote down the description of each. One little pile of business papers had been put by itself; letters were lying open, innocent little account books, memoranda of all kinds. It was like a man's mind turned inside out, with all its careless thoughts, and those futile recollections of no importance which stick fast in corners when all that is worth remembering fades away. The doctor was astonished by the sight, and alarmed as well. He knew that the scrutiny of a couple of innocent girls innocently spying thus into every recess of the thoughts, even of the most virtuous of men, might not be desirable.

"Hallo!" he cried, "you are so very busy, I fear I am an intruder. Is this necessary, do you think? Would it not be better to take all these things home?"

"Oh, doctor, you are our only friend—you can never be an intruder," cried Grace. "Yes, we intended to take everything home; but something has happened since—something that makes every scrap important. We are obliged to do it. It is for the sake of the children!"

"You are giving yourselves a great deal of pain, and you have had enough already," he said, seating himself at the table between them. My dear young ladies, you are sure I don't want to interfere in your family affairs; but I feel responsible to your poor mother for you."

"What does it matter about us? Dr Brewer, we have made a great discovery to-day!"

"I heard you were out," he said. "I was very glad to hear that you had been out—a little change is what you want. A great discovery! Well, so long as it is a pleasant one——"

"I don't know whether it is a pleasant one or not."

"You shall have my opinion if you will trust me with this important secret," said the doctor, smiling. He was a man with daughters of his own. He knew the exaggerations, the excitements of youth; and he was very tender of these fatherless children. His friendly countenance, the very breadth and size of the man was a support to them, as they sat slim and slight on either side of him. But when he said this, they looked at each other with that look of consultation which had amused him so often. The doctor thought it was an unnecessary formula on the part of Grace, who always had her own way; but he liked her the better for thus consulting the silent member of their co-partnership before she spoke. To his surprise, however, that silent member returned a glance of meaning — a sort of unspoken veto upon the intended disclosure.

"We have been to the place where papa was when he caught his cold—the same place; and in the same way."

Here again little Milly, shy and acquiescent as she was, signalled her disapproval. "Don't," she seemed to say, with those soft lips which never before had expressed anything but concurrence. The spectator was much more interested, perversely, than if the sisters had been as usual in perfect accord.

"Then you have found your relations?" he said.

"We don't know if they are relations. Yes, I think so; we had the strangest reception. Doctor, I don't know how to tell you. We are sure there is something underneath — an inheritance, of which papa has been cheated, which we, or rather our Lenny, is the right heir of. I suppose such things are quite common in England?" cried Grace, full of excitement. "You will be able to tell us what people do?"

"An inheritance!" the doctor said, amazed. And then he laughed a little, and shook his head. "No, my dear child, I don't think such things are at all common in England. They happen in novels, but not anywhere else, so far as I know."

This disconcerted the girls for a moment. For to be told that your own story is like a novel is always disagreeable, and throws an air of contempt upon the sternest facts. "It does not matter," said Grace shortly, "however much it may be like a novel, it is nevertheless true. We found the address in papa's letter case—nothing but the address—and we felt sure that was where he had gone, to see old friends, he said. We went there this afternoon thinking we too, perhaps, might find friends, or at least hear something about that last visit. We were received by the strangest, beautiful old lady—oh, she was like a novel if you please!—who would have nothing to say to us. But the others," said Grace, getting somewhat confused, "acknowledged that there was some one who had gone to see them that day, Tuesday, and had left in the rain—who was a relation—who was—or, at least, they said, pretended to be. Only it was quite a different name."

Dr Brewer held up his hands to stop this broken flood of disclosure. "Stop a little, and take me with you," he said. "A beautiful old lady—and

GROVE ROAD, HAMPSTEAD

the others who said—but it was quite a different name. Now, tell me what all this means."

Then they both began to talk together explaining to him. "There was one lady, and her son, who were very kind," Milly said.

"She told us it was an impostor or a madman who had come, and said he was—somebody," cried Grace; "but that *that* person had died long ago; and that our father was far more respectable; and that we could raise a great law-suit if we liked; but the others said if we were *his* daughters, it would make a great difference—oh, a very great difference to them."

"But they were very kind, and kissed us, and promised to come and see us," cried Milly, breathless, coming in again at the end.

"This is a very curious story," said Dr Brewer. "I don't pretend to understand it very well, but so far as I can make out—— What was the name? Of course there are family quarrels now and then, and sons who bring a great deal of trouble upon everybody——"

"That could never be the case with papa," cried Grace proudly; "I am sure he must have been wronged."

"Many an excellent man has been foolish in his youth," said the doctor; "we must not take things too solemnly. If you will tell me the name, perhaps I may recollect if it has figured in the papers."

Here both the girls were up in arms. They confronted him with flaming eyes, and a blaze of anger.

"Doctor, I think you don't understand at all! If you think our dear father, whom we have just lost,"—and here Grace's voice wavered, and Milly dried her eyes—"was likely to do anything that would be in the papers——"

"Why, my dear children," cried the doctor, "how unreasonable you are! Of course, he was in the papers a hundred times over. A man of note in his community—a public man with letters to the Colonial Secretary, and who entertained the Prince, as you told me yourselves——"

Here they looked at each other again, and blushed at their mistake.

"Yes, to be sure," said Grace. "Dr Brewer is right, and we are silly. I was thinking of something else."

"Probably, for instance," said the doctor, "there were advertisements in what people call the agony column, entreating him to go home. You don't know the agony column? Oh, it is very easy to laugh; but there are sometimes appeals there that remind one of sad stories one has known. A doctor, you know, hears a hundred stories. What was the name?"

Once more that consulting look, and once more a blush of excitement tinged with real diffidence, and a little embarrassment of shame. They could not bear to think of a name which was fictitious, of anything that was untrue about their history. "You know," said Grace, hesitating, feeling for the moment as if no inheritance, not even an old castle or even a title, which had vaguely glanced across her mind as a possibility, could make up for this falsehood—" you know, we are not at all sure that it was papa. He never mentioned anything of the kind, nor did we ever hear it before. The name was Crosthwaite. It is not pretty; it is an odd name."

"Crosthwaite—Crosthwaite: where have I heard it? It is not pretty, as you say; it is a north-country name, Yorkshire perhaps, or—where did I hear it? Ah, I remember, some one had been making inquiries down-stairs."

"It was Geoffrey," cried Milly unawares: and then blushed more deeply than she had hitherto blushed either for shame or anger, and caught herself up, and drew back a little, in embarrassment which did not seem to have any adequate cause.

"Then you know the people?" the doctor said in surprise.

"We know only their Christian names," Grace, somewhat startled too, explained eagerly to cover her sister. "The son is Geoffrey, and the old lady is Miss Anna."

"Bless me!" cried the doctor, "this is very peculiar. Oh! but you said there was another lady—a lady and her son? Yes, yes, I see—a Mrs Somebody—and this Miss Anna."

"Mrs Underwood," Grace said.

Dr Brewer's surprise grew more and more. "I know a Geoffrey Underwood," he said, "a young barrister—a very nice young fellow. To be sure! he belongs to two ladies who live up Hampstead way. This is very curious. He is an excellent young fellow. He will tell me at once what the mystery is—if there is any mystery; but, my dear young ladies, I am afraid your romance will come to nothing if Geoffrey Underwood is in it; for you may be sure he is not a young fellow to lend himself to any bad business. Your beautiful old lady may be cracked, you know; she must be off her head—a harmless lunatic perhaps. I very much disapprove of it," said the doctor, with professional warmth; "entirely, in every way—but still there are people who, out of mistaken kindness, insist upon keeping such cases at home—a thing that never ought to be done."

Grace had listened with some dismay, feeling her house of cards tumbling about her ears. "She was not insane, if that is what you mean. They were afraid of her. She was the one who talked the most. I am sure she was not insane; and then Mrs Underwood, too—you remember, Milly?—she said, 'If it is so we are relations;' and then her son, he said, 'It will make the greatest difference to us all.'"

GROVE ROAD, HAMPSTEAD

"He said so? then perhaps after all there is something in it," said Dr Brewer. The doctor began to look serious. "One can never understand the outs and ins of a family. So many people that have a good deal of money to leave make foolish wills. It may be something of that kind. Bless me! poor young Underwood, a fine young fellow. It will be hard upon him. You must excuse me if I see both sides of the case," he added gravely; "young Underwood is——" and here he came to a dead pause.

It would be impossible to imagine anything more uncomfortable than the sensations of these two girls. They were silent for a little, and nothing was said round the table except a faint sound from the doctor of concern and sympathy, accompanied by the shaking of his head. Grace burst forth at last, unable to restrain herself.

"But, doctor, if it belongs to us rightfully, if it ought to come to my brother Lenny—a family estate.—I don't know what it is—perhaps something that has belonged to us for hundreds and hundreds of years, perhaps something that would change his position altogether, and make him somebody of importance: is it not my duty to stand up for my brother, to get him whatever he has a right to—although other people may have to suffer?" the girl cried, with passion.

Milly by this time began to cry quietly, with her

hands over her face; and Grace stood alone, the champion of the family rights.

"Yes, yes," the doctor said—"yes, yes; of course everybody should have their rights; other people must always be a secondary consideration." He added, after a moment's pause, "But don't take up any false ideas about family estates. Young Underwood is sufficiently well off, I have always heard. He has had a good education. I don't suppose he makes very much money by his profession, so he must be able to live without that. But his people are very quiet people. They live quite out of the way; they are scarcely in society at all. Dismiss from your mind all idea of hereditary estates or important position. All the same, money in the funds is very nice—when there is enough of it."

"Money in the funds!" said Grace, her countenance falling; while Milly took one of her hands from her face, and looked over the other like a sort of woebegone and misty Aurora from behind the clouds.

"Nothing more romantic than that, I fear," said Dr Brewer; "but that's a very good thing, a very nice thing. No, life in England is not romantic to speak of; it's a very businesslike affair. If people have enough to live on, it doesn't trouble them very much how it comes. Land is dear. It's very nice if you have enough of it, but it's an expensive luxury. You get better percentage for your money even in the funds—and no risks."

"But, perhaps," said Grace, "as—Geoffrey—is not the right heir—it might be something different. Perhaps if it came back to the old family there might be something more. Sometimes—things pass away, don't they, when it is not the direct line?"

"Peerages?" said Dr Brewer with a laugh. "Oh, yes; but I never heard of property going astray. Money must find its level, you know; it must go somewhere; it cannot just be spilt upon the earth like water and made an end of. It must turn up somewhere. When a man dies intestate, I believe his money goes to the Queen; which is hard, I have always thought. If it were divided among the poorest of his neighbours it would be more sensible. Sometimes a title drops by reason of a failure in the direct line. But I don't suppose you thought——" Here he stopped short, and gave vent to a sudden laugh. "I do believe, my poor dear girl, that this is what was in your mind——"

"I never said there was any such thing in my mind," said Grace, growing crimson. She felt as if she could have sunk into the earth. She had nothing to say to defend herself, except this simple denial, and to hear the doctor laugh was terrible. He laughed so frankly, as at the most apparent nonsense. The girl did not know what to do. Was she such a fool as he thought?

"It is very romantic," he said; "but I fear,

Miss Grace, in modern days such things happen very rarely. Life was a great deal more picturesque in the past. Now people are very thankful for such small mercies as money in the funds."

Grace made no reply. She too felt very much disposed to cry; it seemed cruel that anybody should laugh at them in their circumstances, in their deep crape. The sound of laughter even was out of place in the room from which so lately the chief inhabitant had gone. She felt herself hurt, as well as ashamed, by being made the cause of merriment; and even little Milly, though she had not agreed with her, uncovered her little tearful face, and was indignant in Grace's cause.

"I don't think there is so much to laugh at, Dr Brewer," Milly ventured to say. "You were not there to see what happened. You would have thought it very, very important if you had seen how they looked, and heard what they said."

"I beg your pardon," said the doctor, "was I unmannerly? I didn't mean to be. Why we should laugh at simplicity I cannot tell, but everybody does. I have not the least doubt it was a most natural mistake."

Simplicity! when everybody had always thought her so sensible, so superior to all delusions. Grace shrank back into herself. She would scarcely reply to any further questions.

"But, you know," Dr Brewer said, with great gravity, "it is no laughing matter. Where there is a question of taking their living from another family, you must be very sure of your facts. It is such a hard case that a jury would give every advantage of a doubt to the people assailed. It would prefer to see what they did in the very best light. There would be a prejudice against the claimants, however much *dans leur droit* they might be. The evidence would have to be very exact, as clear as daylight. Any lawyer would tell you this. He would tell you, if your evidence was not beyond question, to accept, or even offer, a compromise. Such things are of every-day occurrence. You may have a strong case, but if you can't support it, and make it all as distinct as clockwork, they will suggest a compromise. Have you found anything among these papers to support the claim you are intending to make?"

"No."

"You say your father never spoke about it, never referred to his former name; gave you not the slightest hint of any rights of his in England?"

"No."

"In short, you have no proof at all?" the doctor said.

"Not any, that we know of," said Grace.

She sat, dogged and obstinate, answering only in monosyllables, or with as few words as possible, sitting bolt upright against the high back of her chair. Her heart had sunk, and her confidence was failing her; but she would not yield, or at least seem to yield.

"That is not very hopeful," said Dr Brewer, "any lawyer would tell you. But you are determined, notwithstanding, to make out your case?"

"Yes," said Grace.

She no longer felt amiably disposed towards the doctor. He had cast down her dream-castle; he had represented her to herself as a vulgar money-seeker; he had overthrown all her romantic hopes of gaining advancement for her family, and making of Lenny a pattern English gentleman, perhaps nobleman. She saw now what a slender foundation she had built it all upon; but as nothing in the world would ever make Grace give in, she hardened herself over her inward confusion, and stood like a rock though her heart was quaking. The doctor made two or three sharp little speeches; but he was half-angry, too, that the girls upon whom he had been spending so much feeling should be so impervious to his influence. He got up hurriedly at last, and said something about still having some patients to see, though it was getting late.

"Good-night," he said. "I should say I would be glad to do anything I could to help you, if I did not think you were embarking upon a most perilous undertaking. I think, permit me to say so, you should take your mother's advice first."

"I shall do nothing mamma will disapprove of," said Grace; and she parted with stateliness from

GROVE ROAD, HAMPSTEAD

this friend who had been the only one to succour them in their trouble.

As for Milly, she was very deprecating and tearful as she held out her two hands to him. "Do not be angry!" she said with her beseeching eyes. It was all the doctor could do not to stoop down and kiss this peace-maker as he went away. He had thought her a little nobody at first, but he did not do so now. "I declare she is as like Laura as one flower is to another," he said to himself as he went down-stairs. Now Laura was the doctor's favourite child—and what more could be said?

When he was gone, Grace returned to her previous occupation with her father's papers; but her heart was gone out of her search. "We might have asked him at least to recommend some lawyer to us," she said, which was the only observation she made to Milly on the subject. Milly, indeed, was dismissed altogether from the employment she had been trusted with before Dr Brewer came in. Grace continued to look over the papers, to put one on this heap, and the other on that; but she no longer required Milly's pen to write down and describe what each was. For at least an hour they sat silent, the younger sister looking wistfully on, the elder rustling the papers, bending over them with puckers of careful consideration over her eyes, affecting to pause now and then to deliberate over one or another. At length Grace gathered them all together, with a sudden impatient movement, and, putting them back into the despatch-box, concluded suddenly without any warning by an outburst of tears.

"To think," she cried, when Milly, greatly alarmed, yet almost glad thus to recover her sister, hurried to her—"to think that we should be going over all these things that were his private things just the other day—not for love, or because it was necessary, but for business, and about money! Oh, how hard we are, how heartless, what poor wretched creatures! I could not have believed it of myself."

"Dear," said Milly, soothing her, "it is because everything is so strange; and to do anything is a little comfort; and for the children's sake."

"I wish now," said Grace, with her head upon her sister's shoulder, "that we had telegraphed at once to mamma."

"Perhaps it would have been better," said Milly; "but you thought it would be so dreadful for her, without any warning."

Grace wept less bitterly when this instance of her own self-denial was suggested to her. "It is so long to wait—so long to wait," she cried. And then a sense of their desolation came over them, and the two forlorn young creatures clung to each other. Their nerves were overwrought, and they were able for no more.

CHAPTER XII

THERE was not very much more happiness under the roof of the house in Grove Road. Geoffrey, as has been said, sat half the night through in his study, with his head in his hands, pondering vainly what he ought to do. Though he said to himself that it was only just that they should produce their proofs, that they should establish their claim before anything was done, he jumped at the conclusion all the same, and took it for granted that the claim would be established, and that his own fate was certain. And after that what was he to do? He was as confused, as downcast as ever, when, in the middle of the night, he made his way through the darkness of the sleeping house and went to bed, but scarcely to rest. His mother, whose thoughts also had kept her awake, and who had cried, and pondered, and dozed, and started up to cry and doze again, heard him come up-stairs, and with difficulty restrained herself from going to him, to see that he was warm in bed, and had taken no harm from his vigil. She did not do it, fortunately remembering that Geoff was not always grateful for her solicitude; but her fears lest he should have cold feet mingled with and aggravated her fears lest he should fall in love, and marry and go from her—and altogether overshadowed her concern about their fortune and the chances that their money might be taken from them. Miss Anna, on her side, was wakeful too. That is, she lay among her pillows in profoundest comfort, with the firelight making the room bright, and candles burning in dainty Dresden candlesticks at her bedside, and one or two favourite books within reach, and turned everything over in her active mind, until she had decided what course to pursue. Not one detail of all the luxury round her would Miss Anna part with without a struggle. She was determined to fight for her fortune to the very last; but if there was any better way than mere brutal fighting, her mind was ready to grasp it and weigh all its possibilities. She, too, heard Geoff, so late, a great deal too late, come up-stairs to bed, but only smiled at it somewhat maliciously, not without an enjoyment of the uneasy thoughts which no doubt had kept him from his rest, and no concern whatever about his cold feet. She lay thus, with her eyes as wakeful as the stars, till she had concluded upon her plan of action. As soon as she had done this she carefully extinguished the candles in an elaborate way of her own, so that there might be no smell, turned round to the fire, which had ceased to flame, and now shot only a ruddy suppressed glow into the curtained darkness—and shutting her eyes fell asleep like a baby.

GROVE ROAD, HAMPSTEAD

But even she, the most comfortable in the house, was far outdone, it need not be said, by the two poor young agitators in the hotel who had filled Grove Road with so many anxieties and cares. Hours before, Grace and Milly, crying and saying their prayers in one breath, had fallen asleep in each other's arms, and knew no more about their troubles nor about the possibilities before them, nor anything else in the world, till the morning sunshine awoke them after eight long hours of perfect repose.

Miss Anna never appeared down-stairs till midday. She had enjoyed a great deal of bad health since she had ceased to be a young woman and queen of hearts. Latterly it had settled into rheumatism, which had made her a little lame, and justified a great deal of indulgence. Her attendants said that even this she could throw off when occasion required. But there could be little pleasure, one would imagine, in making-believe to be lame. Her general delicacy, however, gave rise to a hundred necessities which people in health manage to dispense with. Mrs Underwood and her son had eaten a troubled breakfast long before her dainty meal was carried into her daintier chamber, and she returned to wakeful life under the influence of fragrant coffee and delicate roll, and some elegant trifle of cooked eggs or other light and graceful food. We say cooked eggs with intention, for boiled eggs, or even poached eggs, were vulgarities which Miss Anna would not have tolerated. She ate her pretty breakfast while her sister went through her household duties with a heavy heart, and Geoffrey took his way to town, striding along through the muddy streets, for it had rained all night. A little before noon she sent for Mrs Underwood, who came up with a somewhat haggard countenance, ready to cry at a moment's notice, and with a cap which, in sympathy with her condition of mind, had got awry, and had greatly tried the nerves of the cook, who had a strong sense of humour, and felt her inclination to laugh almost too much for her. This was the first thing Miss Anna remarked when her sister came into the room. She uttered a suppressed shriek of horror.

"Did you give poor Geoff his breakfast with a cap like that upon your head? Good gracious! and then you think it wonderful the poor boy should want to marry and have a trim, neat little wife of his own."

"What is the matter with my cap?" cried Mrs Underwood in alarm, putting up her hands and naturally making bad worse. She almost wept with vexation when she saw herself in one of the many mirrors. "Why didn't somebody tell me?" she said piteously, with dreadful thoughts of Geoff's disgust, and of the comparison he must be making between that trim, neat little wife and a mother with her cap awry.

"Set it right now, and come and sit down here," said Miss Anna.

There could not have been a greater contrast than between these two sisters. One of them seating herself, timid and anxious, by the bed, with no confidence either in her own judgment or in her powers of understanding, or capability of satisfying her imperious critic and companion— her anxious little mind on tip-toe of troubled solicitude to catch what Anna should mean, which was always somewhat difficult to her; while the other, with all her wits about her, seeing everything, noticing everything, lay amid her luxurious pillows and laughed at her sister's agitation.

"I wish I could take things as easily as you do, Anna—oh, I wish I could take them as easy!" Mrs Underwood said.

"You were always a goose," was Miss Anna's remark; but she took the trouble to push aside her curtain and to draw close to the chair at her bedside on which the other sat, before she unfolded to her the plan she had formed — which Mrs Underwood received with great surprise and many holdings up of her hands and wondering exclamations.

"Why, it was just what I thought I ought to do," she said. "It was all in my head, every word. I made it up in my mind to say to them, 'Anna may be against you, but you will never find me against you; and as the house is mine, and I have a right to ask whom I like——'"

"Stick to that," said Miss Anna with a laugh. "It was very impertinent and treacherous of you to think of saying it out of your own head; but now that we have settled it together, stick to that —it is the very thing to say."

"I don't see how you can call it impertinent, Anna: and treacherous!—me—to you! I have always been true to you. I can't think how you can say so. But it is true: the house is mine, however you please to put it. It was left to me expressly by dear papa. Of course, he made sure you would marry; and me a widow with one dear child, it was so natural that he should leave it to me. It will be all we shall have," she added with a sigh, "if this dreadful thing comes true."

"It will never come true if you play your cards well, Mary. You have got it all in your hands," Miss Anna said, "and it will be a fine thought for you that you have saved your family: though you never thought a great deal of your own powers—I will do you that justice."

Mrs Underwood shook her head. "My own family—that is, my boy," she said.

"So it is," said Miss Anna. "Of course I don't count; but you will have the satisfaction, my dear, if you should live to be a hundred, of feeling that you have saved your boy."

GROVE ROAD, HAMPSTEAD

At this Mrs Underwood shook her head once more, and two tears came into her eyes. "He will be lost to me," she said. "Oh, I remember well enough how I felt myself when I married Henry. 'What does he want with his mother? he has got me,' I used to say. I never liked him to go too often to the old lady. And now I am the old lady, and his wife will think the same of me.",

"Let us hope she will be a better Christian than you were," said Miss Anna, with a laugh.

"A better Christian! I hope I have always been a Christian at heart, whatever else I may have failed in. I hope I have always remembered my duty to my Maker," said Mrs Underwood, offended. This assault dried the tears in her eyes. "And, Anna, though I'm sure I am not one to find fault, I don't think that you—never going to church, and reading French novels and things, and making schemes to keep your neighbours out of their rights——"

Miss Anna laughed with genuine enjoyment. "I acknowledge all my sins, my dear," she said. "I am not the person to talk, am I? But, never mind, perhaps there will be no need to hope that Mrs Geoff should be a better Christian than her mother-in-law. Perhaps there will be no Mrs Geoff. It may come to nothing after all."

"Oh, Anna, how cruel you are!" cried Mrs Underwood. "If it comes to nothing, what is to become of my boy?"

GROVE ROAD, HAMPSTEAD

"Anyhow, let us be thankful that you will get a good deal of misery out of it, which will be a satisfaction. Go and put on your bonnet—your best bonnet—and make yourself look nice; we all like you to look nice; and go off, my dear, upon your charitable mission," Miss Anna cried.

Was it a charitable mission? The good woman quite thought so as she drove down the Hampstead slopes and made her way into the heart of London. She was fluttered and anxious about what she was going to do. The possible consequences to Geoff were like a tragedy in front of her; but as for anything else, she was too much confused to realise that this was not the kindest thing that could be done. Two lonely, fatherless children—orphans they might be called, for they had nobody to care for them. It was not right even that two girls of their age should live in a hotel, without so much as a maid to be with them. To offer them a home, to stretch her own protecting wing over them, was the natural thing for a woman to do. Certainly it was the right thing to do. The other question about the property was very vague in her mind. She could see that her sister was scheming to keep it in her own hands, but her mind was so confused about it that she could not feel any guiltiness on the subject. And then the question about Geoff would come uppermost. She wept a good many quiet tears over this as she drove along the streets. She had always felt herself a good Christian, but she had not been pleased when her husband had paid too many visits to the old lady. The old lady! Looking back, Mrs Underwood, with an effort of memory, recollected that the old lady had not been so very aged a person. She was but sixty when she died, and she had lived ten years at least after her son's marriage. "About my age!" This conviction surprised Geoff's mother more than can be described. She was the old lady now; and this girl would grudge her her son's visits, would not let Geoff come to her, would persuade him that his mother was silly, that she was old-fashioned, that she wanted a great deal too much attention. She had done all that in her day, and had not thought it any harm.

These were her thoughts as she went to Piccadilly, crossing through all those endless streets. When she came near the hotel some one passed her quickly, holding up an umbrella, so that she could not see his face. But her heart gave a thump at the sight of him. If it was not Geoff she had never seen any one so like him. Down to the very coat he wore, the spats which she had herself buttoned for him, his walk—all was Geoff. Had he been here forestalling her? Had he come and made his own advances already, without losing a moment? Her heart sank, but a wild curiosity took possession of her. She would see for herself how he had been received, what had happened. What could happen but that this girl, any girl, would throw herself at the first word into the arms of Geoff? It was not often a girl had such a chance. "Look at Anna," she said to herself, "so pretty, so clever, and never married at all." Besides, since Anna's time there were, everybody said, twice as many women as there used to be, and a man like Geoff, if such a thing was to be found, was more and more precious than ever before. Ah, there could be no doubt how he would be received. Perhaps by this time it was all settled, and the girls were talking of her as the old lady, and planning how she was to be kept at arm's length. She wept once more, then dried her eyes, and armed herself for what might be awaiting her. What if that little thing should rush into her arms and tell her—giving her kisses that would not be genuine, that would mean no affection to her? But even that she would have to put up with. She remembered—with how many compunctions, though thirty years too late—how the old lady—poor old lady!—had made little attempts to propitiate her, and tell her pretty things that Henry had said of her, and give her to believe that nothing but praise and sweetness was ever spoken of her between the mother and the son. It would be her turn now to show herself in the best light to her daughter-in-law, to conciliate her, and appeal to her tolerance. Alas! how time goes on, turning triumph into humiliation, and the first into the last.

CHAPTER XIII

GEOFF had not thought it necessary to say anything about his intention, but he had made up his mind during the vigil of the night to act for himself. He did not go to the chambers, which he shared with a friend, or to his club for his letters, or to any of his usual haunts; but went direct to Piccadilly, which is a long way from Grove Road. A long walk is sometimes an advantage when you are going to have a decisive interview; but Geoffrey, it is to be feared, did not do himself much good by thinking of the hostile party whom he was about to meet. They were not only not disagreeable to him, but the very sight of them stilled every warlike inclination in his breast. Not only he did not want to fight with them, but his desire was to take up their cause and fight it for them, against himself and all belonging to him—which it will readily be perceived was not a way to do any good. He saw them only too clearly in his mind's eye: the one sister standing a little in advance of the other; the eyes of Grace shining with courage and high spirit, while those softer lights under Milly's soft brows rose upon him from time to time, always with a new eloquence of appeal. "If she were to ask me for my head, I think I would give it her," Geoff said to himself; but there was no chance that she would ask for his head. He thought of them as he had seen them first, seated close by each other, turning two wistful, pale faces and eyes wet with tears upon him as he stood at the door, alarmed by his own intrusion. Their black dresses and their piteous looks had made an impression upon him which would never be effaced; and he had heard their story with a knot in his throat, ready to weep for very sympathy. When the same wonderful pair had arrived at Grove Road, he had been too much startled to know what to do or say. But now he was going to them with all his wits about him, no surprise possible, to open up all the question, and discuss it amicably, and help them, if it was possible to help those whose cause was so entirely in opposition to his own.

Grace and Milly were together as usual in the sitting-room, which had become by this time so intolerable to them. They were both very much surprised when he came in. They rose to their feet in wonder and partial dismay. They had been talking over all their affairs, and had come to a kind of conclusion between themselves; but this was a circumstance upon which they had not calculated. They had thought it very unlikely that they should hear anything more of Grove Road unless they themselves took the initiative. They

GROVE ROAD, HAMPSTEAD

gazed at each other with their usual mutual consultation, bewildered; but as soon as they came to themselves they too were very anxious to be polite to the enemy.

"I hope you will not think me intrusive," he said.

"Oh, no; we do not know any one—" This was intended to mean that a visitor was welcome; but the speech was broken off in consequence of the embarrassment of the speaker.

"If what we think is true, we—my mother and I—should be more to you than anybody else in England," Geoff said.

"But if what we think is true," cried Grace, "or rather what you think—for we know nothing—we are enemies, are we not?"

"I don't see why we should be. I have come to tell you all I know. You ought to have at least what information we can give you in order to find out who you really are, Miss——"

"Yorke," cried Grace, "Yorke! that is our name; and as for finding out who we are, that is quite unnecessary. We may be strangers here," the girl cried, holding her head high. "We have been very unhappy and very unfortunate, oh, miserable here! But when we are at home everybody knows who we are. We are as well known as you or any one. The Yorkes of Quebec—you have only to ask any Canadian. If you think it is necessary to find out a family for us, you are very, very much mistaken! England is not all the world. We are unknown only here."

Her eyes flashed, her cheeks coloured as she spoke; all her pride was roused; and Milly held up her head proudly too. They had not been used to be nobodies, and they did not understand nor feel disposed to submit to it. This was a totally different thing from claiming their rights.

"I beg your pardon," he said. "You know I don't mean anything disrespectful; but you know also that there is another question. It is not as Miss Yorke that there can be any question between you and me. It is as the daughter of my mother's cousin, Leonard Crosthwaite. Will you let me explain to you how the matter stands between us, if you are his children? This is how it is. Abraham Crosthwaite, an old unmarried uncle, died twenty years ago, leaving his money to Leonard, who had disappeared some time before. It was an old will, and it was supposed by everybody that Uncle Abraham had altered it in behalf of his nieces, Anna, and Mary, who is my mother. But he did not alter it; and when he died this was the state of affairs. Leonard Crosthwaite had not been heard of for ten years: everybody thought him dead; he had been advertised for, and had not replied. My mother and Aunt Anna were the next of kin. They succeeded without a question. Everybody had expected them to succeed. Uncle Abraham had announced over and over again his intention to give them everything he had. My mother had taken care of him for some years; of Aunt Anna he had always been proud. I never in my life heard any question of their rights, until all at once, a fortnight since, some one appeared at our house calling himself Leonard Crosthwaite——"

"Mr Geoffrey, papa would never have said he was any one, unless it had been true."

"I cast no doubt upon that. I tell you only of our wonder, our alarm. My mother thought she recognised something in him like her cousin. Aunt Anna from the first said no; but you will take these statements for what they are worth. Aunt Anna would naturally resist anything that threatened to interfere with her comfort. My mother, on the other hand, is easily persuaded. I, of course, could say nothing on one side or the other. The gentleman I saw had every appearance of being a gentleman, and a man of truth and honour——"

Milly gave him a grateful glance behind her sister—a glance of tender thanks which made his heart beat. As for Grace, she bowed her head with a sort of stately assent.

"He was to come back; but we heard no more of him, until I came here to this hotel, and was entirely puzzled, as you know. I saw you, and thought you were very kind to interest yourselves about a person whom you had never heard of. When I saw you yesterday at Hampstead, I thought again it was kindness merely—that you had heard of the man of whom I was in search——"

"You must have thought us very extraordinary to interfere."

"I thought you," he said somewhat incoherently;—"but it does not matter what I thought you. Circumstances make us, as you say, almost enemies, who might have been—who ought to have been, dear friends."

They both looked at him with melting eyes. "Yes," said Grace, with a beautiful flush of sympathy, "cousins, almost like brothers and sisters. And perhaps, that may be still!" she cried. "Listen, this is what we had made up our minds to——"

"Let me say out my say first," he said with a not very cheerful smile. "You are strangers, and you are too young to know how to manage such a complicated case. If you are Crosthwaites, and my cousin Leonard's daughters, it will be best for us in the long run, as well as for you, that it should be proved—that the question should be settled. And you cannot know of yourselves what is necessary. I have brought you the names of two good lawyers—respectable, honourable men, either of whom will advise you wisely." He took out a piece of paper as he spoke and handed it to

Grace. "With either of these you will be safe," he said.

The girls looked at each other for a moment; then Grace rose up and held out her hand to her adversary, seeing him through wet eyes. "Cousin Geoffrey," she said, "I am sure you must be of the same blood with our father, for this is exactly what he would have done. Let us call you cousin: it is all we want, Milly and I. We had made up our minds this morning to forget it altogether, never to say another word or think of it any more."

Milly's hand was held out too, though more timidly. She did not say anything, but she looked a great deal more than Grace had said, he thought. He had risen too in a tremulous state of excitement and generous enthusiasm. It was only his left hand that he had to give to the younger sister, but even in that fact there seemed to both of them something special—a closer approach.

"I do not know what to say," he said, "dear, brave, generous girls! To have you will be worth a great deal more than the money. We are friends for ever, whatever may come of it." Then he kissed first one hand and then the other with quivering lips, the girls, blushing both, drawing close to each other, abashed, yet touched beyond description with a kind of sacred joy and awe. The emotion was exquisite, novel beyond anything in their experience; and the young man, thus suddenly bound to them, was as much affected as they.

"But we cannot accept this, all the same," he said at last. "I should say all the less:—it must be investigated, and everything found out that can be found out."

"We do not wish it; we will not have it," the girls cried both together. But Geoffrey shook his head.

"You have nobody else to look after your interests. I am your next friend," he said. "Don't you know that is how we do in English law? Those who are too young or too helpless to plead for themselves plead by their next friend. And that is the most fit office for me."

"Then that makes England a little like what we thought it: not like the cruel, cruel place," cried Grace, "that it has been to Milly and me."

"It has been cruel," he said tenderly, with a voice which had tears in it, like their eyes. And there was not much more said, for they were all touched to that point at which words become vulgar and unmeaning. He went away shortly after, his heart swelling with tender brotherliness, friendship, and all the enthusiasm of generosity. The mere suggestion of their sacrifice had made him capable of that which had seemed so terrible to him an hour ago. He went out with his heart beating, full of high purpose and inspiration, quite happy, though that which had made him so miserable yesterday appeared now assured and certain. Such is the unreasonableness of youth.

When he had gone the girls turned to each other half laughing, half crying. They were happy too in this little encounter of generosity and impulsive feeling. "That is what we thought Englishmen were like," said Grace.

"And he is the first Englishman we have known," said Milly.

"Very different from Dr Brewer," cried the elder sister.

Milly looked up, wondering, with a little "Oh!" of startled, almost wounded feeling. To compare Geoffrey to Dr Brewer! — or to any one, she whispered deep down in her being, out of hearing even of herself.

They had scarcely recovered from the commotion of this crisis when some one again knocked at the door. "It will be *that* doctor," Grace said under her breath; and she was in no hurry to reply. It was only upon a second summons that she went forward slowly, reluctantly to open the door. And there outside stood Geoffrey's mother, somewhat fluttered, somewhat red, not knowing very well how to meet the two enemies of her peace. She came in with a little eagerness and kissed them both; and then she delivered herself breathlessly of her mission.

"I said I would come and see you to-day. Oh, my dears! I am afraid you thought Anna was not very kind yesterday. She is an invalid, you know; she has tempers now and then. Oh, I don't mean you to think she has a bad temper or is unkind. Nothing at all like that; but only—you can imagine if she had a bad night or a little extra ache. We ought all to be very forbearing, you know, and put up with people who are often in pain. Dear children! when I see you here in an inn, and think how many empty rooms we have got at home—there are more rooms, a great many more rooms than you would think in the Grove Road houses. And though Anna lives with me, the house, you know—the house is mine."

They did not know very well what answer to make, but they put her in the best chair the room contained, and sat round her listening, which was, of course, the best thing to do.

"Yes, the house is mine. I am the real mistress of it, though Anna often takes a great deal upon her; but I don't mind, I really don't mind. And when I have set my heart upon anything she never interferes. Do you know what I have come for now? I have come to take you both back with me home."

"Home!" the girls drew a long breath after the word. They seemed scarcely able to realise to themselves what it meant.

"Yes, home. I have set my heart upon it. If you are Leonard Crosthwaite's daughters—I declare," cried Mrs Underwood, her real feelings breaking in through all the flutter of words that had been put into her mouth—"I declare I don't know whether I wish you to be Crosthwaites or not! Two nice girls—two dear girls; I am sure you have been nicely brought up, and that your mother is a nice woman. Poor dear!" said the kind soul, wiping her eyes and forgetting her rôle altogether. "My heart bleeds for her, poor dear!"

This brought the girls, who could doubt, clinging round her, hanging about her. Their soft touch, their tender faces went to her heart. No woman who is good for anything, not even the jealous mother of an only son, defending him from all feminine wolves, can resist the contact of innocent girls—creatures of her own kind. It was a novel pleasure to Mrs Underwood, who never had a daughter, and had always been an exclusively devoted parent, absorbed in her son. She put one arm round each and kissed them again, this time in all truth and tenderness, and with her heart full of natural feeling. "Will she have heard of it yet?" she said in a tone of tender awe.

"Oh, not for nearly a week yet," the girls cried. And Mrs Underwood wept in sympathy.

"Poor dear! Oh, God help her, poor dear! I know what it is myself; but I was with him till the last moment. She will think if she had been here it would never have happened. Oh, God help her, poor dear! Then," she added a minute after, as if this had been a reason, "you must get your boxes ready and come with me at once, my poor children; I cannot leave you here. I tell you I don't know whether I shall be glad or sorry, if it is settled that you are Leonard Crosthwaite's children. Sorry, I suppose, because I shall lose my money; but now that I know you I should be almost as sorry to lose you."

This, though it was sudden, was real and true; for the kind woman felt that she had done them injustice. They were not dangerous adventuresses, hunting Geoff, but good girls, breaking their hearts for their mother, and counting the days till she should hear that terrible news. Mrs Underwood jumped into enthusiasm for them because she had been so much afraid of them before.

"You shall not lose either us or the money," said Grace. "We had resolved before Mr Geoffrey was here, that we should do nothing more and think nothing more about it. If papa had meant us to do anything he would have said so. We made up our minds to this—this morning, before Mr Geoffrey was here."

"My dears!" said Mrs Underwood, bewildered. She had no head for business, and she could not understand more than one thing at a time. She withdrew her arm a little and said doubtfully, 'Then Geoffrey has been here?"

"He came—in the most generous, noble way. I am so glad, I am so thankful," cried Grace, "and so is Milly—that we had quite made up our minds before."

Mrs Underwood breathed forth a sigh of resignation. "I must hear all about this after," she said, faltering; "but, my dears, the fly is standing at the door, and it is no use keeping it waiting. Put up your things as quickly as you can. Anna thinks—I mean I feel quite sure that you ought not to be staying at an inn in your circumstances. If your luggage is too heavy for the fly the heavy boxes can be sent afterwards. Of course you have all your coloured things, poor dears; and to go into such deep mourning with nobody to advise you! The best thing will be to bring just what is necessary. Run and put your things together and I will wait here."

Then there passed between Milly and Grace a final consultation, several volumes in one glance. "Do you really mean that we are to go with you—to go home with you? Do you really want to have us?" said Grace with quivering lips.

"Oh, my dear, of course, of course I want you! And Anna—well, we need never mind Anna. You will amuse her too. She is very fond of clever people, and you are clever; at least *you* are clever, my dear," Mrs Underwood said, patting Grace upon the shoulder; "and you are the little silly one, you will just do for me," she said, putting her arm through Milly's. Then her countenance clouded over. The girls did not know what to make of it.

GROVE ROAD, HAMPSTEAD

They could not hear the voice which was in Mrs Underwood's ears—her own voice, saying, "I wonder why he should always be going to see the old lady—when he has me?" She gazed into Milly's face and wondered wistfully whether it would frown at her, and find fault with Geoff for his attention to his mother. "It is nothing, my dear, nothing," she said, recovering herself; "a little pain that I am quite used to. Go and get ready, like dear children; it will be such a surprise for Geoff."

Thus Mrs Underwood carried out Miss Anna's plans. That lady smiled when she heard the arrival, the boxes carried up-stairs, the sound of the young voices in the house. She thought it was all her doing, and that Geoff was a young precisian and his mother a fool, and she herself the only member of the family capable of doing anything in its defence.

CHAPTER XIV

IT was, as his mother foresaw, a great surprise for Geoff, to see Grace and Milly established under her wing when he reached home. They seemed to have each got her corner of the drawing-room, as if they had been there all their lives. The windows with that great distance stretching blue and far underneath, and the smoke, which was London, at their feet, attracted them both—a standing wonder and miracle; but Milly had brought down her little work-basket, and placed it on a corner of Mrs Underwood's special table, and there she had settled herself as if she belonged to it; while Grace had got to the books which stood in low bookcases on either side of the fireplace. For the first hour Geoffrey really believed, with a wonder which he could hardly restrain, that his mother had broken loose from her life-long bondage to her sister, and that this bold step had really been taken by herself on her own responsibility. It was herself who undeceived him on this point. When the dressing-bell rang, and the girls went up-stairs to prepare for dinner, he put his arm round her and thanked and praised her. "It was like yourself to do it, mother," he said warmly.

"When you follow your own kind heart, you always do what is best."

"Yes, my dear," said Mrs Underwood, faltering; "indeed, indeed, I hope it is for the best. At least, that has been my meaning, dear. And Anna said——"

"Anna?" cried Geoff, with a cloud coming over his face.

"She thought it was the only wise thing. But she is not to be supposed to know anything about it," his mother said, lowering her voice and holding up a finger at him. "You must be very careful. If she looks as if she did not like it, you are not to take any notice. I was not to tell anybody she had a hand in it; but of course I never meant to conceal it from you."

Geoff was so angry and disconcerted, and so sick of the domestic fraud into which his mother had been beguiled, that he went off to his room without a word, leaving her sadly put out, but quite unable to divine what could have offended him. However, by the time he had changed his dress, Geoff, all alone in his room, burst out into a sudden laugh. "She is an old witch," he said to himself; "she is as clever as—the old gentleman himself." He was ashamed of the artifice, but could not help being diverted by the skill of that unseen helms-woman who managed everything her own way.

Miss Anna came to dinner as usual, leaning on

her stick, and she received the girls with stately surprise, as if their presence was quite unlooked for but gradually unbent, and by degrees grew brilliant in her talk, and amused and delighted them. Geoffrey looked on with a mixture of shame, amusement, and contempt, at this pretended thawing and acceptance of what she could not prevent. She acted her part admirably, though now and then he surprised a glance of satisfaction and secret triumph which made him furious. But she kept up her show of reluctance so far that no one was invited into her boudoir that evening. They went back to the drawing-room again after dinner, where Geoffrey found both the girls standing within the half-drawn curtains of the window, looking down upon the London lights. They stood close together, talking low, talking of the great city all muffled and mysterious in mist, and smoke, and darkness, at their feet. When Geoffrey joined them, they stopped their conversation. "I am afraid I have interrupted you," he said.

"Oh no, no! We can't help talking of one thing. It is wearisome to other people; but after all it is only a few days. We were wondering where it was that *he* is lying," said Milly.

Geoff pointed out to them as well as he could where the spot was.

"We have so often talked of seeing London, and thought what it would be like and what we

GROVE ROAD, HAMPSTEAD

should like most in it," said Grace. "We little thought——"

He seemed to be taken into their confidence as they broke off and stood gazing with brimming eyes towards the place where their father lay.

"And now you will have no association with London but that of pain," he said.

There was a pause, and then it was Milly who replied, " People have been very kind to us. We can never forget the kindness wherever we may be."

To this Grace assented with a little reservation. "Yes, we shall never forget Grove Road—your mother and you, Mr Geoffrey."

"What!" said Geoff, "are you drawing back already? I was Cousin Geoffrey this morning; and I do not think I have done anything to forfeit the name."

There was a little murmur of apology from both; and there is no telling how long they might have lingered there, with the light and warmth behind them, and the wide world of sky and air, and distant mighty multitudinous life before, had not Mrs Underwood come forward anxiously to see what was going on. She had begun to feel herself deserted, and to remember again what she had once felt and said about the old lady. She had not so much as thought of the old lady since she brought them into the house; but now the murmur of voices behind the curtain; the natural, inevitable manner in which Geoff found his way there, the solitude into which she was herself thrown, brought back all her alarm. "Geoff," she said, "you must not keep them in the cold: there is a great draught from that window: we always have the curtains drawn. Come in, my dears, come in to the light; there has been so much rain that it is quite cold to-night."

They came directly, obedient to the call; there was no undutifulness, no resistance. They must have felt they were doing wrong, they obeyed so quickly, she thought. But then Mrs Underwood had a very happy hour. Geoffrey took up the evening paper which had been brought in for him —Miss Anna having previously finished it and sent it with a message that there was nothing in it— while Grace returned to her examination of the books, and Milly settled herself by Mrs Underwood's side. She was glad to see that he could still think of politics, although they were here. Miss Anna, in order that she might come down gradually from her eminence, had left the door of communication open between her room and this one, and sometimes launched a word at them, stimulating their somewhat languid talk. For neither Mrs Underwood nor Milly were great talkers; they sat together, finding great fellowship in this mere vicinity, now and then exchanging a word as they lent each other the scissors or the thread. And Geoff read his newspaper calmly in this calm interior, where there was still no appearance of any power or passion which might either break old ties or form new.

Thus the soft evening sped along. It gave Mrs Underwood a little tremor to see that when Geoff laid aside his paper he went to the table at which Grace was seated with a number of books round her, and began an earnest conversation. But she reflected within herself that it was not Grace but the little one, and took comfort. Perhaps she would not have been so much consoled had she known what the subject of the conversation was. Grace was so buried in the books which she had collected from the shelves, that she scarcely noticed, till he spoke, the shadow which was hovering between her and the light.

"I want to tell you," he said—and she started, looking up at him with a little impatience, yet—as remembering the calls of politeness, and that she was his mother's guest—with a smile—"I have laid the whole matter before the lawyer whose name I gave you to-day," Geoffrey said.

"The whole matter!—there is no whole matter; nothing but guesses and perhapses. We do not want anything more said about it, Cousin Geoff."

"But we must have something more said about it, Cousin Grace. Who can tell? It might be dragged to light in the third or fourth generation," he said with a smile. "Your grandson might question the right of mine, to any small remnant that may be left by that time."

"I will answer for my grandson," said Grace.

"But I cannot answer for mine; probably he will be a headstrong, hot-headed fellow. No, it must be settled now. Mr Furnival wants to know what evidence you have, one way or another; if you have anything that throws light on the subject: any clue to the past or information about the family or name? You may trust everything to his hands."

"But I told you we had no information whatever —none. I never heard the name before. My brother is called Leonard, that is the only thing; and there are one or two memoranda of papa's."

"These will be of the utmost value."

"I don't think you will find them of any value at all. One is in his little diary that he kept during the voyage. I do not like to give it into any stranger's hands. No, there is nothing private in it; but only the little things that—that are more hard to look at than great ones," said Grace "Little, little things that we did every day—that we never shall do any more."

There was a pause, and then he said, insisting gently, "You must not think me troublesome and pertinacious; but you may be sure it will be handled with reverence, and given back to you without delay."

"You can't think how little it is, it is nothing,"

she said; but finally she consented to bring all the scraps together and place them in Geoff's hands. They were not much when they were put together. First, the entry in the diary: "Same name in directory at old address. To go first thing and enquire." Then the still more hieroglyphical notes written on the same paper which contained the address, "Left July '45. U.A. died '55. Due with interest for twenty years—but forgiven;" and the repeated 3 Grove Road, written over his blotting-book, and repeated on at least two pieces of paper. Geoff folded them carefully up, and sealed them into a packet. His mind was heavy, but his heart was light. He saw moral confirmation indisputable in these scraps of writing. It seemed to him that in no way could his mother retain her fortune against a claim so certain; but he saw at the same time that there could be no legal proof, and that his aunt would be triumphant and retain hers. Was not this the best solution of the matter that could be? He did not see his way yet about his own work and ability to make up to his mother for what she must lose; therefore his mind was troubled and in difficulty still; but to know that when he came home at night he should find Milly shyly smiling at Mrs Underwood's side, taking her place as if in her own home, beguiled the young man out of all his cares. Whatever happened, nothing could take from him this sweet evening, and other sweet evenings like it.

GROVE ROAD, HAMPSTEAD

A week of close domestic intercourse, long evenings spent together, how rapidly acquaintance grows under such circumstances! They made the most delightful family party, moving from one room to another in the long delicious evenings, cheerful, though still subdued by the recent grief which was so ready to revive in the girls' eyes at any chance allusion. This made a tenderness in their intercourse which nothing else could have done. Even Miss Anna was tender of the young mourners, and it was she who most steadily exerted her powers to cheer them, and win from them smiles, and even laughter, and a hundred little returns towards amusement, towards the brighter impulses of life. But perhaps what they enjoyed most was to stand behind the half-drawn curtain in the evenings, and gaze out on London, and talk, with tears which no one rebuked, which Geoff, their only companion, if any reliance could be placed upon his voice, was often very near sharing. They told him about their father, about the household at home, about their first glorious morning in London, when they had gone to Westminster and feared no evil; and Geoff listened with sympathy, with tender curiosity, with all the youthful freemasonry which understands almost without a word. While these talks were going on, Mrs Underwood, stranded as it were outside, would sit fidgeting in her chair, longing to interfere, thinking within herself of the old lady left alone, and scarcely able to restrain her trembling anxiety, lest things should go too far, and her doom be sealed. Miss Anna, on the contrary, watched over the young people, going and coming with that little pat of her stick upon the floor, and restraining her sister. "You simpleton," she would say in a whisper, "don't you see everything is going to a wish? What could you desire more? They are getting acquainted; they are getting on as fast as possible.' "Oh, but Anna!" poor Mrs Underwood would say, getting up and sitting down again. "My boy, my boy!" "Oh, hold your tongue, you silly woman! Your boy is happier than he ever was in his life," said the imperious sister, sitting down to keep watch over Geoff's tranquillity. Mrs Underwood dared not stir, with Miss Anna guarding her like this; but she moaned within herself and shook her head. It was all a conspiracy to take her son from her. She liked the little one well enough—nay, very much, as she sat on the low chair, and talked a little now and then, and was always ready with the scissors. Mrs Underwood had a way of losing hers, and she had never had a daughter to find them for her, to know by instinct when she wanted them for her work as Milly did. That was all very pleasant. And it might be good as a family arrangement; Anna thought so, and Anna knew best; but to tell her that her boy had never been so happy—though she had devoted herself to him all her life—this was indeed too much to bear.

CHAPTER XV

A WEEK after their settlement at Grove Road, while the girls were expecting every day to receive at least by telegraph some news from their mother, Geoffrey made his appearance in the middle of the day, and with a face of much serious meaning. He asked his mother and her guests to come with him to Miss Anna's room; and then having gathered them all around him, he took out some papers and made a little speech to them with great seriousness. "I thought it was of the utmost importance that we should all know exactly how we stood," he said, "and I put the whole case into Mr Furnival's hands. We all trust him who know him, and Grace and Milly were willing to take him on my word. He has had all the facts before him for some days; with such scraps of evidence as you could furnish us with," he added, turning to Grace: "and he took counsel's opinion. I informed him that it would be in any case an amicable suit to settle our respective rights. I have brought you their opinions now."

"I thought there was something going on," said Miss Anna, "something underhand, a conspiracy, concealed from me."

GROVE ROAD, HAMPSTEAD

"Conspiracies are not in my way," Geoffrey said. "Perhaps you would like me to read what they say. It confirms my own opinion—though perhaps my advice would have been different."

He spread out his papers on the table, and the women round him turned their eyes to him with expressions as different as their characters: his mother proud of the position her boy was assuming, yet a little nervous as to how Anna would take it, and suspicious of the look which she thought she detected him directing towards Milly; Grace a little reserved, holding her head erect, looking at him with an interest which had not much curiosity in it, but a rising impulse of resistance—although she could not tell as yet what it was she was to resist; Milly with milder interest and a gentle admiration of Geoff which was like a shy shadow of his mother's. But Miss Anna, all alert, turned eagerly towards him as if she would have snatched the papers out of his hands, her dark eyes blazing, her whole figure full of energy and latent wrath, which she was ready to pour out upon him should the lawyers' opinion go against her own.

"I need not read it word for word," said Geoff; "I will give it afterwards to my cousin Grace. The lawyers think, after close consideration, that there is—no case——." (Here there was a movement on the part of Miss Anna and a quick "I told you so.") "Wait a little," said Geoffrey, "They say there is scarcely any case to go to a jury; but they say also that if it did go to a jury the strong moral probability and the touching character of all the circumstances might lead to a verdict for the claimants notwithstanding the weakness of the evidence. Law would be against it; but the jury might be for it."

"I understand that reasoning," said Miss Anna: "most men are fools, and jurymen are men—therefore it is likely that fools being the judges, the verdict would be preposterous. Is that all your wiseacres have got to say?"

"Not quite," said Geoff; "the lawyers advise a compromise."

"A compromise? I object—I object at once. I will not hear of it. Let it go into court. If I am compelled to yield to the sentiment of a dozen British idiots, I must do so; but consent to rob myself, for no reason? oh no, no! I will never do that."

"Aunt Anna, you are not the only person concerned."

"I am," she said; "I have the largest share. I am the eldest. Your mother has never gone against me in her life, and she will not now."

"Anna," said Mrs Underwood tremulously, "I always have followed your advice—oh, always, it is quite true; but Geoff, you know—Geoff is a man now; and he has been bred up to the law, and he ought to know better, far better than we do."

"Should he? but he doesn't; he's a poor weak sentimental creature not strong enough to be either one thing or another, a swindler or an honest man. He naturally takes refuge in compromises. I haven't known him so long without knowing that. I believe the lawyer's opinion is his own, it is so like him. A compromise? no! I will have no compromise," cried Miss Anna, striking her stick upon the floor.

"And we reject it too," cried Grace—"we will have nothing, nothing! we settled upon all that before we came here. If we had not decided so, we should never have come."

"Let it go to a jury if you like," said Miss Anna, paying no attention to this. "I am not afraid. I take the risk of sentiment. Yes, of course, they are a pack of sentimental fools: two pretty girls in deep mourning will get anything out of a British jury. Still I'll risk it. But nothing, nothing in the world will make me consent to a compromise."

Grace had risen to her feet, with her usual eagerness of impulse, "Do you not hear me—do you not understand me, Miss Anna? We will take nothing; we will have no compromises, no more talk even, not a word said. We will have nothing, nothing to do with it! We have a right to be heard as well as you——"

"And I think I also have a right to be heard,"

cried Geoff—he was calm between the excitement of the others; "I am not without a voice. Whatever you say, justice must be done, and justice suggests this course. Yes, Aunt Anna, whatever you say, I have a right to be heard. It is for our own comfort, without thought of them."

"I want no such comfort," she cried. "I gave in to your mother's nonsense, and allowed them to be asked here. I allowed them to be asked because they were——"

"Aunt Anna! do you wish me to tell them in so many words why you wanted them——?"

"Geoff, Geoff!" cried his mother, in alarm.

The girls paid but little attention to this quarrel as it raged. They did not comprehend even what it was about. "We had better go away as this is not our affair," Grace said, with a stately little bow. And Milly, too, rose to go with her sister—when the conflict around suddenly ceased, and the two girls, who seemed to have been pushed aside by the other more energetic emotions, suddenly became again the centre of the scene, and the chief persons in it. What was it? only the entrance of old Simmons with a yellow envelope in his hand.

The others stopped short in their conflict. They acknowledged with a little awe the presence of something greater which had come into their midst. They looked on in silence while the girls, clinging together, read their telegram. Then there was a little pause.

"We must go home at once," said Grace, as well as she could speak for tears. "We do not require to wait. There are steamers every day, I suppose. Would you answer this for us, Cousin Geoffrey? and say we want no one. We will come."

It required some power of divination to make out the last words, which were almost choked with the weeping to which Milly had entirely given way.

"Go at once?" said Miss Anna, "without an escort—without seeing anything?"

The girls gave her, both together, an indignant look; and then they turned and went out of the room, moving in one step, like one creature, with a soft sweep as of wings. So at least Geoffrey thought, looking after them with the tenderest pity in his eyes. They did not walk but disappeared, flying to be alone and get some comfort from their tears.

"What does the telegram say—who sends it—is it long or short—is it from the mother herself, is it—?" Miss Anna put out her hand and tried to take it from Geoff. Both the ladies were full of curiosity. Mrs Underwood, indeed, in sympathy with the trouble of the girls, dried her eyes as she looked up eagerly for news—but Miss Anna owned no trace of tears. She was full of interest and keen curiosity. "Give it me. The very wording of it will tell us something more about them," she cried.

GROVE ROAD, HAMPSTEAD

Geoff's first movement was to hurry away, carrying this communication with him; but he paused as a new idea took possession of him. He was too good a man to be altogether a free agent. He paused, and looked at the mother upon whom he knew he was about to inflict a great blow. She was not a wise woman, and the instinct of curiosity which had possession of her at the moment was not one to please that critical faculty which is so exaggerated in youth. He did not like to see in her eyes even a shadow of the hungry appetite for news which burned in her sister's. Nevertheless, he read the telegram slowly.

"Your terrible news just received. Mother utterly prostrated. Wire if wish me to come for you—otherwise return first ship."

The name of the sender was a strange one—it was evidently an uncle or some relation who could speak with authority. Geoff paid no attention to what the ladies said, but went on. "Mother, I am going to say something which will vex you. You must try to remember that I am old enough to take care of myself. I am going with them, to take them to their mother."

"Geoff—Geoff—by sea!—to America!" Mrs Underwood gasped; she could not get her breath.

"Of course it must be by sea if he goes to America," said Miss Anna. "There is no land passage invented yet."

"It is my plain duty," said Geoff, colouring a

little, "if, as I believe, they are our near relations; and in any case there is a question between us which they are too young in their generosity to settle. We cannot take advantage of the generosity of two children, mother——"

"Oh, Geoff! but for you to go — to go to America—a long voyage, and at this time of the year——"

"The equinoctials coming on," put in Miss Anna quickly.

"The equin——, yes; nothing but storms and shipwrecks, and every kind of danger. If you mean me never to have a night's rest more—to go distracted every wind that blows—to have neither peace nor comfort of my life! Oh, Geoff! all that, for them that you never had seen a fortnight ago! and me, your mother, that have never had another thought but you for eight-and-twenty years——"

"Surely, mother," cried poor Geoff, "there is no need to put it so tragically. I am not going to abandon you. I am only going to do what half the men of my age do for pleasure—and I shall have a real motive in it. In the first place, a duty to Grace and Milly: if they were your children, how should you like them to go over the sea all alone, when a great idle fellow calling himself their cousin was here doing nothing? And then this business, which otherwise may worry us for years, which we never can be sure about—for if these dear girls, in the generosity of their hearts, refuse to have anything to do with it, who can tell that their mother, their brothers will be of the same mind?"

Mrs Underwood had fallen into tears and broken exclamations. She was incapable of any connected words. "Oh Geoff—my boy—all I have—all I have in the world!" and "a sea voyage—a sea voyage to America," was all she said.

Miss Anna got up to her feet, and struck her stick emphatically upon the floor. "Listen, Mary! I have said your son was soft, and a dawdle like yourself. I retract. He's a clever fellow, and sees the rights of a matter when it's put before him. There, Geoff! go, and you have my blessing. I'll give you a hundred pounds, too, if you want it, that you may have a pleasant trip. Your mother's talking nonsense. I never knew her lose a night's rest, except when you were teething; and then that was your doing, not hers, for you squalled all night. Go, my boy, and success to you. It's the wisest thing you ever thought of in your life."

"Oh, Anna!" cried her sister, "how can you be so cruel?" "She had dried her eyes at these accusations, and sat up with a flushed countenance. "If you knew, if you only knew half what a mother goes through! Do you think I have always told you when I lay awake thinking of him—or any one? Geoff, I have never denied you anything; but I think this will break my heart!"

"Mother," said Geoff, half pleading, half angry, "I run no more risk than half the women's sons in England—no risk at all; you make me feel a fool to talk like this."

"Never mind," said Miss Anna, while Mrs Underwood relapsed into weeping; "I'll bring her round. Go off at once, there is plenty of time, and see about your berths. You'll find her quite reconciled to it when you come back."

"But, Aunt Anna, I don't understand the change on your part. You who rejected all idea of a compromise——"

Aunt Anna laughed. "I have no objection to one kind of compromise. Bring us back that little dove-eyed thing as Mrs Geoff. I'd rather have had the other; but you could never have managed her. Settle my money upon Milly in her marriage settlements; and don't mind about our absence from the ceremony. Go and see Niagara, and all that, and bring us back your wife—that's the kind of compromise I want; that's all I stipulate for, Geoff."

"If I can, Aunt Anna."

"Pooh—can! With a week under the same roof, and a fortnight in the same ship. Rubbish! If you can't, you are a poorer creature than I thought. Go, go, off with you, Geoff—before your mother comes to herself."

GROVE ROAD, HAMPSTEAD

"Where is Geoff going? Oh, Anna, help me, help me! don't let him go. Geoff!" cried Mrs Underwood.

Upon which Miss Anna confronted her sister with her most imposing looks. "Mary! don't be a fool. The boy is doing precisely what he ought to do. I never had such a good opinion of him before; let him alone. He is fifty times better able to take care of himself than you are to take care of him. Here's the telegram; let us see what it says."

"It says, I suppose, just what he read to us, Anna," said the other, frightened into some degree of self-denial, and with a little curiosity re-awakening in her blurred overflowing eyes.

"A thing never says anything to you when it's read aloud. Here it is. 'Stephen Salisbury, Quebec, to Grace Yorke, Montague Hotel, London.' (Then it was sent on from the hotel.) 'Terrible news received; mother prostrated; wire if wish me to come.' Of course it must be the mother's brother. The people must be well off, Mary. There cannot be any doubt about that. You see he says he will come if they want him; and even the message shows it. The man would never have sent such a long message if he had not been well off."

"I always knew that," said Mrs Underwood feebly, "from what Grace and Milly said. Why shouldn't their uncle (if it is their uncle) come for them? I don't know why they should be in such a hurry to get away?"

"It is a great deal better that Geoff should go with them," Miss Anna said. "Pluck up a heart; or if you can't do that, get a little common-sense, Mary; common-sense will do just as well. Why should anything happen to a Cunard steamer because your boy happens to be in it more than another? Do you think God has a special spite against *you*?"

"Oh, Anna!" cried her sister, horrified; "me? I know God is merciful and good: but——"

"But you would rather not trust Geoff in His hands, lest He should take a cruel advantage? That is the way of people like you."

"I never said so; I never thought so. I—I hope I have always put my trust in God."

"But you think, all the same, if He had a chance like this, that He would like to do you an ill turn? Oh, I understand what you mean. I have heard a great many people—pious, devout people—speak just like you."

Mrs Underwood relapsed into speechless misery. Against such an accusation as this, what could she say? She who never missed church, nor ceased to profess her belief in Providence. She was silenced altogether. She wept and sighed the name of Geoff now and then; but there was nothing more to say.

Geoff went down to the City without loss of a

moment. He secured berths in a steamer which was to sail in three days; and with a bound of pleasure and conscious pride in his heart found himself engaged for his passage across the Atlantic. He went home very soberly, but with the blood coursing in his veins. He had taken such an initiative now as he had never been able to take in all his life before. He had emancipated himself at last. It was, however, with a little apprehension that he turned homeward. Whether his mother would impede his way with weeping, whether the sisters would reject his escort, he could not tell; but his fears in both cases were unnecessary. Mrs Underwood had been reduced to subjection some time before he got home. And as for Grace and Milly, they were neither excited about his proposal nor disposed to refuse it. They took it as the most natural thing in the world. There was a gleam of brightness, he thought, in Milly's face, but Grace paid very little attention. Geoffrey was a little cast down when he perceived that they saw nothing at all heroic in his mission, nothing that anybody would think twice about. But he had to console himself with Miss Anna's declaration that a fortnight on board ship would settle all questions. He himself felt a great confidence that everything would come right in the end.

Thus the difficulty was brought to a conclusion, in a way little contemplated by the Canadian who once had been Leonard Crosthwaite, and had broken his heart for his cousin Anna. When the young people were gone, the two ladies from Grove Road made a little pilgrimage to the great, grey, dismal London cemetery in which all that remained of him lay—where Mrs Underwood laid some flowers, and Anna gazed with eyes that looked as if they could penetrate the very secrets of the grave, upon the mound under which the lover of her youth slept in peace. What were the thoughts that had lain concealed within his breast for thirty years, yet which had brought him, carrying fear and confusion which he little anticipated, to her dwelling, the first day he spent in England, no one could tell. He had carried all that mystery with him to the other world.

And after a while Geoffrey Underwood came safely back from the terrible voyage which had so much alarmed his mother, bringing with him, exactly as Miss Anna had foreseen and commanded, his young wife. She was far too young a wife, her mother thought, to venture so far; but Milly did not think so. How to do without Grace, and to think for herself, was more difficult to Milly than the distance and the voyage. But she did what was a great deal easier than thinking for herself—she transferred all the responsibility to her husband. Nothing could be handsomer than the marriage settlement which Miss Anna made.

GROVE ROAD, HAMPSTEAD

She made the little bride her own representative, with the larger share of the fortune. And the Canadian family were well pleased, and asked no more. Indeed, all that Mrs Yorke desired was that nothing should be said about this strange illumination thrown at the last upon the husband who had been hers for twenty years, and who now seemed to be stolen from her and changed into another man. She would not listen to any explanations on the subject; the sound of the other name was odious to her. She took even from her boy, Leonard, that name of his which came from his father's old life, and jealously called him Robert, which was his second name.

Almost a year elapsed before the young pair came home. They arrived on a bright April afternoon, when the sun was shining over the great smoke. The windows were open: the lawn all green with spring, and set in a frame of English primroses, looked as fresh as the bride herself, who recognised it, and the difference in it, with a little cry of pleasure. Mrs Underwood threw herself, as was natural, upon the wonderful son who had been delivered from the seas, who had not been drowned, or swallowed by a whale, who had come safely through marriage, and all the other terrific dangers to which he had been exposed; but Miss Anna walked across the room

GROVE ROAD, HAMPSTEAD

with a little stately limp, casting aside her stick, and took little Milly in her arms. "Welcome!" she said, "little girl with the dove's eyes. I always said I would accept one, but only one, compromise!"

A CATALOGUE OF BOOKS AND ANNOUNCEMENTS OF METHUEN AND COMPANY PUBLISHERS : LONDON 36 ESSEX STREET W.C.

CONTENTS

	PAGE
FORTHCOMING BOOKS, .	2
POETRY, . .	9
ENGLISH CLASSICS,	11
ILLUSTRATED BOOKS, .	12
HISTORY, . . .	13
BIOGRAPHY, . .	15
GENERAL LITERATURE,	17
SCIENCE, . .	20
THEOLOGY AND PHILOSOPHY, .	20
LEADERS OF RELIGION, .	22
FICTION, . . .	22
BOOKS FOR BOYS AND GIRLS, .	32
UNIVERSITY EXTENSION SERIES,	33
SOCIAL QUESTIONS OF TO-DAY,	35
CLASSICAL TRANSLATIONS, .	36
EDUCATIONAL BOOKS,	37

MARCH 1896

MARCH 1896.

MESSRS. METHUEN'S
ANNOUNCEMENTS

―――●―――

Poetry and Belles Lettres

LANG AND CRAIGIE

THE POEMS OF ROBERT BURNS. Edited by ANDREW LANG and W. A. CRAIGIE. With Portrait. *Demy 8vo.* 6s.
Also 50 copies on hand-made paper. *Demy 8vo.* 21s. *net.*

This edition will contain a carefully collated Text, numerous Notes, critical and textual, a critical and biographical Introduction, and a Glossary.
The publishers hope that it will be the most complete and handsome edition ever issued at the price.

W. M. DIXON

A PRIMER OF TENNYSON. By W. M. DIXON, M.A., Professor of English Literature at Mason College. *Cr. 8vo.* 2s. 6d.

This book consists of (1) a succinct but complete biography of Lord Tennyson; (2) an account of the volumes published by him in chronological order, dealing with the more important poems separately; (3) a concise criticism of Tennyson in his various aspects as lyrist, dramatist, and representative poet of his day; (4) a bibliography. Such a complete book on such a subject, and at such a moderate price, should find a host of readers.

W. A. CRAIGIE

A PRIMER OF BURNS. By W. A. CRAIGIE. *Cr. 8vo.* 2s. 6d.

This book is planned on a method similar to the 'Primer of Tennyson.' It has also a glossary. It will be issued in time for the Burns Centenary.

English Classics

THE LIVES OF THE ENGLISH POETS. By SAMUEL JOHNSON, LL.D. With an Introduction by JOHN HEPBURN MILLAR, and a Portrait. 3 *vols.* *Crown 8vo, buckram.* 10s. 6d.

SHAKESPEARE'S POEMS. Edited by GEORGE WYNDHAM, M.P. *Crown 8vo.* 3s. 6d.

Theology and Philosophy

E. C. S. GIBSON

THE XXXIX. ARTICLES OF THE CHURCH OF ENGLAND. Edited with an Introduction by E. C. S. GIBSON, M.A., Vicar of Leeds, late Principal of Wells Theological College. *In two volumes. Demy 8vo.* 7s. 6d. each. *Vol. I.*

This is the first volume of a treatise on the xxxix. Articles, and contains the Introduction and Articles i.-viii.

R. L. OTTLEY

THE DOCTRINE OF THE INCARNATION. By R. L. OTTLEY, M.A., late fellow of Magdalen College, Oxon., Principal of Pusey House. *In two volumes. Demy 8vo.* 15s.

This is the first volume of a book intended to be an aid in the study of the doctrine of the Incarnation. It deals with the leading points in the history of the doctrine, its content, and its relation to other truths of Christian faith.

L. T. HOBHOUSE

THE THEORY OF KNOWLEDGE. By L. T. HOBHOUSE, Fellow and Tutor of Corpus College, Oxford. *Demy 8vo.* 21s.

'The Theory of Knowledge' deals with some of the fundamental problems of Metaphysics and Logic, by treating them in connection with one another. PART I. begins with the elementary conditions of knowledge such as Sensation and Memory, and passes on to Judgment. PART II. deals with Inference in general, and Induction in particular. PART III. deals with the structural conceptions of Knowledge, such as Matter, Substance, and Personality. The main purpose of the book is constructive, but it is also critical, and various objections are considered and met.

MESSRS. METHUEN'S ANNOUNCEMENTS

W. H. FAIRBROTHER

THE PHILOSOPHY OF T. H. GREEN. By W. H. FAIR-
BROTHER, M.A., Lecturer at Lincoln College, Oxford. *Crown 8vo.*
3s. 6d.

This volume is expository, not critical, and is intended for senior students at the Universities, and others, as a statement of Green's teaching and an introduction to the study of Idealist Philosophy.

F. W. BUSSELL

THE SCHOOL OF PLATO: its Origin and Revival under the Roman Empire. By F. W. BUSSELL, M.A., Fellow and Tutor of Brasenose College, Oxford. *Demy 8vo. Two volumes.* 7s. 6d. *each. Vol. I.*

In these volumes the author has attempted to reach the central doctrines of Ancient Philosophy, or the place of man in created things, and his relation to the outer world of Nature or Society, and to the Divine Being. The first volume comprises a survey of the entire period of a thousand years, and examines the cardinal notions of the Hellenic, Hellenistic, and Roman ages from this particular point of view.

In succeeding divisions the works of Latin and Greek writers under the Empire will be more closely studied, and detailed essays will discuss their various systems, *e.g.* Cicero, Manilius, Lucretius, Seneca, Aristides, Appuleius, and the Neo-Platonists of Alexandria and Athens.

History and Biography

EDWARD GIBBON

THE DECLINE AND FALL OF THE ROMAN EMPIRE.
By EDWARD GIBBON. A New Edition, edited with Notes, Appendices, and Maps by J. B. BURY, M.A., Fellow of Trinity College, Dublin. *In Seven Volumes. Crown 8vo.* 6s. *each. Vol. I.*

The time seems to have arrived for a new edition of Gibbon's great work—furnished with such notes and appendices as may bring it up to the standard of recent historical research. Edited by a scholar who has made this period his special study, and issued in a convenient form and at a moderate price, this edition should fill an obvious void. The volumes will be issued at intervals of a few months.

MESSRS. METHUEN'S ANNOUCEMENTS

F. W. JOYCE

THE LIFE OF SIR FREDERICK GORE OUSELEY. By F. W. JOYCE, M.A. With Portraits and Illustrations. *Crown 8vo.* 7s. 6d.

This book will be interesting to a large number of readers who care to read the Life of a man who laboured much for the Church, and especially for the improvement of ecclesiastical music.

CAPTAIN HINDE

THE FALL OF THE CONGO ARABS. By SIDNEY L. HINDE. With Portraits, Illustrations, and Plans. *Demy 8vo.* 12s. 6d.

This volume deals with the recent Belgian Expedition to the Upper Congo, which developed into a war between the State forces and the Arab slave-raiders in Central Africa. Two white men only returned alive from the three years' war— Commandant Dhanis and the writer of this book, Captain Hinde. During the greater part of the time spent by Captain Hinde in the Congo he was amongst cannibal races in little-known regions, and, owing to the peculiar circumstances of his position, was enabled to see a side of native history shown to few Europeans. The war terminated in the complete defeat of the Arabs, seventy thousand of whom perished during the struggle.

General Literature

L. WHIBLEY

GREEK OLIGARCHIES: THEIR ORGANISATION AND CHARACTER. By L. WHIBLEY, M.A., Fellow of Pembroke College, Cambridge. *Crown 8vo.* 6s.

This book is a study of the Oligarchic Constitutions of Greece, treated historically and from the point of view of political philosophy.

C. H. PEARSON

ESSAYS AND CRITICAL REVIEWS. By C. H. PEARSON, M.A., Author of 'National Life and Character.' Edited, with a Biographical Sketch, by H. A. STRONG, M.A., LL.D. With a Portrait. *Demy 8vo.* 7s. 6d.

This volume contains the best critical work of Professor Pearson, whose remarkable book on 'National Life and Character' created intense interest.

W. CUNNINGHAM
MODERN CIVILISATION IN SOME OF ITS ECONOMIC ASPECTS. By W. CUNNINGHAM, D.D., Fellow of Trinity College, Cambridge. *Crown 8vo.* 2s. 6d. [*Social Questions Series.*

A book on economics treated from the standpoint of morality.

F. W. THEOBALD
INSECT LIFE. By F. W. THEOBALD, M.A. *Illustrated. Crown 8vo.* 2s. 6d. [*Univ. Extension Series.*

Classical Translations

CICERO—De Natura Deorum. Translated by F. BROOKS, M.A. *Crown 8vo, buckram.* 3s. 6d.

Fiction

THE NOVELS OF MARIE CORELLI
FIRST COMPLETE AND UNIFORM EDITION
Large crown 8vo. 6s.

MESSRS. METHUEN beg to announce that they will in May commence the publication of a New and Uniform Edition of MARIE CORELLI's Romances. This Edition will be revised by the Author, and will contain new Prefaces. The volumes will be issued at short intervals in the following order:—

1. A ROMANCE OF TWO WORLDS. 2. VENDETTA
3. THELMA. 4. ARDATH.
5. THE SOUL OF LILITH. 6. WORMWOOD.
7. BARABBAS. 8. THE SORROWS OF SATAN.

BARING GOULD
THE BROOM-SQUIRE. By S. BARING GOULD, Author of 'Mehalah,' 'Noémi,' etc. Illustrated by FRANK DADD. *Crown 8vo.* 6s.

The scene of this romance is laid on the Surrey hills, and the date is that of the famous Hindhead murder in 1786.

GILBERT PARKER
THE SEATS OF THE MIGHTY. By GILBERT PARKER, Author of 'When Valmond came to Pontiac,' 'Pierre and his People,' etc. *Crown 8vo.* 6s.

A Romance of the Anglo-French War of 1759.

EMILY LAWLESS
HURRISH. By the Honble. EMILY LAWLESS, Author of 'Maelcho,' 'Grania,' etc. *Crown 8vo.* 6s.

A reissue of Miss Lawless' most popular novel, uniform with 'Maelcho.'

MRS. OLIPHANT
THE TWO MARYS. By MRS. OLIPHANT. *Crown 8vo.* 6s.

MRS. WALFORD
SUCCESSORS TO THE TITLE. By MRS. WALFORD, Author of 'Mr. Smith,' etc. *Crown 8vo.* 6s.

JOHN DAVIDSON
MRS. ARMSTRONG'S AND OTHER CIRCUMSTANCES. By JOHN DAVIDSON, Author of 'The Ballad of a Nun,' etc. *Crown 8vo.* 6s.

A collection of stories by Mr. John Davidson, whose fine verses are well known.

J. BLOUNDELLE BURTON
IN THE DAY OF ADVERSITY. By J. BLOUNDELLE BURTON, Author of 'The Desert Ship,' etc. *Crown 8vo.* 6s.

A historical romance.

HENRY JOHNSTON
DR. CONGALTON'S LEGACY. By HENRY JOHNSTON, Author of 'Kilmallie,' etc. *Crown 8vo.* 6s.

A story of Scottish life.

J. H. FINDLATER
THE GREEN GRAVES OF BALGOWRIE. By JANE H. FINDLATER. *Crown 8vo.* 6s.

A story of Scotland.

J. L. PATON

A HOME IN INVERESK. By J. L. PATON. *Crown 8vo.* 6s.

A story of Scotland and British Columbia.

M. A. OWEN

THE DAUGHTER OF ALOUETTE. By MARY A. OWEN. *Crown 8vo.* 6s.

A story of life among the American Indians.

RONALD ROSS

THE SPIRIT OF STORM. By RONALD ROSS, Author of 'The Child of Ocean.' *Crown 8vo.* 6s.

A romance of the Sea.

J. A. BARRY

TALES OF THE SEA. By J. A. BARRY. Author of 'Steve Brown's Bunyip.' *Crown 8vo.* 6s.

H. A. MORRAH

A SERIOUS COMEDY. By H. A. MORRAH. *Crown 8vo.* 6s.

A LIST OF

Messrs. Methuen's
PUBLICATIONS

―――◆―――

Poetry

Rudyard Kipling. BARRACK-ROOM BALLADS; And Other Verses. By RUDYARD KIPLING. *Ninth Edition.* Crown 8vo. 6s.

> 'Mr. Kipling's verse is strong, vivid, full of character. . . . Unmistakable genius rings in every line.'—*Times.*

> 'The disreputable lingo of Cockayne is henceforth justified before the world; for a man of genius has taken it in hand, and has shown, beyond all cavilling, that in its way it also is a medium for literature. You are grateful, and you say to yourself, half in envy and half in admiration: "Here is a *book*; here, or one is a Dutchman, is one of the books of the year."'—*National Observer.*

> '"Barrack-Room Ballads" contains some of the best work that Mr. Kipling has ever done, which is saying a good deal. "Fuzzy-Wuzzy," "Gunga Din," and "Tommy," are, in our opinion, altogether superior to anything of the kind that English literature has hitherto produced.'—*Athenæum.*

> 'The ballads teem with imagination, they palpitate with emotion. We read them with laughter and tears; the metres throb in our pulses, the cunningly ordered words tingle with life; and if this be not poetry, what is?'—*Pall Mall Gazette.*

Henley. LYRA HEROICA: An Anthology selected from the best English Verse of the 16th, 17th, 18th, and 19th Centuries. By WILLIAM ERNEST HENLEY. *Crown 8vo. Buckram, gilt top.* 6s.

> 'Mr. Henley has brought to the task of selection an instinct alike for poetry and for chivalry which seems to us quite wonderfully, and even unerringly, right.'—*Guardian.*

"Q." THE GOLDEN POMP : A Procession of English Lyrics from Surrey to Shirley, arranged by A. T. QUILLER COUCH. *Crown 8vo. Buckram. 6s.*

'A delightful volume : a really golden "Pomp."'—*Spectator.*
'Of the many anthologies of "old rhyme" recently made, Mr. Couch's seems the richest in its materials, and the most artistic in its arrangement. Mr. Couch's notes are admirable; and Messrs. Methuen are to be congratulated on the format of the sumptuous volume.'—*Realm.*

"Q." GREEN BAYS : Verses and Parodies. By "Q.," Author of 'Dead Man's Rock,' etc. *Second Edition. Crown 8vo.* 3s. 6d.

'The verses display a rare and versatile gift of parody, great command of metre, and a very pretty turn of humour.'—*Times.*

H. C. Beeching. LYRA SACRA : An Anthology of Sacred Verse. Edited by H. C. BEECHING, M.A. *Crown 8vo. Buckram, gilt top. 6s.*

'An anthology of high excellence.'—*Athenæum.*
'A charming selection, which maintains a lofty standard of excellence.'—*Times.*

Yeats. AN ANTHOLOGY OF IRISH VERSE. Edited by W. B. YEATS. *Crown 8vo.* 3s. 6d.

'An attractive and catholic selection.'—*Times.*
'It is edited by the most original and most accomplished of modern Irish poets, and against his editing but a single objection can be brought, namely, that it excludes from the collection his own delicate lyrics.'—*Saturday Review.*

Mackay. A SONG OF THE SEA : MY LADY OF DREAMS, AND OTHER POEMS. By ERIC MACKAY, Author of 'The Love Letters of a Violinist.' *Second Edition. Fcap. 8vo, gilt top.* 5s.

'Everywhere Mr. Mackay displays himself the master of a style marked by all the characteristics of the best rhetoric. He has a keen sense of rhythm and of general balance ; his verse is excellently sonorous.'—*Globe.*
'Throughout the book the poetic workmanship is fine.'—*Scotsman.*

Ibsen. BRAND. A Drama by HENRIK IBSEN. Translated by WILLIAM WILSON. *Second Edition. Crown 8vo.* 3s. 6d.

'The greatest world-poem of the nineteenth century next to "Faust." It is in the same set with "Agamemnon," with "Lear," with the literature that we now instinctively regard as high and holy.'—*Daily Chronicle.*

'A. G." VERSES TO ORDER. By "A. G." *Cr. 8vo.* 2s. 6d. net.

A small volume of verse by a writer whose initials are well known to Oxford men.
A capital specimen of light academic poetry. These verses are very bright and engaging, easy and sufficiently witty.'—*St. James's Gazette.*

Hosken. VERSES BY THE WAY. By J. D. HOSKEN. *Crown 8vo.* 5s.

MESSRS. METHUEN'S LIST   11

Gale. CRICKET SONGS. By NORMAN GALE. *Crown 8vo. Linen.* 2s. 6d.

'Simple, manly, and humorous. Every cricketer should buy the book.'—*Westminster Gazette.*
'Cricket has never known such a singer.'—*Cricket.*

Langbridge. BALLADS OF THE BRAVE: Poems of Chivalry, Enterprise, Courage, and Constancy, from the Earliest Times to the Present Day. Edited, with Notes, by Rev. F. LANGBRIDGE. *Crown 8vo. Buckram.* 3s. 6d. *School Edition.* 2s. 6d.

'A very happy conception happily carried out. These "Ballads of the Brave" are intended to suit the real tastes of boys, and will suit the taste of the great majority.'—*Spectator.*   'The book is full of splendid things.'—*World.*

English Classics

Edited by W. E. HENLEY.

Messrs. Methuen are publishing, under this title, some of the masterpieces of the English tongue, which, while well within the reach of the average buyer, shall be at once an ornament to the shelf of him that owns, and a delight to the eye of him that reads.

'This new edition of a great classic might make an honourable appearance in any library in the world. Printed by Constable on laid paper, bound in most artistic and restful-looking fig-green buckram, with a frontispiece portrait, the book might well be issued at three times its present price.'—*Irish Independent.*

'Very dainty volumes are these; the paper, type, and light-green binding are all very agreeable to the eye. *Simplex munditiis* is the phrase that might be applied to them.'—*Globe.*

'The volumes are strongly bound in green buckram, are of a convenient size, and pleasant to look upon, so that whether on the shelf, or on the table, or in the hand the possessor is thoroughly content with them.'—*Guardian.*

'The paper, type, and binding of this edition are in excellent taste, and leave nothing to be desired by lovers of literature.'—*Standard.*

'Two handsome and finely-printed volumes, light to hold, pleasing to look at, easy to read.'—*National Observer.*

THE LIFE AND OPINIONS OF TRISTRAM SHANDY.
By LAWRENCE STERNE. With an Introduction by CHARLES WHIBLEY, and a Portrait. 2 *vols.* 7s.

THE COMEDIES OF WILLIAM CONGREVE. With an Introduction by G. S. STREET, and a Portrait. 2 *vols.* 7s.

THE ADVENTURES OF HAJJI BABA OF ISPAHAN
By JAMES MORIER. With an Introduction by E. G. BROWNE, M.A., and a Portrait. 2 *vols.* 7s.

THE LIVES OF DONNE, WOTTON, HOOKER, HERBERT, AND SANDERSON. By IZAAK WALTON. With an Introduction by VERNON BLACKBURN, and a Portrait. 3s. 6d.

THE LIVES OF THE ENGLISH POETS. By SAMUEL JOHNSON, LL.D. With an Introduction by J. H. MILLAR, and a Portrait. 3 vols. 10s. 6d.

Illustrated Books

Jane Barlow. THE BATTLE OF THE FROGS AND MICE, translated by JANE BARLOW, Author of 'Irish Idylls,' and pictured by F. D. BEDFORD. Small 4to. 6s. net.

S. Baring Gould. A BOOK OF FAIRY TALES retold by S. BARING GOULD. With numerous illustrations and initial letters by ARTHUR J. GASKIN. Second Edition. Crown 8vo. Buckram. 6s.

'Mr. Baring Gould has done a good deed, and is deserving of gratitude, in re-writing in honest, simple style the old stories that delighted the childhood of "our fathers and grandfathers." We do not think he has omitted any of our favourite stories, the stories that are commonly regarded as merely "old fashioned." As to the form of the book, and the printing, which is by Messrs. Constable, it were difficult to commend overmuch.—*Saturday Review.*

S. Baring Gould. OLD ENGLISH FAIRY TALES. Collected and edited by S. BARING GOULD. With Numerous Illustrations by F. D. BEDFORD. Second Edition. Crown 8vo. Buckram. 6s.

This volume consists of some of the old English stories which have been lost to sight, and they are fully illustrated by Mr. Bedford.

'Nineteen stories which will probably be new to everybody, who is not an antiquarian or a bibliographer. A book in which children will revel.'—*Daily Telegraph.*

'Of the fairy tales, first place must be given to the collection of "Old English Fairy Tales" of Mr. S. Baring Gould, in introducing which the author expresses his surprise that no collection had before been attempted and adapted to the reading of children of the old delightful English folk-tales and traditionary stories. He has gone to the most ancient sources, and presents to young readers in this volume a series of seventeen, told in his own way, and illustrated by F. D. Bedford. We can conceive of no more charming gift-book for children than this volume.'—*Pall Mall Gazette.*

'The only collection of really *old* English fairy tales that we have.'—*Woman.*

'A charming volume, which children will be sure to appreciate. The stories have been selected with great ingenuity from various old ballads and folk-tales, and, having been somewhat altered and readjusted, now stand forth, clothed in Mr. Baring-Gould's delightful English, to enchant youthful readers. All the tales are good.'—*Guardian.*

S. Baring Gould. A BOOK OF NURSERY SONGS AND RHYMES. Edited by S. BARING GOULD, and Illustrated by the Students of the Birmingham Art School. *Buckram, gilt top. Crown 8vo.* 6s.

' The volume is very complete in its way, as it contains nursery songs to the number of 77, game-rhymes, and jingles. To the student we commend the sensible introduction, and the explanatory notes. The volume is superbly printed on soft, thick paper, which it is a pleasure to touch ; and the borders and pictures are, as we have said, among the very best specimens we have seen of the Gaskin school.' — *Birmingham Gazette.*

' One of the most artistic Christmas books of the season. Every page is surrounded by a quaint design, and the illustrations are in the same spirit. The collection itself is admirably done, and provides a prodigious wealth of the rhymes generations of English people have learned in tender years. A more charming volume of its kind has not been issued this season.' — *Record.*

' A perfect treasure.' — *Black and White.*

' The collection of nursery rhymes is, since it has been made by Mr. Baring Gould, very complete, and among the game-rhymes we have found several quite new ones. The notes are just what is wanted.' — *Bookman.*

H. C. Beeching. A BOOK OF CHRISTMAS VERSE. Edited by H. C. BEECHING, M.A., and Illustrated by WALTER CRANE. *Crown 8vo.* 5s.

A collection of the best verse inspired by the birth of Christ from the Middle Ages to the present day. Mr. Walter Crane has designed several illustrations and the cover. A distinction of the book is the large number of poems it contains by modern authors, a few of which are here printed for the first time.

' "A Book of Christmas Verse," selected by so good a judge of poetry as Mr. Beeching, and picturesquely illustrated by Mr. Crane, is likely to prove a popular Christmas book, more especially as it is printed by Messrs. Constable, with their usual excellence of typography.' — *Athenæum.*

' A very pleasing anthology, well arranged and well edited.' — *Manchester Guardian.*

' A beautiful anthology.' — *Daily Chronicle.*

' An anthology which, from its unity of aim and high poetic excellence, has a better right to exist than most of its fellows.' — *Guardian.*

' As well-chosen and complete a collection as we have seen.' — *Spectator.*

History

Flinders Petrie. A HISTORY OF EGYPT, FROM THE EARLIEST TIMES TO THE PRESENT DAY. Edited by W. M. FLINDERS PETRIE, D.C.L., LL.D., Professor of Egyptology at University College. *Fully Illustrated. In Six Volumes. Crown 8vo.* 6s. *each.*

Vol. I. PREHISTORIC TO EIGHTEENTH DYNASTY. W. M. F. Petrie. *Second Edition.*

' A history written in the spirit of scientific precision so worthily represented by Dr. Petrie and his school cannot but promote sound and accurate study, and supply a vacant place in the English literature of Egyptology.' — *Times.*

Flinders Petrie. EGYPTIAN TALES. Edited by W. M.
FLINDERS PETRIE. Illustrated by TRISTRAM ELLIS. *In Two Volumes. Crown 8vo.* 3s. 6d. *each.*

'A valuable addition to the literature of comparative folk-lore. The drawings are really illustrations in the literal sense of the word.'—*Globe.*

'It has a scientific value to the student of history and archæology.'—*Scotsman.*

'Invaluable as a picture of life in Palestine and Egypt.'—*Daily News.*

Flinders Petrie. EGYPTIAN DECORATIVE ART. By W. M. FLINDERS PETRIE, D.C.L. With 120 Illustrations. *Crown 8vo.* 3s. 6d.

'Professor Flinders Petrie is not only a profound Egyptologist, but an accomplished student of comparative archæology. In these lectures, delivered at the Royal Institution, he displays both qualifications with rare skill in elucidating the development of decorative art in Egypt, and in tracing its influence on the art of other countries. Few experts can speak with higher authority and wider knowledge than the Professor himself, and in any case his treatment of his subject is full of learning and insight.'—*Times.*

S. Baring Gould. THE TRAGEDY OF THE CÆSARS. The Emperors of the Julian and Claudian Lines. With numerous Illustrations from Busts, Gems, Cameos, etc. By S. BARING GOULD, Author of 'Mehalah,' etc. *Third Edition. Royal 8vo.* 15s.

'A most splendid and fascinating book on a subject of undying interest. The great feature of the book is the use the author has made of the existing portraits of the Caesars, and the admirable critical subtlety he has exhibited in dealing with this line of research. It is brilliantly written, and the illustrations are supplied on a scale of profuse magnificence.'—*Daily Chronicle.*

'The volumes will in no sense disappoint the general reader. Indeed, in their way, there is nothing in any sense so good in English. . . . Mr. Baring Gould has presented his narrative in such a way as not to make one dull page.'—*Athenæum.*

Clark. THE COLLEGES OF OXFORD: Their History and their Traditions. By Members of the University. Edited by A. CLARK, M.A., Fellow and Tutor of Lincoln College. *8vo.* 12s. 6d.

'A work which will certainly be appealed to for many years as the standard book on the Colleges of Oxford.'—*Athenæum.*

Perrens. THE HISTORY OF FLORENCE FROM 1434 TO 1492. By F. T. PERRENS. Translated by HANNAH LYNCH. *8vo.* 12s. 6d.

A history of Florence under the domination of Cosimo, Piero, and Lorenzo de Medicis.

'This is a standard book by an honest and intelligent historian, who has deserved well of all who are interested in Italian history.'—*Manchester Guardian.*

E. L. S. Horsburgh. THE CAMPAIGN OF WATERLOO. By E. L. S. HORSBURGH, B.A. *With Plans. Crown 8vo. 5s.*
A brilliant essay—simple, sound, and thorough.'—*Daily Chronicle.*
'A study, the most concise, the most lucid, the most critical that has been produced.' —*Birmingham Mercury.*
'A careful and precise study, a fair and impartial criticism, and an eminently readable book.'—*Admiralty and Horse Guards Gazette.*

George. BATTLES OF ENGLISH HISTORY. By H. B. GEORGE, M.A., Fellow of New College, Oxford. *With numerous Plans. Second Edition. Crown 8vo. 6s.*
'Mr. George has undertaken a very useful task—that of making military affairs intelligible and instructive to non-military readers—and has executed it with laudable intelligence and industry, and with a large measure of success.'—*Times.*
'This book is almost a revelation; and we heartily congratulate the author on his work and on the prospect of the reward he has well deserved for so much conscientious and sustained labour.'—*Daily Chronicle.*

Browning. A SHORT HISTORY OF MEDIÆVAL ITALY A.D. 1250-1530. By OSCAR BROWNING, Fellow and Tutor of King's College, Cambridge. *Second Edition. In Two Volumes. Crown 8vo. 5s. each.*
VOL. I. 1250-1409.—Guelphs and Ghibellines.
VOL. II. 1409-1530.—The Age of the Condottieri.
A vivid picture of mediæval Italy.'—*Standard.*
'Mr. Browning is to be congratulated on the production of a work of immense labour and learning.'—*Westminster Gazette.*

O'Grady. THE STORY OF IRELAND. By STANDISH O'GRADY, Author of 'Finn and his Companions.' *Cr. 8vo. 2s. 6d.*
'Most delightful, most stimulating. Its racy humour, its original imaginings, make it one of the freshest, breeziest volumes.'—*Methodist Times.*
A survey at once graphic, acute, and quaintly written.'—*Times.*

Biography

Robert Louis Stevenson. VAILIMA LETTERS. By ROBERT LOUIS STEVENSON. With an Etched Portrait by WILLIAM STRANG, and other Illustrations. *Second Edition. Crown 8vo. Buckram. 7s. 6d.*
Also 125 copies on hand-made paper. *Demy 8vo. 25s. net.*
'The book is, on the one hand, a new revelation of a most lovable personality, and, on the other, it abounds in passages of the most charming prose—personal, descriptive, humorous, or all three; exquisite vignettes of Samoan scenery, passages of joy in recovered health, to be followed—alas, too soon—by depression, physical and mental; little revelations of literary secrets, such as of the origin of "David Balfour," or of the scheme of the books not yet published; amusing stories about the household, and altogether a picture of a character and surroundings that have never before been brought together since Britons took to writing books and travelling across the seas. The Vailima Letters are rich in all the varieties of that charm which have secured for Stevenson the affection of many others besides "journalists, fellow-novelists, and boys."'—*The Times.*
'Few publications have in our time been more eagerly awaited than these "Vailima

Letters," giving the first fruits of the correspondence of Robert Louis Stevenson. But, high as the tide of expectation has run, no reader can possibly be disappointed in the result.'—*St. James's Gazette.*

'For the student of English literature these letters indeed are a treasure. They are more like "Scott's Journal" in kind than any other literary autobiography.' —*National Observer.*

'One of the most noteworthy and most charming of the volumes of letters that have appeared in our time or in our language.'—*Scotsman.*

'Eagerly as we awaited this volume, it has proved a gift exceeding all our hopes—a gift, I think, almost priceless. It unites in the rarest manner the value of a familiar correspondence with the value of an intimate journal.'—A. T. Q. C., in *Speaker.*

Collingwood. THE LIFE OF JOHN RUSKIN. By W. G. COLLINGWOOD, M.A., Editor of Mr. Ruskin's Poems. With numerous Portraits, and 13 Drawings by Mr. Ruskin. *Second Edition.* 2 vols. 8vo. 32s.

'No more magnificent volumes have been published for a long time. . . .'—*Times.*

'It is long since we have had a biography with such delights of substance and of form. Such a book is a pleasure for the day, and a joy for ever.'—*Daily Chronicle.*

'A noble monument of a noble subject. One of the most beautiful books about one of the noblest lives of our century.'—*Glasgow Herald.*

Waldstein. JOHN RUSKIN: a Study. By CHARLES WALDSTEIN, M.A., Fellow of King's College, Cambridge. With a Photogravure Portrait after Professor HERKOMER. *Post 8vo.* 5s.

'A thoughtful, impartial, well-written criticism of Ruskin's teaching, intended to separate what the author regards as valuable and permanent from what is transient and erroneous in the great master's writing.'—*Daily Chronicle.*

W. H. Hutton. THE LIFE OF SIR THOMAS MORE. By W. H. HUTTON, M.A., Author of 'William Laud.' *With Portraits. Crown 8vo.* 5s.

'Mr. Wm. Holden Hutton has in a neat volume of less than 300 pages, told the story of the life of More, and he has placed it in such a well-painted setting of the times in which he lived, and so accompanied it by brief outlines of his principal writings, that the book lays good claim to high rank among our biographies. The work, it may be said, is excellently, even lovingly, written.' —*Scotsman.*

'An excellent monograph.'—*Times.*

'A most complete presentation.'—*Daily Chronicle.*

Kaufmann. CHARLES KINGSLEY. By M. KAUFMANN, M.A. *Crown 8vo. Buckram.* 5s.

A biography of Kingsley, especially dealing with his achievements in social reform.

'The author has certainly gone about his work with conscientiousness and industry.'— *Sheffield Daily Telegraph.*

Robbins. THE EARLY LIFE OF WILLIAM EWART GLADSTONE. By A. F. ROBBINS. *With Portraits. Crown 8vo.* 6s.

'Considerable labour and much skill of presentation have not been unworthily expended on this interesting work.'—*Times.*

Clark Russell. THE LIFE OF ADMIRAL LORD COLLINGWOOD. By W. CLARK RUSSELL, Author of 'The Wreck of the Grosvenor.' With Illustrations by F. BRANGWYN. *Second Edition. Crown 8vo.* 6s.

'A most excellent and wholesome book, which we should like to see in the hands of every boy in the country.'—*St. James's Gazette.*
'A really good book.'—*Saturday Review.*
'A most excellent and wholesome book, which we should like to see in the hands of every boy in the country.'—*St. James's Gazette.*

Southey. ENGLISH SEAMEN (Howard, Clifford, Hawkins, Drake, Cavendish). By ROBERT SOUTHEY. Edited, with an Introduction, by DAVID HANNAY. *Crown 8vo.* 6s.

'Admirable and well-told stories of our naval history.'—*Army and Navy Gazette.*
'A brave, inspiring book.'—*Black and White.*
'The work of a master of style, and delightful all through.'—*Daily Chronicle.*

General Literature

S. Baring Gould. OLD COUNTRY LIFE. By S. BARING GOULD, Author of 'Mehalah,' etc. With Sixty-seven Illustrations by W. PARKINSON, F. D. BEDFORD, and F. MASEY. *Large Crown 8vo, cloth super extra, top edge gilt,* 10s. 6d. *Fifth and Cheaper Edition.* 6s.

'"Old Country Life," as healthy wholesome reading, full of breezy life and movement, full of quaint stories vigorously told, will not be excelled by any book to be published throughout the year. Sound, hearty, and English to the core.'—*World.*

S. Baring Gould. HISTORIC ODDITIES AND STRANGE EVENTS. By S. BARING GOULD, Author of 'Mehalah,' etc. *Third Edition. Crown 8vo.* 6s.

'A collection of exciting and entertaining chapters. The whole volume is delightful reading.'—*Times.*

S. Baring Gould. FREAKS OF FANATICISM. By S. BARING GOULD, Author of 'Mehalah,' etc. *Third Edition. Crown 8vo.* 6s.

'Mr. Baring Gould has a keen eye for colour and effect, and the subjects he has chosen give ample scope to his descriptive and analytic faculties. A perfectly fascinating book.'—*Scottish Leader.*

S. Baring Gould. A GARLAND OF COUNTRY SONG:
English Folk Songs with their Traditional Melodies. Collected and arranged by S. BARING GOULD and H. FLEETWOOD SHEPPARD. *Demy 4to.* 6s.

S. Baring Gould. SONGS OF THE WEST: Traditional Ballads and Songs of the West of England, with their Traditional Melodies. Collected by S. BARING GOULD, M.A., and H. FLEETWOOD SHEPPARD, M.A. Arranged for Voice and Piano. In 4 Parts (containing 25 Songs each), *Parts I., II., III.,* 3s. each. *Part IV.,* 5s. *In one Vol., French morocco,* 15s.

'A rich collection of humour, pathos, grace, and poetic fancy.'—*Saturday Review.*

S. Baring Gould. YORKSHIRE ODDITIES AND STRANGE EVENTS. *Fourth Edition. Crown 8vo.* 6s.

S. Baring Gould. STRANGE SURVIVALS AND SUPERSTITIONS. With Illustrations. By S. BARING GOULD. *Crown 8vo. Second Edition.* 6s.

'We have read Mr. Baring Gould's book from beginning to end. It is full of quaint and various information, and there is not a dull page in it.'—*Notes and Queries.*

S. Baring Gould. THE DESERTS OF SOUTHERN FRANCE. By S. BARING-GOULD. With numerous Illustrations by F. D. BEDFORD, S. HUTTON, etc. *2 vols. Demy 8vo.* 32s.

This book is the first serious attempt to describe the great barren tableland that extends to the south of Limousin in the Department of Aveyron, Lot, etc., a country of dolomite cliffs, and cañons, and subterranean rivers. The region is full of prehistoric and historic interest, relics of cave-dwellers, of mediæval robbers, and of the English domination and the Hundred Years' War.

'His two richly-illustrated volumes are full of matter of interest to the geologist, the archæologist, and the student of history and manners.'—*Scotsman.*

'It deals with its subject in a manner which rarely fails to arrest attention.'—*Times.*

W. E. Gladstone. THE SPEECHES AND PUBLIC ADDRESSES OF THE RT. HON. W. E. GLADSTONE, M.P. Edited by A. W. HUTTON, M.A., and H. J. COHEN, M.A. With Portraits. *8vo. Vols. IX. and X.* 12s. 6d. each.

Henley and Whibley. A BOOK OF ENGLISH PROSE. Collected by W. E. HENLEY and CHARLES WHIBLEY. *Cr. 8vo.* 6s.

'A unique volume of extracts—an art gallery of early prose.'—*Birmingham Post.*
'An admirable companion to Mr. Henley's "Lyra Heroica."'—*Saturday Review.*
'Quite delightful. The choice made has been excellent, and the volume has been most admirably printed by Messrs. Constable. A greater treat for those not well acquainted with pre-Restoration prose could not be imagined.'—*Athenæum.*

Wells. OXFORD AND OXFORD LIFE. By Members of the University. Edited by J. WELLS, M.A., Fellow and Tutor of Wadham College. *Crown 8vo.* 3s. 6d.

This work contains an account of life at Oxford—intellectual, social, and religious—a careful estimate of necessary expenses, a review of recent changes, a statement of the present position of the University, and chapters on Women's Education, aids to study, and University Extension.

'We congratulate Mr. Wells on the production of a readable and intelligent account of Oxford as it is at the present time, written by persons who are possessed of a close acquaintance with the system and life of the University.'—*Athenæum.*

W. B. Worsfold. SOUTH AFRICA : Its History and its Future. By W. BASIL WORSFOLD, M.A. *With a Map. Crown 8vo.* 6s.

'An intensely interesting book.'—*Daily Chronicle.*

'A monumental work compressed into a very moderate compass. The early history of the colony, its agricultural resources, literature, and gold and diamond mines are all clearly described, besides the main features of recent Kaffir and Boer campaigns; nor (to bring his record quite up to date) does the author fail to devote a chapter to Mr. Cecil Rhodes, the Chartered Company, and the Boer Convention of 1884. Additional information from sources not usually accessible is to be found in the notes at the end of the book, as well as a historical summary, a statistical appendix, and other matters of special interest at the present moment.' —*World.*

Ouida. VIEWS AND OPINIONS. By OUIDA. *Crown 8vo. Second Edition.* 6s.

'Ouida is outspoken, and the reader of this book will not have a dull moment. The book is full of variety, and sparkles with entertaining matter.'—*Speaker.*

J. S. Shedlock. THE PIANOFORTE SONATA : Its Origin and Development. By J. S. SHEDLOCK. *Crown 8vo.* 5s.

'This work should be in the possession of every musician and amateur, for it not only embodies a concise and lucid history of the origin of one of the most important forms of musical composition, but, by reason of the painstaking research and accuracy of the author's statements, it is a very valuable work for reference.' —*Athenæum.*

Bowden. THE EXAMPLE OF BUDDHA: Being Quotations from Buddhist Literature for each Day in the Year. Compiled by E. M. BOWDEN. With Preface by Sir EDWIN ARNOLD. *Third Edition.* 16mo. 2s. 6d.

Bushill. PROFIT SHARING AND THE LABOUR QUESTION. By T. W. BUSHILL, a Profit Sharing Employer. *Crown 8vo.* 2s. 6d.

John Beever. PRACTICAL FLY-FISHING, Founded on Nature, by JOHN BEEVER, late of the Thwaite House, Coniston. A New Edition, with a Memoir of the Author by W. G. COLLINGWOOD, M.A. *Crown 8vo.* 3s. 6d.

A little book on Fly-Fishing by an old friend of Mr. Ruskin.

Science

Freudenreich. DAIRY BACTERIOLOGY. A Short Manual for the Use of Students. By Dr. ED. VON FREUDENREICH. Translated from the German by J. R. AINSWORTH DAVIS, B.A., F.C.P. *Crown 8vo.* **2s. 6d.**

Chalmers Mitchell. OUTLINES OF BIOLOGY. By P. CHALMERS MITCHELL, M.A., F.Z.S. *Fully Illustrated. Crown 8vo.* **6s.**

A text-book designed to cover the new Schedule issued by the Royal College of Physicians and Surgeons.

Massee. A MONOGRAPH OF THE MYXOGASTRES. By GEORGE MASSEE. With 12 Coloured Plates. *Royal 8vo.* **18s. net.**

'A work much in advance of any book in the language treating of this group of organisms. It is indispensable to every student of the Myxogastres. The coloured plates deserve high praise for their accuracy and execution.'—*Nature.*

Theology and Philosophy

Driver. SERMONS ON SUBJECTS CONNECTED WITH THE OLD TESTAMENT. By S. R. DRIVER, D.D., Canon of Christ Church, Regius Professor of Hebrew in the University of Oxford. *Crown 8vo.* **6s.**

A welcome companion to the author's famous 'Introduction.' No man can read these discourses without feeling that Dr. Driver is fully alive to the deeper teaching of the Old Testament.'—*Guardian.*

Cheyne. FOUNDERS OF OLD TESTAMENT CRITICISM: Biographical, Descriptive, and Critical Studies. By T. K. CHEYNE, D.D., Oriel Professor of the Interpretation of Holy Scripture at Oxford. *Large crown 8vo.* **7s. 6d.**

This important book is a historical sketch of O. T. Criticism in the form of biographical studies from the days of Eichhorn to those of Driver and Robertson Smith. It is the only book of its kind in English.
'A very learned and instructive work.'—*Times.*

Prior. CAMBRIDGE SERMONS. Edited by C. H. PRIOR, M.A., Fellow and Tutor of Pembroke College. *Crown 8vo.* **6s.**

A volume of sermons preached before the University of Cambridge by various preachers, including the Archbishop of Canterbury and Bishop Westcott.
'A representative collection. Bishop Westcott's is a noble sermon.'—*Guardian.*

Beeching. SERMONS TO SCHOOLBOYS. By H. C. BEECHING, M.A., Rector of Yattendon, Berks. With a Preface by Canon SCOTT HOLLAND. *Crown 8vo.* **2s. 6d.**

Seven sermons preached before the boys of Bradfield College.

MESSRS. METHUEN'S LIST 21

Layard. RELIGION IN BOYHOOD. Notes on the Religious Training of Boys. With a Preface by J. R. ILLINGWORTH. By E. B. LAYARD, M.A. 18*mo*. 1*s*.

C. J. Shebbeare. THE GREEK THEORY OF THE STATE AND THE NONCONFORMIST CONSCIENCE: a Socialistic Defence of some Ancient Institutions. By CHARLES JOHN SHEBBEARE, B.A., Christ Church, Oxford. *Crown 8vo.* 2*s*. 6*d*.

F. S. Granger. THE WORSHIP OF THE ROMANS. By F. S. GRANGER, M.A., Litt.D., Professor of Philosophy at University College, Nottingham. *Crown 8vo.* 6*s*.

The author has attempted to delineate that group of beliefs which stood in close connection with the Roman religion, and among the subjects treated are Dreams, Nature Worship, Roman Magic, Divination, Holy Places, Victims, etc. Thus the book is, apart from its immediate subject, a contribution to folk-lore and comparative psychology.

'A scholarly analysis of the religious ceremonies, beliefs, and superstitions of ancient Rome, conducted in the new instructive light of comparative anthropology.'—*Times*.

'This is an analytical and critical work which will assist the student of Romish history to understand the factors which went to build up the remarkable characteristics of the old Romans especially in matters appertaining to religion.'—*Oxford Review*.

Devotional Books.

With Full-page Illustrations. Fcap. 8vo. Buckram. 3s. 6d. Padded morocco, 5s.

THE IMITATION OF CHRIST. By THOMAS À KEMPIS. With an Introduction by DEAN FARRAR. Illustrated by C. M. GERE, and printed in black and red.

'Amongst all the innumerable English editions of the "Imitation," there can have been few which were prettier than this one, printed in strong and handsome type by Messrs. Constable, with all the glory of red initials, and the comfort of buckram binding.'—*Glasgow Herald*.

THE CHRISTIAN YEAR. By JOHN KEBLE. With an Introduction and Notes by W. LOCK, M.A., Sub-Warden of Keble College, Ireland Professor at Oxford, Author of the 'Life of John Keble.' Illustrated by R. ANNING BELL.

'The present edition is annotated with all the care and insight to be expected from Mr. Lock. The progress and circumstances of its composition are detailed in the Introduction. There is in an interesting Appendix on the MSS. of the "Christian Year," and another giving the order in which the poems were written. A "Short Analysis of the Thought" is prefixed to each, and any difficulty in the text is explained in a note. When we add to all this that the book is printed in clear, black type on excellent paper, and bound in dull red buckram, we shall have said enough to vindicate its claim to a place among the prettiest gift-books of the season.'—*Guardian*.

'The most acceptable edition of this ever popular work with which we are acquainted.'—*Globe*.

'An edition which should be recognised as the best extant. . . . The edition is one which John Henry Newman and the late Dean Church would have handled with meet and affectionate remembrance.'—*Birmingham Post*.

Leaders of Religion

Edited by H. C. BEECHING, M.A. *With Portraits, crown 8vo.*

A series of short biographies of the most prominent leaders of religious life and thought of all ages and countries.

The following are ready—

3/6

CARDINAL NEWMAN. By R. H. HUTTON.
JOHN WESLEY. By J. H. OVERTON, M.A.
BISHOP WILBERFORCE. By G. W. DANIEL, M.A.
CARDINAL MANNING. By A. W. HUTTON, M.A.
CHARLES SIMEON. By H. C. G. MOULE, M.A.
JOHN KEBLE. By WALTER LOCK, M.A.
THOMAS CHALMERS. By Mrs. OLIPHANT.
LANCELOT ANDREWES. By R. L. OTTLEY, M.A.
AUGUSTINE OF CANTERBURY. By E. L. CUTTS, D.D.
WILLIAM LAUD. By W. H. HUTTON, M.A.
JOHN KNOX. By F. M'CUNN.
JOHN HOWE. By R. F. HORTON, D.D.

Other volumes will be announced in due course.

Fiction

SIX SHILLING NOVELS

Marie Corelli. BARABBAS: A DREAM OF THE WORLD'S TRAGEDY. By MARIE CORELLI, Author of 'A Romance of Two Worlds,' 'Vendetta,' etc. *Twenty-first Edition. Crown 8vo. 6s.*

'The tender reverence of the treatment and the imaginative beauty of the writing have reconciled us to the daring of the conception, and the conviction is forced on us that even so exalted a subject cannot be made too familiar to us, provided it be presented in the true spirit of Christian faith. The amplifications of the Scripture narrative are often conceived with high poetic insight, and this "Dream of the World's Tragedy" is, despite some trifling incongruities, a lofty and not inadequate paraphrase of the supreme climax of the inspired narrative.'—*Dublin Review.*

Marie Corelli. THE SORROWS OF SATAN. By MARIE CORELLI. *Crown 8vo. Seventeenth Edition. 6s.*

'There is in Marie Corelli's work a spark of the Divine. Her genius is neither common nor unclean. She has a far-reaching and gorgeous imagination; she feels the beautiful intensely, and desires it. She believes in God and in good; she hopes for the kindest and the best; she is dowered with "the scorn of scorn, the hate of hate, the love of love." There is to be discerned in her work that sense of the unseen which is the glad but solemn prerogative of the pure in heart. Again, she is a keen observer, a powerful, fearless, caustic satirist; she makes an effective protest, and enforces a grave warning against the follies and shams and vices of the age.'—Report of a sermon delivered on 'The Sorrows of Satan,' by the Rev. A. R. HARRISON, Vicar, in Tettenhall Church, Wolverhampton, on Sunday, November 12.—*Midland Evening News.*

'A very powerful piece of work. . . . The conception is magnificent, and is likely to win an abiding place within the memory of man. . . . The author has immense command of language, and a limitless audacity. . . . This interesting and remarkable romance will live long after much of the ephemeral literature of the day is forgotten. . . . A literary phenomenon . . . novel, and even sublime.'—W. T. STEAD in the *Review of Reviews.*

Anthony Hope. THE GOD IN THE CAR. BY ANTHONY HOPE, Author of 'A Change of Air,' etc. *Seventh Edition. Crown 8vo. 6s.*

'A very remarkable book, deserving of critical analysis impossible within our limit; brilliant, but not superficial; well considered, but not elaborated; constructed with the proverbial art that conceals, but yet allows itself to be enjoyed by readers to whom fine literary method is a keen pleasure; true without cynicism, subtle without affectation, humorous without strain, witty without offence, inevitably sad, with an unmorose simplicity.'—*The World.*

Anthony Hope. A CHANGE OF AIR. By ANTHONY HOPE, Author of 'The Prisoner of Zenda,' etc. *Third Edition. Crown 8vo. 6s.*

'A graceful, vivacious comedy, true to human nature. The characters are traced with a masterly hand.'—*Times.*

Anthony Hope. A MAN OF MARK. By ANTHONY HOPE, Author of 'The Prisoner of Zenda,' 'The God in the Car,' etc. *Third Edition. Crown 8vo. 6s.*

'Of all Mr. Hope's books, "A Man of Mark" is the one which best compares with "The Prisoner of Zenda." The two romances are unmistakably the work of the same writer, and he possesses a style of narrative peculiarly seductive, piquant, comprehensive, and—his own.'—*National Observer.*

Anthony Hope. THE CHRONICLES OF COUNT ANTONIO. By ANTHONY HOPE, Author of 'The Prisoner of Zenda,' 'The God in the Car,' etc. *Third Edition. Crown 8vo. 6s.*

'It is a perfectly enchanting story of love and chivalry, and pure romance. The outlawed Count is the most constant, desperate, and withal modest and tender of lovers, a peerless gentleman, an intrepid fighter, a very faithful friend, and a most magnanimous foe. In short, he is an altogether admirable, lovable, and delightful hero. There is not a word in the volume that can give offence to the most fastidious taste of man or woman, and there is not, either, a dull paragraph in it. The book is everywhere instinct with the most exhilarating spirit of adventure, and delicately perfumed with the sentiment of all heroic and honourable deeds of history and romance.'—*Guardian.*

Conan Doyle. ROUND THE RED LAMP. By A. CONAN DOYLE, Author of 'The White Company,' 'The Adventures of Sherlock Holmes,' etc. *Fourth Edition. Crown 8vo.* 6s.

'The book is, indeed, composed of leaves from life, and is far and away the best view that has been vouchsafed us behind the scenes of the consulting-room. It is very superior to "The Diary of a late Physician."'—*Illustrated London News.*

Stanley Weyman. UNDER THE RED ROBE. By STANLEY WEYMAN, Author of 'A Gentleman of France.' With Twelve Illustrations by R. Caton Woodville. *Eighth Edition. Crown 8vo.* 6s.

'A book of which we have read every word for the sheer pleasure of reading, and which we put down with a pang that we cannot forget it all and start again.'—*Westminster Gazette.*
'Every one who reads books at all must read this thrilling romance, from the first page of which to the last the breathless reader is haled along. An inspiration of manliness and courage.'—*Daily Chronicle.*
'A delightful tale of chivalry and adventure, vivid and dramatic, with a wholesome modesty and reverence for the highest.'—*Globe.*

Mrs. Clifford. A FLASH OF SUMMER. By MRS. W. K. CLIFFORD, Author of 'Aunt Anne,' etc. *Second Edition. Crown 8vo.* 6s.

'The story is a very sad and a very beautiful one, exquisitely told, and enriched with many subtle touches of wise and tender insight. Mrs. Clifford's gentle heroine is a most lovable creature, contrasting very refreshingly with the heroine of latter-day fiction. The minor characters are vividly realised. "A Flash of Summer" is altogether an admirable piece of work, wrought with strength and simplicity. It will, undoubtedly, add to its author's reputation—already high—in the ranks of novelists.'—*Speaker.*
'We must congratulate Mrs. Clifford upon a very successful and interesting story, told throughout with finish and a delicate sense of proportion, qualities which, indeed, have always distinguished the best work of this very able writer.'—*Manchester Guardian.*

Emily Lawless. MAELCHO: a Sixteenth Century Romance. By the Hon. EMILY LAWLESS, Author of 'Grania,' 'Hurrish,' etc. *Second Edition. Crown 8vo.* 6s.

'A really great book.'—*Spectator.*
'There is no keener pleasure in life than the recognition of genius. Good work is commoner than it used to be, but the best is as rare as ever. All the more gladly, therefore, do we welcome in "Maelcho" a piece of work of the first order, which we do not hesitate to describe as one of the most remarkable literary achievements of this generation. Miss Lawless is possessed of the very essence of historical genius.'—*Manchester Guardian.*

E. F. Benson. DODO: A DETAIL OF THE DAY. By E. F. BENSON. *Sixteenth Edition. Crown 8vo.* 6s.

'A delightfully witty sketch of society.'—*Spectator.*
'A perpetual feast of epigram and paradox.'—*Speaker.*
'By a writer of quite exceptional ability.'—*Athenæum.*
'Brilliantly written.'—*World.*

MESSRS. METHUEN'S LIST 25

E. F. Benson. THE RUBICON. By E. F. BENSON, Author of 'Dodo.' *Fifth Edition. Crown 8vo. 6s.*

'Well written, stimulating, unconventional, and, in a word, characteristic.'— *Birmingham Post.*

'An exceptional achievement; a notable advance on his previous work.'—*National Observer.*

M. M. Dowie. GALLIA. By MÉNIE MURIEL DOWIE, Author of 'A Girl in the Carpathians.' *Third Edition. Crown 8vo. 6s.*

'The style is generally admirable, the dialogue not seldom brilliant, the situations surprising in their freshness and originality, while the subsidiary as well as the principal characters live and move, and the story itself is readable from title-page to colophon.'—*Saturday Review.*

'A very notable book; a very sympathetically, at times delightfully written book. —*Daily Graphic.*

MR. BARING GOULD'S NOVELS

'To say that a book is by the author of "Mehalah" is to imply that it contains a story cast on strong lines, containing dramatic possibilities, vivid and sympathetic descriptions of Nature, and a wealth of ingenious imagery.'—*Speaker.*

'That whatever Mr. Baring Gould writes is well worth reading, is a conclusion that may be very generally accepted. His views of life are fresh and vigorous, his language pointed and characteristic, the incidents of which he makes use are striking and original, his characters are life-like, and though somewhat exceptional people, are drawn and coloured with artistic force. Add to this that his descriptions of scenes and scenery are painted with the loving eyes and skilled hands of a master of his art, that he is always fresh and never dull, and under such conditions it is no wonder that readers have gained confidence both in his power of amusing and satisfying them, and that year by year his popularity widens.'—*Court Circular.*

Baring Gould. URITH: A Story of Dartmoor. By S. BARING GOULD. *Third Edition. Crown 8vo. 6s.*

'The author is at his best.'—*Times.*

'He has nearly reached the high water-mark of "Mehalah."'—*National Observer.*

Baring Gould. IN THE ROAR OF THE SEA: A Tale of the Cornish Coast. By S. BARING GOULD. *Fifth Edition. 6s.*

'One of the best imagined and most enthralling stories the author has produced.' —*Saturday Review.*

Baring Gould. MRS. CURGENVEN OF CURGENVEN. By S. BARING GOULD. *Fourth Edition. 6s.*

'A novel of vigorous humour and sustained power.'—*Graphic.*

'The swing of the narrative is splendid.'—*Sussex Daily News.*

Baring Gould. CHEAP JACK ZITA. By S. BARING GOULD. *Third Edition. Crown 8vo. 6s.*

'A powerful drama of human passion.'—*Westminster Gazette.*

'A story worthy the author.'—*National Observer.*

S. Baring Gould. THE QUEEN OF LOVE. By S. BARING GOULD. *Fourth Edition. Crown 8vo. 6s.*

'The scenery is admirable, and the dramatic incidents are most striking.'—*Glasgow Herald.*
'Strong, interesting, and clever.'—*Westminster Gazette.*
'You cannot put it down until you have finished it.'—*Punch.*
'Can be heartily recommended to all who care for cleanly, energetic, and interesting fiction.'—*Sussex Daily News.*

S. Baring Gould. KITTY ALONE. By S. BARING GOULD, Author of 'Mehalah,' 'Cheap Jack Zita,' etc. *Fourth Edition. Crown 8vo. 6s.*

'A strong and original story, teeming with graphic description, stirring incident, and, above all, with vivid and enthralling human interest.'—*Daily Telegraph.*
'Brisk, clever, keen, healthy, humorous, and interesting.'—*National Observer.*
'Full of quaint and delightful studies of character.'—*Bristol Mercury.*

S. Baring Gould. NOÉMI: A Romance of the Cave-Dwellers. By S. BARING GOULD. Illustrated by R. CATON WOODVILLE. *Third Edition. Crown 8vo. 6s.*

'"Noémi" is as excellent a tale of fighting and adventure as one may wish to meet. All the characters that interfere in this exciting tale are marked with properties of their own. The narrative also runs clear and sharp as the Loire itself.'—*Pall Mall Gazette.*
'Mr. Baring Gould's powerful story is full of the strong lights and shadows and vivid colouring to which he has accustomed us.'—*Standard.*

Mrs. Oliphant. SIR ROBERT'S FORTUNE. By MRS. OLIPHANT. *Crown 8vo. 6s.*

'Full of her own peculiar charm of style and simple, subtle character-painting comes her new gift, the delightful story before us. The scene mostly lies in the moors, and at the touch of the authoress a Scotch moor becomes a living thing, strong, tender, beautiful, and changeful. The book will take rank among the best of Mrs. Oliphant's good stories.'—*Pall Mall Gazette.*

W. E. Norris. MATTHEW AUSTIN. By W. E. NORRIS, Author of 'Mademoiselle de Mersac,' etc. *Fourth Edition. Crown 8vo. 6s.*

'"Matthew Austin" may safely be pronounced one of the most intellectually satisfactory and morally bracing novels of the current year.'—*Daily Telegraph.*

W. E. Norris. HIS GRACE. By W. E. NORRIS, Author of 'Mademoiselle de Mersac.' *Third Edition. Crown 8vo. 6s.*

Mr. Norris has drawn a really fine character in the Duke of Hurstbourne, at once unconventional and very true to the conventionalities of life, weak and strong in a breath, capable of inane follies and heroic decisions, yet not so definitely portrayed as to relieve a reader of the necessity of study on his own behalf.'—*Athenæum.*

W. E. Norris. THE DESPOTIC LADY AND OTHERS. By W. E. NORRIS, Author of 'Mademoiselle de Mersac.' *Crown 8vo.* 6s.

'A budget of good fiction of which no one will tire.'—*Scotsman.*
'An extremely entertaining volume—the sprightliest of holiday companions.'—*Daily Telegraph.*

Gilbert Parker. PIERRE AND HIS PEOPLE. By GILBERT PARKER. *Third Edition. Crown 8vo.* 6s.

'Stories happily conceived and finely executed. There is strength and genius in Mr. Parker's style.'—*Daily Telegraph.*

Gilbert Parker. MRS. FALCHION. By GILBERT PARKER, Author of 'Pierre and His People.' *Second Edition. Crown 8vo.* 6s.

'A splendid study of character.'—*Athenæum.*
'But little behind anything that has been done by any writer of our time.'—*Pall Mall Gazette.*
'A very striking and admirable novel.'—*St. James's Gazette.*

Gilbert Parker. THE TRANSLATION OF A SAVAGE. By GILBERT PARKER. *Crown 8vo.* 6s.

'The plot is original and one difficult to work out; but Mr. Parker has done it with great skill and delicacy. The reader who is not interested in this original, fresh, and well-told tale must be a dull person indeed.'—*Daily Chronicle.*
'A strong and successful piece of workmanship. The portrait of Lali, strong, dignified, and pure, is exceptionally well drawn.'—*Manchester Guardian.*

Gilbert Parker. THE TRAIL OF THE SWORD. By GILBERT PARKER. *Third Edition. Crown 8vo.* 6s.

'Everybody with a soul for romance will thoroughly enjoy "The Trail of the Sword."'—*St. James's Gazette.*
'A rousing and dramatic tale. A book like this, in which swords flash, great surprises are undertaken, and daring deeds done, in which men and women live and love in the old straightforward passionate way, is a joy inexpressible to the reviewer, brain-weary of the domestic tragedies and psychological puzzles of every-day fiction; and we cannot but believe that to the reader it will bring refreshment as welcome and as keen.'—*Daily Chronicle.*

Gilbert Parker. WHEN VALMOND CAME TO PONTIAC: The Story of a Lost Napoleon. By GILBERT PARKER. *Third Edition. Crown 8vo.* 6s.

'Here we find romance—real, breathing, living romance, but it runs flush with our own times, level with our own feelings. Not here can we complain of lack of inevitableness or homogeneity. The character of Valmond is drawn unerringly; his career, brief as it is, is placed before us as convincingly as history itself. The book must be read, we may say re-read, for any one thoroughly to appreciate Mr. Parker's delicate touch and innate sympathy with humanity.'—*Pall Mall Gazette.*
'The one work of genius which 1895 has as yet produced.'—*New Age.*

Gilbert Parker. AN ADVENTURER OF THE NORTH: The Last Adventures of 'Pretty Pierre.' By GILBERT PARKER. *Crown 8vo.* 6s.

'The present book is full of fine and moving stories of the great North, and it will add to Mr. Parker's already high reputation.'—*Glasgow Herald.*

'The new book is very romantic and very entertaining—full of that peculiarly elegant spirit of adventure which is so characteristic of Mr. Parker, and of that poetic thrill which has given him warmer, if less numerous, admirers than even his romantic story-telling gift has done.'—*Sketch.*

H. G. Wells. THE STOLEN BACILLUS, and other Stories. By H. G. WELLS, Author of 'The Time Machine.' *Crown 8vo.* 6s.

'The ordinary reader of fiction may be glad to know that these stories are eminently readable from one cover to the other, but they are more than that; they are the impressions of a very striking imagination, which it would seem, has a great deal within its reach.'—*Saturday Review.*

Arthur Morrison. TALES OF MEAN STREETS. By ARTHUR MORRISON. *Third Edition. Crown 8vo.* 6s.

'Told with consummate art and extraordinary detail. He tells a plain, unvarnished tale, and the very truth of it makes for beauty. In the true humanity of the book lies its justification, the permanence of its interest, and its indubitable triumph.'—*Athenæum.*

'A great book. The author's method is amazingly effective, and produces a thrilling sense of reality. The writer lays upon us a master hand. The book is simply appalling and irresistible in its interest. It is humorous also; without humour it would not make the mark it is certain to make.'—*World.*

J. Maclaren Cobban. THE KING OF ANDAMAN: A Saviour of Society. By J. MACLAREN COBBAN, Author of 'The Red Sultan,' etc. *Second Edition. Crown 8vo.* 6s.

'An unquestionably interesting book. It would not surprise us if it turns out to be the most interesting novel of the season, for it contains one character, at least, who has in him the root of immortality, and the book itself is ever exhaling the sweet savour of the unexpected. . . . Plot is forgotten and incident fades, and only the really human endures, and throughout this book there stands out in bold and beautiful relief its high-souled and chivalric protagonist, James the Master of Hutcheon, the King of Andaman himself.'—*Pall Mall Gazette.*

A most original and refreshing story. The supreme charm of the book lies in the genial humour with which the central character is conceived. James Hutcheon is a personage whom it is good to know and impossible to forget. He is beautiful within and without, whichever way we take him.'—*Spectator.*

'"The King of Andaman" has transcended our rosiest expectations. If only for the brilliant portraits of 'the Maister,' and his false friend Fergus O'Rhea, the book deserves to be read and remembered. The sketches of the Chartist movement are wonderfully vivid and engrossing, while the whole episode of James Hutcheon's fantastic yet noble scheme is handled with wonderful spirit and sympathy. "The King of Andaman," in short, is a book which does credit not less to the heart than the head of its author.'—*Athenæum.*

'The fact that Her Majesty the Queen has been pleased to gracefully express to the author of "The King of Andaman" her interest in his work will doubtless find for it many readers.'—*Vanity Fair.*

Julian Corbett. A BUSINESS IN GREAT WATERS. By JULIAN CORBETT, Author of 'For God and Gold,' 'Kophetua XIIIth.,' etc. *Crown 8vo.* 6s.

'In this stirring story Mr. Julian Corbett has done excellent work, welcome alike for its distinctly literary flavour, and for the wholesome tone which pervades it. Mr. Corbett writes with immense spirit, and the book is a thoroughly enjoyable one in all respects. The salt of the ocean is in it, and the right heroic ring resounds through its gallant adventures, in which pirates, smugglers, sailors, and refugees are mingled in picturesque confusion, with the din of battle and the soft strains of love harmoniously clashing an accompaniment. We trust that Mr. Corbett will soon give us another taste of his qualities in a novel as exciting, as dramatic, and as robustly human, as "A Business in Great Waters."'—*Speaker.*

C. Phillips Woolley. THE QUEENSBERRY CUP. A Tale of Adventure. By CLIVE PHILLIPS WOOLLEY, Author of 'Snap,' Editor of 'Big Game Shooting.' *Illustrated. Crown 8vo.* 6s.

This is a story of amateur pugilism and chivalrous adventure, written by an author whose books on sport are well known.

'A book which will delight boys: a book which upholds the healthy schoolboy code of morality.'—*Scotsman.*

'A brilliant book. Dick St. Clair, of Caithness, is an almost ideal character—a combination of the mediæval knight and the modern pugilist.'—*Admiralty and Horseguards Gazette.*

'If all heroes of boy's books were as truly heroic as Dick St. Clair, the winner of the Queensberry Cup, we should have nothing to complain of in literature specially written for boys.'—*Educational Review.*

Robert Barr. IN THE MIDST OF ALARMS. By ROBERT BARR, Author of 'From Whose Bourne,' etc. *Third Edition. Crown 8vo.* 6s.

'A book which has abundantly satisfied us by its capital humour.'—*Daily Chronicle.*

'Mr. Barr has achieved a triumph whereof he has every reason to be proud.'—*Pall Mall Gazette.*

L. Daintrey. THE KING OF ALBERIA. A Romance of the Balkans. By LAURA DAINTREY. *Crown 8vo.* 6s.

'Miss Daintrey seems to have an intimate acquaintance with the people and politics of the Balkan countries in which the scene of her lively and picturesque romance is laid. On almost every page we find clever touches of local colour which differentiate her book unmistakably from the ordinary novel of commerce. The story is briskly told, and well conceived.'—*Glasgow Herald.*

Mrs. Pinsent. CHILDREN OF THIS WORLD. By ELLEN F. PINSENT, Author of 'Jenny's Case.' *Crown 8vo.* 6s.

'Mrs. Pinsent's new novel has plenty of vigour, variety, and good writing. There are certainty of purpose, strength of touch, and clearness of vision.'—*Athenæum.*

Clark Russell. MY DANISH SWEETHEART. By W. CLARK RUSSELL, Author of 'The Wreck of the Grosvenor,' etc. *Illustrated. Third Edition. Crown 8vo.* 6s.

G. Manville Fenn. AN ELECTRIC SPARK. By G. MANVILLE FENN, Author of 'The Vicar's Wife,' 'A Double Knot,' etc. *Second Edition. Crown 8vo.* 6s.

'A simple and wholesome story.'—*Manchester Guardian.*

Pryce. TIME AND THE WOMAN. By RICHARD PRYCE, Author of 'Miss Maxwell's Affections,' 'The Quiet Mrs. Fleming,' etc. *Second Edition. Crown 8vo.* 6s.

'Mr. Pryce's work recalls the style of Octave Feuillet, by its clearness, conciseness, its literary reserve.'—*Athenæum.*

Mrs. Watson. THIS MAN'S DOMINION. By the Author of 'A High Little World.' *Second Edition. Crown 8vo.* 6s.

Marriott Watson. DIOGENES OF LONDON and other Sketches. By H. B. MARRIOTT WATSON, Author of 'The Web of the Spider.' *Crown 8vo. Buckram.* 6s.

'By all those who delight in the uses of words, who rate the exercise of prose above the exercise of verse, who rejoice in all proofs of its delicacy and its strength, who believe that English prose is chief among the moulds of thought, by these Mr. Marriott Watson's book will be welcomed.'—*National Observer.*

Gilchrist. THE STONE DRAGON. By MURRAY GILCHRIST. *Crown 8vo. Buckram.* 6s.

'The author's faults are atoned for by certain positive and admirable merits. The romances have not their counterpart in modern literature, and to read them is a unique experience.'—*National Observer.*

THREE-AND-SIXPENNY NOVELS

Edna Lyall. DERRICK VAUGHAN, NOVELIST. By EDNA LYALL, Author of 'Donovan,' etc. *Forty-first Thousand. Crown 8vo.* 3s. 6d.

Baring Gould. ARMINELL: A Social Romance. By S. BARING GOULD. *New Edition. Crown 8vo.* 3s. 6d.

Baring Gould. MARGERY OF QUETHER, and other Stories. By S. BARING GOULD. *Crown 8vo.* 3s. 6d.

Baring Gould. JACQUETTA, and other Stories. By S. BARING GOULD. *Crown 8vo.* 3s. 6d.

Miss Benson. SUBJECT TO VANITY. By MARGARET BENSON. *With numerous Illustrations. Second Edition. Crown 8vo.* 3s. 6d.

'A charming little book about household pets by a daughter of the Archbishop of Canterbury.'—*Speaker.*

'A delightful collection of studies of animal nature. It is very seldom that we get anything so perfect in its kind. . . . The illustrations are clever, and the whole book a singularly delightful one.'—*Guardian.*

MESSRS. METHUEN'S LIST 31

Mary Gaunt. THE MOVING FINGER: Chapters from the Romance of Australian Life. By MARY GAUNT, Author of 'Dave's Sweetheart.' *Crown 8vo.* 3s. 6d.

'Rich in local colour, and replete with vigorous character sketches. They strike us as true to the life.'—*Times.*
'Unmistakably powerful. Tragedies in the bush and riot in the settlement are portrayed for us in vivid colour and vigorous outline.'—*Westminster Gazette.*

Gray. ELSA. A Novel. By E. M'QUEEN GRAY. *Crown 8vo.* 3s. 6d.

J. H. Pearce. JACO TRELOAR. By J. H. PEARCE, Author of 'Esther Pentreath.' *New Edition. Crown 8vo.* 3s. 6d.

The Spectator' speaks of Mr. Pearce as '*a writer of exceptional power*'; the 'Daily Telegraph' calls the book '*powerful and picturesque*'; the 'Birmingham Post' asserts that it is '*a novel of high quality.*'

X. L. AUT DIABOLUS AUT NIHIL, and Other Stories. By X. L. *Second Edition. Crown 8vo.* 3s. 6d.

'Distinctly original and in the highest degree imaginative. The conception is almost as lofty as Milton's.'—*Spectator.*
'Original to a degree of originality that may be called primitive—a kind of passionate directness that absolutely absorbs us.'—*Saturday Review.*
'Of powerful interest. There is something startlingly original in the treatment of the themes. The terrible realism leaves no doubt of the author's power.'—*Athenæum.*

O'Grady. THE COMING OF CUCULAIN. A Romance of the Heroic Age of Ireland. By STANDISH O'GRADY, Author of 'Finn and his Companions.' Illustrated. *Crown 8vo.* 3s. 6d.

'The suggestions of mystery, the rapid and exciting action, are superb poetic effects.'—*Speaker.*
'For light and colour it resembles nothing so much as a Swiss dawn.'—*Manchester Guardian.*

Constance Smith. A CUMBERER OF THE GROUND. By CONSTANCE SMITH, Author of 'The Repentance of Paul Wentworth,' etc. *New Edition. Crown 8vo.* 3s. 6d.

Author of 'Vera.' THE DANCE OF THE HOURS. By the Author of 'Vera.' *Crown 8vo.* 3s. 6d.

Esmè Stuart. A WOMAN OF FORTY. By ESMÈ STUART, Author of 'Muriel's Marriage,' 'Virginie's Husband,' etc. *New Edition. Crown 8vo.* 3s. 6d.

'The story is well written, and some of the scenes show great dramatic power.'—*Daily Chronicle.*

Fenn. THE STAR GAZERS. By G. MANVILLE FENN, Author of 'Eli's Children,' etc. *New Edition. Cr. 8vo.* 3s. 6d.

'A stirring romance.'—*Western Morning News.*
'Told with all the dramatic power for which Mr. Fenn is conspicuous.'—*Bradford Observer.*

MESSRS. METHUEN'S LIST

Dickinson. A VICAR'S WIFE. By EVELYN DICKINSON.
Crown 8vo. 3s. 6d.

Prowse. THE POISON OF ASPS. By R. ORTON PROWSE.
Crown 8vo. 3s. 6d.

R. Pryce. THE QUIET MRS. FLEMING. By R. PRYCE.
Crown 8vo. 3s. 6d.

Lynn Linton. THE TRUE HISTORY OF JOSHUA DAVIDSON, Christian and Communist. By E. LYNN LINTON. *Eleventh Edition. Post 8vo.* 1s.

HALF-CROWN NOVELS
A Series of Novels by popular Authors

2/6

1. THE PLAN OF CAMPAIGN. By F. MABEL ROBINSON.
2. DISENCHANTMENT. By F. MABEL ROBINSON.
3. MR. BUTLER'S WARD. By F. MABEL ROBINSON.
4. HOVENDEN, V.C. By F. MABEL ROBINSON.
5. ELI'S CHILDREN. By G. MANVILLE FENN.
6. A DOUBLE KNOT. By G. MANVILLE FENN.
7. DISARMED. By M. BETHAM EDWARDS.
8. A LOST ILLUSION. By LESLIE KEITH.
9. A MARRIAGE AT SEA. By W. CLARK RUSSELL.
10. IN TENT AND BUNGALOW. By the Author of 'Indian Idylls.'
11. MY STEWARDSHIP. By E. M'QUEEN GRAY.
12. A REVEREND GENTLEMAN. By J. M. COBBAN.
13. A DEPLORABLE AFFAIR. By W. E. NORRIS.
14. JACK'S FATHER. By W. E. NORRIS.
15. A CAVALIER'S LADYE. By Mrs. DICKER.
16. JIM B.

Books for Boys and Girls
A Series of Books by well-known Authors, well illustrated. Crown 8vo.

3/6

1. THE ICELANDER'S SWORD. By S. BARING GOULD.
2. TWO LITTLE CHILDREN AND CHING. By EDITH E. CUTHELL.
3. TODDLEBEN'S HERO. By M. M. BLAKE.
4. ONLY A GUARD ROOM DOG. By EDITH E. CUTHELL.

MESSRS. METHUEN'S LIST 33

5. THE DOCTOR OF THE JULIET. By HARRY COLLINGWOOD.
6. MASTER ROCKAFELLAR'S VOYAGE. By W. CLARK RUSSELL.
7. SYD BELTON : Or, The Boy who would not go to Sea. By G. MANVILLE FENN.

The Peacock Library

A Series of Books for Girls by well-known Authors, handsomely bound in blue and silver, and well illustrated. Crown 8vo. 3/6

1. A PINCH OF EXPERIENCE. By L. B. WALFORD.
2. THE RED GRANGE. By Mrs. MOLESWORTH.
3. THE SECRET OF MADAME DE MONLUC. By the Author of 'Mdle Mori.'
4. DUMPS. By Mrs. PARR, Author of 'Adam and Eve.'
5. OUT OF THE FASHION. By L. T. MEADE.
6. A GIRL OF THE PEOPLE. By L. T. MEADE.
7. HEPSY GIPSY. By L. T. MEADE. 2s. 6d.
8. THE HONOURABLE MISS. By L. T. MEADE.
9. MY LAND OF BEULAH. By Mrs. LEITH ADAMS.

University Extension Series

A series of books on historical, literary, and scientific subjects, suitable for extension students and home-reading circles. Each volume is complete in itself, and the subjects are treated by competent writers in a broad and philosophic spirit.

Edited by J. E. SYMES, M.A.,
Principal of University College, Nottingham.

Crown 8vo. Price (with some exceptions) 2s. 6d.

The following volumes are ready:—

THE INDUSTRIAL HISTORY OF ENGLAND. By H. DE B. GIBBINS, M.A., late Scholar of Wadham College, Oxon., Cobden Prizeman. *Fourth Edition. With Maps and Plans.* 3s.

'A compact and clear story of our industrial development. A study of this concise but luminous book cannot fail to give the reader a clear insight into the principal phenomena of our industrial history. The editor and publishers are to be congratulated on this first volume of their venture, and we shall look with expectant interest for the succeeding volumes of the series.'—*University Extension Journal.*

A HISTORY OF ENGLISH POLITICAL ECONOMY. By L. L. PRICE, M.A., Fellow of Oriel College, Oxon. *Second Edition.*

PROBLEMS OF POVERTY: An Inquiry into the Industrial Conditions of the Poor. By J. A. HOBSON, M.A. *Second Edition.*

VICTORIAN POETS. By A. SHARP.

THE FRENCH REVOLUTION. By J. E. SYMES, M.A.

PSYCHOLOGY. By F. S. GRANGER, M.A., Lecturer in Philosophy at University College, Nottingham.

THE EVOLUTION OF PLANT LIFE: Lower Forms. By G. MASSEE, Kew Gardens. *With Illustrations.*

AIR AND WATER. Professor V. B. LEWES, M.A. *Illustrated.*

THE CHEMISTRY OF LIFE AND HEALTH. By C. W. KIMMINS, M.A. Camb. *Illustrated.*

THE MECHANICS OF DAILY LIFE. By V. P. SELLS, M.A. *Illustrated.*

ENGLISH SOCIAL REFORMERS. H. DE B. GIBBINS, M.A.

ENGLISH TRADE AND FINANCE IN THE SEVENTEENTH CENTURY. By W. A. S. HEWINS, B.A.

THE CHEMISTRY OF FIRE. The Elementary Principles of Chemistry. By M. M. PATTISON MUIR, M.A. *Illustrated.*

A TEXT-BOOK OF AGRICULTURAL BOTANY. By M. C. POTTER, M.A., F.L.S. *Illustrated.* 3s. 6d.

THE VAULT OF HEAVEN. A Popular Introduction to Astronomy. By R. A. GREGORY. *With numerous Illustrations.*

METEOROLOGY. The Elements of Weather and Climate. By H. N. DICKSON, F.R.S.E., F.R. Met. Soc. *Illustrated.*

A MANUAL OF ELECTRICAL SCIENCE. By GEORGE J. BURCH, M.A. *With numerous Illustrations.* 3s.

THE EARTH. An Introduction to Physiography. By EVAN SMALL, M.A. *Illustrated.*

INSECT LIFE. By F. W. THEOBALD, M.A. *Illustrated.*

ENGLISH POETRY FROM BLAKE TO BROWNING. By W. M. DIXON, M.A.

ENGLISH LOCAL GOVERNMENT. By E JENKS, M.A., Professor of Law at University College, Liverpool.

Social Questions of To-day

Edited by H. DE B. GIBBINS, M.A.

Crown 8vo. 2s. 6d.   **2/6**

A series of volumes upon those topics of social, economic, and industrial interest that are at the present moment foremost in the public mind. Each volume of the series is written by an author who is an acknowledged authority upon the subject with which he deals.

The following Volumes of the Series are ready:—

TRADE UNIONISM—NEW AND OLD. By G. HOWELL, Author of 'The Conflicts of Capital and Labour.' *Second Edition.*

THE CO-OPERATIVE MOVEMENT TO-DAY. By G. J. HOLYOAKE, Author of 'The History of Co-operation.'

MUTUAL THRIFT. By Rev. J. FROME WILKINSON, M.A., Author of 'The Friendly Society Movement.'

PROBLEMS OF POVERTY: An Inquiry into the Industrial Conditions of the Poor. By J. A. HOBSON, M.A. *Second Edition.*

THE COMMERCE OF NATIONS. By C. F. BASTABLE, M.A., Professor of Economics at Trinity College, Dublin.

THE ALIEN INVASION. By W. H. WILKINS, B.A., Secretary to the Society for Preventing the Immigration of Destitute Aliens.

THE RURAL EXODUS. By P. ANDERSON GRAHAM.

LAND NATIONALIZATION. By HAROLD COX, B.A.

A SHORTER WORKING DAY. By H. DE B. GIBBINS and R. A. HADFIELD, of the Hecla Works, Sheffield.

BACK TO THE LAND: An Inquiry into the Cure for Rural Depopulation. By H. E. MOORE.

TRUSTS, POOLS AND CORNERS: As affecting Commerce and Industry. By J. STEPHEN JEANS, M.R.I., F.S.S.

THE FACTORY SYSTEM. By R. COOKE TAYLOR.

THE STATE AND ITS CHILDREN. By GERTRUDE TUCKWELL.

WOMEN'S WORK. By LADY DILKE, MISS BULLEY, and MISS WHITLEY.

MUNICIPALITIES AT WORK. The Municipal Policy of Six Great Towns, and its Influence on their Social Welfare. By FREDERICK DOLMAN.

SOCIALISM AND MODERN THOUGHT. By M. KAUFMANN.

THE HOUSING OF THE WORKING CLASSES. By R. F. BOWMAKER.

Classical Translations

Edited by H. F. FOX, M.A., Fellow and Tutor of Brasenose College, Oxford.

Messrs. Methuen are issuing a New Series of Translations from the Greek and Latin Classics. They have enlisted the services of some of the best Oxford and Cambridge Scholars, and it is their intention that the Series shall be distinguished by literary excellence as well as by scholarly accuracy.

ÆSCHYLUS—Agamemnon, Chöephoroe, Eumenides. Translated by LEWIS CAMPBELL, LL.D., late Professor of Greek at St. Andrews. 5s.

CICERO—De Oratore I. Translated by E. N. P. MOOR, M.A., Assistant Master at Clifton. 3s. 6d.

CICERO—Select Orations (Pro Milone, Pro Murena, Philippic II., In Catilinam). Translated by H. E. D. BLAKISTON, M.A., Fellow and Tutor of Trinity College, Oxford. 5s

CICERO—De Natura Deorum. Translated by F. BROOKS, M.A., late Scholar of Balliol College, Oxford. 3s. 6d.

LUCIAN—Six Dialogues (Nigrinus, Icaro-Menippus, The Cock, The Ship, The Parasite, The Lover of Falsehood). Translated by S. T. IRWIN, M.A., Assistant Master at Clifton; late Scholar of Exeter College, Oxford. 3s. 6d.

SOPHOCLES—Electra and Ajax. Translated by E. D. A. MORSHEAD, M.A., late Scholar of New College, Oxford; Assistant Master at Winchester. 2s. 6d.

TACITUS—Agricola and Germania. Translated by R. B. TOWNSHEND, late Scholar of Trinity College, Cambridge. 2s. 6d.

Educational Books

CLASSICAL

TACITI AGRICOLA. With Introduction, Notes, Map, etc. By R. F. DAVIS, M.A., Assistant Master at Weymouth College. *Crown 8vo.* 2*s.*

TACITI GERMANIA. By the same Editor. *Crown 8vo.* 2*s.*

HERODOTUS: EASY SELECTIONS. With Vocabulary. By A. C. LIDDELL, M.A., Assistant Master at Nottingham High School. *Fcap. 8vo.* 1*s.* 6*d.*

SELECTIONS FROM THE ODYSSEY. By E. D. STONE, M.A., late Assistant Master at Eton. *Fcap. 8vo.* 1*s.* 6*d.*

PLAUTUS: THE CAPTIVI. Adapted for Lower Forms by J. H. FREESE, M.A., late Fellow of St. John's, Cambridge. 1*s.* 6*d.*

DEMOSTHENES AGAINST CONON AND CALLICLES. Edited with Notes, and Vocabulary, by F. DARWIN SWIFT, M.A., formerly Scholar of Queen's College, Oxford; Assistant Master at Denstone College. *Fcap. 8vo.* 2*s.*

GERMAN

A COMPANION GERMAN GRAMMAR. By H. DE B. GIBBINS, M.A., Assistant Master at Nottingham High School. *Crown 8vo.* 1*s.* 6*d.*

GERMAN PASSAGES FOR UNSEEN TRANSLATION. By E. M'QUEEN GRAY. *Crown 8vo.* 2*s.* 6*d.*

SCIENCE

THE WORLD OF SCIENCE. Including Chemistry, Heat, Light, Sound, Magnetism, Electricity, Botany, Zoology, Physiology, Astronomy, and Geology. By R. ELLIOT STEEL, M.A., F.C.S. 147 Illustrations. *Second Edition. Crown 8vo.* 2*s.* 6*d.*

'Mr. Steel's Manual is admirable in many ways. The book is well calculated to attract and retain the attention of the young.'—*Saturday Review.*

'If Mr. Steel is to be placed second to any for this quality of lucidity, it is only to Huxley himself; and to be named in the same breath with this master of the craft of teaching is to be accredited with the clearness of style and simplicity of arrangement that belong to thorough mastery of a subject.'—*Parents' Review.*

ELEMENTARY LIGHT. By R. E. STEEL. With numerous Illustrations. *Crown 8vo.* 4*s.* 6*d.*

ENGLISH

ENGLISH RECORDS. A Companion to the History of England. By H. E. MALDEN, M.A. *Crown 8vo.* 3s. 6d.

A book which aims at concentrating information upon dates, genealogy, officials, constitutional documents, etc., which is usually found scattered in different volumes.

THE ENGLISH CITIZEN: HIS RIGHTS AND DUTIES. By H. E. MALDEN, M.A. 1s. 6d.

'The book goes over the same ground as is traversed in the school books on this subject written to satisfy the requirements of the Education code. It would serve admirably the purposes of a text-book, as it is well based in historical facts, and keeps quite clear of party matters.'—*Scotsman.*

METHUEN'S COMMERCIAL SERIES.

BRITISH COMMERCE AND COLONIES FROM ELIZABETH TO VICTORIA. By H. DE B. GIBBINS, M.A., Author of 'The Industrial History of England,' etc. etc. 2s.

COMMERCIAL EXAMINATION PAPERS. By H. DE B. GIBBINS, M.A. 1s. 6d.

THE ECONOMICS OF COMMERCE. By H. DE B. GIBBINS, M.A. 1s. 6d.

A MANUAL OF FRENCH COMMERCIAL CORRESPONDENCE. By S. E. BALLY, Modern Language Master at the Manchester Grammar School. 2s.

A FRENCH COMMERCIAL READER. By S. E. BALLY. 2s.

COMMERCIAL GEOGRAPHY, with special reference to Trade Routes, New Markets, and Manufacturing Districts. By L. W. LYDE, M.A., of the Academy, Glasgow. 2s.

A PRIMER OF BUSINESS. By S. JACKSON, M.A. 1s. 6d.

COMMERCIAL ARITHMETIC. By F. G. TAYLOR, M.A. 1s. 6d.

WORKS BY A. M. M. STEDMAN, M.A.

INITIA LATINA: Easy Lessons on Elementary Accidence. *Second Edition. Fcap. 8vo.* 1s.

FIRST LATIN LESSONS. *Fourth Edition. Crown 8vo.* 2s.

FIRST LATIN READER. With Notes adapted to the Shorter Latin Primer and Vocabulary. *Second Edition.* Crown 8vo. 1s. 6d.

EASY SELECTIONS FROM CAESAR. Part I. The Helvetian War. 18mo. 1s.

EASY SELECTIONS FROM LIVY. Part I. The Kings of Rome. 18mo. 1s. 6d.

EASY LATIN PASSAGES FOR UNSEEN TRANSLATION. *Third Edition.* Fcap. 8vo. 1s. 6d.

EXEMPLA LATINA. First Lessons in Latin Accidence. With Vocabulary. Crown 8vo. 1s.

EASY LATIN EXERCISES ON THE SYNTAX OF THE SHORTER AND REVISED LATIN PRIMER. With Vocabulary. *Fourth Edition.* Crown 8vo. 2s. 6d. Issued with the consent of Dr. Kennedy.

THE LATIN COMPOUND SENTENCE: Rules and Exercises. Crown 8vo. 1s. 6d. With Vocabulary. 2s.

NOTANDA QUAEDAM: Miscellaneous Latin Exercises on Common Rules and Idioms. *Second Edition.* Fcap. 8vo. 1s. 6d. With Vocabulary, 2s.

LATIN VOCABULARIES FOR REPETITION: Arranged according to Subjects. *Fourth Edition.* Fcap. 8vo. 1s. 6d.

A VOCABULARY OF LATIN IDIOMS AND PHRASES. 18mo. 1s.

STEPS TO GREEK. 18mo. 1s.

EASY GREEK PASSAGES FOR UNSEEN TRANSLATION. Fcap. 8vo. 1s. 6d.

EASY GREEK EXERCISES ON ELEMENTARY SYNTAX. (*In preparation.*)

GREEK VOCABULARIES FOR REPETITION. Arranged according to Subjects. *Second Edition.* Fcap. 8vo. 1s. 6d.

GREEK TESTAMENT SELECTIONS. For the use of Schools. *Third Edition.* With Introduction, Notes, and Vocabulary. Fcap. 8vo. 2s. 6d.

STEPS TO FRENCH. 18mo. 8d.

FIRST FRENCH LESSONS. Crown 8vo. 1s.

EASY FRENCH PASSAGES FOR UNSEEN TRANSLATION. Second Edition. Fcap. 8vo. 1s. 6d.

EASY FRENCH EXERCISES ON ELEMENTARY SYNTAX. With Vocabulary. Crown 8vo. 2s. 6d.

FRENCH VOCABULARIES FOR REPETITION: Arranged according to Subjects. Third Edition. Fcap. 8vo. 1s.

SCHOOL EXAMINATION SERIES.

EDITED BY A. M. M. STEDMAN, M.A.

Crown 8vo. 2s. 6d.

FRENCH EXAMINATION PAPERS IN MISCELLANEOUS GRAMMAR AND IDIOMS. By A. M. M. STEDMAN, M.A. Sixth Edition.

A KEY, issued to Tutors and Private Students only, to be had on application to the Publishers. Second Edition. Crown 8vo. 6s. net.

LATIN EXAMINATION PAPERS IN MISCELLANEOUS GRAMMAR AND IDIOMS. By A. M. M. STEDMAN, M.A. Fourth Edition. Key issued as above. 6s. net.

GREEK EXAMINATION PAPERS IN MISCELLANEOUS GRAMMAR AND IDIOMS. By A. M. M. STEDMAN, M.A. Third Edition. Key issued as above. 6s. net.

GERMAN EXAMINATION PAPERS IN MISCELLANEOUS GRAMMAR AND IDIOMS. By R. J. MORICH, Manchester. Third Edition. KEY issued as above. 6s. net.

HISTORY AND GEOGRAPHY EXAMINATION PAPERS. By C. H. SPENCE, M.A., Clifton Coll.

SCIENCE EXAMINATION PAPERS. By R. E. STEEL, M.A., F.C.S., Chief Natural Science Master, Bradford Grammar School. In two vols. Part I. Chemistry; Part II. Physics.

GENERAL KNOWLEDGE EXAMINATION PAPERS. By A. M. M. STEDMAN, M.A. Second Edition. KEY issued as above. 7s. net.

www.ingramcontent.com/pod-product-compliance
Lightning Source LLC
Chambersburg PA
CBHW030342230426
43664CB00007BA/508